HOW GOD
BECOMES
REAL

HOW GOD BECOMES REAL

Kindling the Presence of Invisible Others

❖

T. M. LUHRMANN

PRINCETON UNIVERSITY PRESS

PRINCETON AND OXFORD

Requests for permission to reproduce material from this work
should be sent to permissions@press.princeton.edu

Published by Princeton University Press
41 William Street, Princeton, New Jersey 08540
99 Banbury Road, Oxford OX2 6JX

press.princeton.edu

First paperback printing, 2022
Paper ISBN 978-0-691-23444-1

The Library of Congress has cataloged the cloth edition as follows:

Names: Luhrmann, T. M. (Tanya M.), 1959– author.
Title: How God becomes real : kindling the presence of invisible others /
    T. M. Luhrmann.
Description: Princeton, New Jersey : Princeton University Press, 2020. |
    Includes bibliographical references and index.
Identifiers: LCCN 2020022662 (print) | LCCN 2020022663 (ebook) |
    ISBN 9780691164465 (acid-free paper) | ISBN 9780691211985 (ebook)
Subjects: LCSH: Spirituality. | Presence of God.
Classification: LCC BL624 .L84 2020 (print) | LCC BL624 (ebook) |
    DDC 202/.117—dc23
LC record available at https://lccn.loc.gov/2020022662
LC ebook record available at https://lccn.loc.gov/2020022663

British Library Cataloging-in-Publication Data is available

Editorial: Fred Appel and Jenny Tan
Production Editorial: Natalie Baan
Text and Cover Design: Leslie Flis
Production: Erin Suydam
Publicity: Kate Hensley and Kathryn Stevens
Copyeditor: Hank Southgate

Cover art: *The Angels Presenting to God the Souls of the Elect.*
From a fifteenth-century miniature. Illustration in *Military and Religious Life
in the Middle Ages* by Paul Lacroix (published ca. 1880) / Alamy Stock Photo

This book has been composed in Minion Pro

in memory of my mother

CONTENTS

CONTENTS

PREFACE

We are all in the gutter, but some of us are looking at the stars.

—Oscar Wilde, *Lady Windemere's Fan*

When I ponder why faith endures, I am struck by how little our theories consider two straightforward features of religion. First, religion is a practice in which people go to effort to make contact with an invisible other. Second, people who are religious want change. They want to feel differently than they do. Yet instead of exploring these features, most theories of religion begin by treating belief in an invisible other both as taken for granted and as a cognitive mistake. They assume that a prayer for rain is actually a prayer for rain and that it fails. Then these theories go on to explain why apparently foolish beliefs can be held by sensible people. People are afraid of aloneness and so project a parent (Freud); the experience of the social is so powerful that people have symbolized it as God (Durkheim); people dream and have odd experiences that seem evidence of something supernatural (Tylor, James); people have evolved an attributional style such that when they think quickly and automatically they intuit the presence of an invisible other (Boyer, Barrett); translations of nature stories have slipped and stumbled so much over the course of time that a "disease of language" led to mythologies about otherworldly beings (Müller). These theories presume that belief is direct and unproblematic—that in most cultures, people simply take spirit and the supernatural to be there.

That doesn't make sense. Gods and spirits cannot be seen. You cannot shake their hands, look them in the eye, or hear their voice when they speak. It seems odd to assume that people just take for granted that they are present. Moreover, people sometimes have elaborate ideas about what these invisible beings will deliver to them, and these promises often fall short. In many cases, gods are supposed to know one's thoughts and determine one's fate, and in many cases they promise justice and rewards to those who worship them. Yet even for the faithful, life can sometimes feel arbitrary and unfair. We should not assume that it is easy to feel that such powerful, benevolent, invisible beings are simply available and responsive.

If we start not with a presumption of belief, but with the question of whether the effort people invest in their faith helps them to feel that their gods and spirits are real, we are forced to focus on what people do when they worship gods and spirits, and on how those practices themselves might affect those who engage in them. Then we can ask whether the practices themselves help to make the beliefs compelling. And once we allow ourselves to ask whether people everywhere need to persuade themselves that their gods are real, religious rituals suddenly make more sense. After all, if spirits are believed to be unproblematically present— simply there, responsive and available—why do you need an all-night drumming ceremony to call them forth? If God is always present and aware, why does anyone need to pray?

I argue here that the puzzle of religion is not the problem of false be- lief, but the question of how gods and spirits become and remain real to people and what this real-making does for humans. This is not a claim that gods are not real or that people who are religious feel doubt. Many people of faith never express doubt; they talk as if it were obvious that their gods are real. Yet they go to great lengths in their worship. They build grand cathedrals at vast cost in labor, time, and money. They spend days, even weeks, preparing for rituals, assembling food, building rit- ual sites, and gathering participants. They create theatrical effects in sa- cred spaces—the dim lighting in temples, the elaborate staging in evan- gelical megachurches—that enhance a sense of otherness but are not commanded in the sacred texts. They fast. They wear special clothes. They chant for hours. They set out to pray without ceasing.

Of course, one might say: they believe, and so they build the cathe- drals. I am asking what we might learn if we shift our focus: if, rather than presuming that people worship because they believe, we ask instead whether people believe because they worship. I suggest that prayer and ritual and worship help people to shift from knowing in the abstract that the invisible other is real to feeling that gods and spirits are present in the moment, aware and willing to respond. I will call this "real-making," and I think that the satisfactions of its process explain—in part—why faiths endure.

By "real-making," I mean that the task for a person of faith is to believe not just that gods and spirits are there in some abstract way, like dark energy, but that these gods and spirits matter in the here and now. I mean not just that you know that they are real, the way you know that the floor is real (or would, if you paused to think about it), but that they feel real the way your mother's love feels real. I mean that people of faith come to feel inwardly and intimately that gods or spirits are involved with them. For humans to sustain their involvement with entities who are invisible and matter in a good way to their lives, I suggest that a god must be made real again and again against the evident features of an obdurate world. Humans must somehow be brought to a point from which the altar becomes more than gilded wood, so that the icon's eyes look back at them, ablaze.

This book describes some of the ways through which invisible others come to feel real to humans. I focus my anthropological attention on the mind, or on inner awareness, because knowing the unseen involves the imagination: the human ability to conceive of that which is not available to the senses. As Maurice Bloch (2008) reminds us, the capacity to imagine makes religion possible. Much of what I describe involves microprocesses of attention, ways of using the mind so that the invisible other can be grasped—sometimes more vividly, sometimes more indirectly, but always in a way that enables the person of faith to hold on to the possibility of presence. I call these acts of real-making "kindling," because they are small events, like the twigs and tinder from which a great fire can be lit, that shape where and how the fire burns. The microprocesses of attending—socially shaped, locally specific—kindle divine presence for a person of faith by using the mind to shift attention from the world as it is to the world as it should be, as understood within that faith. I will argue that the kindling processes through which invisible others come to feel real changes people and that the change becomes a powerful motivation for their faith.

This book lays out a set of hypotheses that emerged from my previous ethnographic work with evangelical Christians. I have explored many other faiths—British magic, American Santeria, Indian Zoroastrianism, and others. It was, however, in the evangelical tradition that I saw a process of real-making that I set out to understand in depth. Much of what I saw there occurs in other religions. Much is different, of course.

But the problem that spirits are invisible is common to many social worlds. Here I ask whether the basic processes I saw at work in the religions I know may illuminate something about religion in other social worlds.

The basic claim is this: *that god or spirit—the invisible other—must be made real for people, and that this real-making changes those who do it.* When I look at the social practices that surround what we call religion, I see a set of behaviors that change a practitioner's felt sense of what is real. These behaviors both enable what is unseen to feel more present and alter the person who performs them.

Each chapter of *How God Becomes Real* lays out a step in the argument—a proposition, or a hypothesis. Each chapter leaves open how widely the hypothesis can be generalized to other religions and other social worlds. Readers will disagree with each other. No one has ever settled the question of what counts as religion, nor whether gods are necessarily invisible, nor whether a football fanatic is engaged in the same kind of activity as a devout Catholic. There is also the problem of whether real-making is more important for the "big gods" (as Ara Norenzayan [2013] describes them) who are powerful, omniscient, and moral, than for the "little gods" who hang around particular trees or rivers and whose powers are limited. But I do think that the practices I describe here are common to many, many religions, and that these practices explain something about how unseen and invisible others come to be experienced as present.

And so the book is an invitation—a provocation, as we say these days. It lays out some hypotheses and asks you, the reader, how much of what we call religion they explain. Here is a list of these main hypotheses. It is a roadmap to the chapters of this book.

First: *People don't (easily) have faith in gods and spirits.* People do not, in fact, behave as if gods and spirits are real in the way that everyday objects are real. The great realization of the cognitive science of religion is that people quickly, easily, and automatically generate ideas about agents they can't see when they are scared or startled. But to have a sustained commitment to the reality of invisible agents, the deeply held feeling that gods and spirits are real in a way that matters, someone must interpret the world through a special way of thinking, expecting, and remembering. I will call this a faith frame. That faith frame coexists alongside the ordinary ways people make sense of the world, and sometimes contradicts them. The priest says, *this is my body*, but it looks like a dry cracker. The sermon insists, *my God can do anything*, but God didn't stop the divorce. And so faith is hard—particularly when an invisible other is supposed to love you, care for you, and keep you safe.

Second: *Detailed stories help to make gods and spirits feel real.* Detailed stories make the faith frame more accessible and help people to experience invisible others as more real. The work of making an invisible other feel present begins with a good story, and good stories are compelling because they have rich and specific detail. Good, detailed stories—vividly imagined worlds—enable suspended disbelief. They also introduce invisible others as characters who interact with people, and they set out ways to talk with these others and to experience them as talking back.

Third: *Talent and training matter.* What people do and what they bring to what they do affect the way they experience gods and spirits. People who are able to become absorbed in what they imagine are more likely to have powerful experiences of an invisible other. Practice also helps. People who practice being absorbed in what they imagine during prayer or ritual are also more likely to have such experiences. This absorption blurs the boundary between the inner world and the outer world, which makes it easier for people to turn to a faith frame to make sense of the world and to experience invisible others as present in a way they feel with their senses.

Fourth: *The way people think about their minds also matters.* The intimate evidence for gods and spirits often comes from a domain felt to be in between the mind and the world, from the space betwixt a person's inner awareness and the sensible world—the thought that does not feel like yours, the voice that feels whispered on the wind, the person who feels there and yet beyond the reach of sight. How people in a particular social world represent the mind itself—how they map the human terrain of thinking, feeling, intending, and desiring into a cultural model—shapes the way they attend to these odd moments so that the moments feel more or less sensory, more or less external, more or less real, more or less like evidence of gods and spirits.

Fifth: *The sense of response is "kindled."* A person's sense of an invisible other's presence is not only kindled from the tinder of these small practices of attention, but kindled in a particular way. The fire reignites more easily, but also in more specific ways. The chapter lays out a theory of what kindles spiritual presence and how. These moments when someone hears a god, sees a spirit, or feels the presence of the dead are important because they become evidence, for the person of faith, that does not rely on the testimony of others. Such moments make it easier to reach for a faith frame to make sense of the world.

Sixth: *Prayer practice changes the way people attend to their thoughts.* Prayer is a specific way of using a faith frame, and it changes people because it changes the way they attend to their own awareness, their inner worlds. Prayer is an act of thinking about thinking. Prayer shifts the way those who pray attend to their own thoughts in much the same way that cognitive behavioral therapists teach their clients to alter the attention they pay to theirs. Prayer is the first extended example of how real-making changes people.

Seventh: *People create relationships with gods and spirits.* This is the second extended example of how real-making changes people. As people practice, as the invisible other becomes more real to them, people remake themselves in relationship with that other. These relationships can be intensely intimate and drenched in feeling—something not quite captured by the word "belief." When real-making works, it makes that god real in a particular way, and people create particular relationships with that god that have in some ways the back-and-forth qualities that all social relationships do. That now-real god will change what feels real to people in other ways, sometimes in ways dramatically different from those in other faiths who have relationships with different gods. These relationships anchor the faith frame in the ordinary world and make it matter.

This is not an atheist's book. It is not a believer's book. It is an anthropologist's book and a work of the anthropology of mind, that filter through which humans become aware of their world. Nothing I say here speaks for or against the genuine reality of gods and spirits. What anthropologists can see is the human side of the relationship with the invisible other. The complexity and ambiguity of that relationship are as apparent to the person of faith as they are to the skeptic. We all of us see through a glass darkly, and none of us have direct access to the Real.

What I offer here is an account of how people change when they make gods and spirits real and develop a relationship with an unseen presence that feels alive.

Note: Each chapter has a short essay in the Bibliographic Essays and Notes section that includes richer scholarly discussions and more detailed empirical analyses of the material for interested readers.

HOW GOD
BECOMES
REAL

1

THE FAITH FRAME

Belief has always struck me as the wrong question, especially
when it is offered as a diagnostic for determining the realness of
the gods.

—Robert Orsi, *Between Heaven and Earth*

Devout modern Christians talk constantly about not being faithful
enough. They bemoan how hard it is to keep God's love at the front of
their minds. They complain about forgetting about God between Sunday services. They apologize for not being able to trust God to solve their
problems. I remember a man weeping in front of a church over not having sufficient faith that God would replace the job he had lost. When you
pay attention, you can see that church services are about reminding
people to take God seriously and to behave in ways that will enable God
to have an impact on their lives: to pray, to read the Bible, to be Christ-
like. And then people say that they go back home and yell at their kids
and feel foolish because they have forgotten that they meant to be like
Jesus. They report that they run out of time to pray. They confess that
they do not behave as if God can help them. They worry that they do
not really understand or commit as they should.

In fact, when you look carefully, you can see that church is about
changing people's mental habits Sunday by Sunday so that they feel that
God is more real, more relevant, and more present for them—so that
they believe more than they did when they walked in and hold on to
those beliefs a little longer after they walk out. It is one of the clearest
messages in Christianity: *You may think you believe in God, but really
you don't. You don't take God seriously enough. You don't act as if he's
there. Mark 9:24: Lord, I believe; help my unbelief.*

This apparent paradox—believers as the unbelieving—stood out to me when I was doing ethnographic fieldwork with charismatic evangelical Protestants in Chicago and in the San Francisco South Bay (Luhrmann, *When God Talks Back*). Here were committed believers, most of whom asserted God's reality with firm conviction and many of whom had acted and voted according to those convictions (as they understood them) in ways that had real consequences. Yet as I watched and listened carefully as an ethnographer, it became clear to me that they treated the invisible other at the heart of their faith quite differently than they treated visible, everyday things like barking dogs and orange peels. They said that God spoke to them, but they were often skeptical of other people's reports of hearing God's word, particularly when that word had specific outcomes. As one pastor said in church, "If you hear God say that you should be calm, take it as God! If God tells you to quit your job and move to Los Angeles, I want you to be praying with me, with your housegroup, and with your prayer circle to discern whether you heard God accurately." People never asked God to write their term papers or to go shopping for them, even though they said that nothing was impossible with God. They said again and again that God's power and love were infinite, but they often felt helpless and unlovable; they often said that they forgot to pray for help when they should have prayed; and they often struggled with apparently unanswered prayers. They talked about the mystery of faith, and how little they understood of why God seemed to answer some prayers but not others, and why God allowed such pain in their lives.

My observations suggested that it took these staunch evangelicals effort to keep God present and salient in their lives; that their belief in this invisible other was different in some way than their belief in the everyday reality of visible objects, or even invisible objects like electricity or microbes; and that it was particularly hard to sustain a straightforward faith in God's deep love because the world so often seemed to deny it.

I saw that these Christians went to church at least once a week. They tried to read their Bibles every day, and they explained the details of their lives through biblical stories. They thought they should pray at least thirty minutes a day. Many of them spent an evening each week with a small group of other congregants, where they prayed and sang and talked about the Bible. They said again and again that unless you did all those things, your faith would wither and die—that unless people went to efforts to keep God front and center in their awareness, God would simply disappear for them. They never said any of those things about the kitchen table or other ordinary objects in the everyday natural world. There is an obduracy about the world of the visible that means that when inferences about invisible others are not supported by experience, the commitment to them can fade away—and believers know it.

This is not the way many anthropologists talk about belief. To be fair, Christians often state their beliefs with absolute conviction. It is easy for an observer to say, these people neither doubt nor question. They praise the Lord at every other sentence, so why would one even wonder about their confidence in the realness of God? "I believe in Christianity," C. S. Lewis wrote, "as I believe that the Sun has risen, not only because I see it but because by it I see everything else" (1962: 165).

Perhaps because they hear statements like these at home, many anthropologists often write as if their subjects never entertain hesitations about the supernatural and never doubt that the supernatural is straightforwardly as real as the ground they walk on. Anthropologists, often describing people who are not Western and whose societies have never been secular to readers they presume to be both secular and Western, write sentences like these:

> [The Andaman Islanders] believe that the spirits feed on the flesh of dead men and women. (Radcliffe-Brown [1922] 2013: 140)

> Chiefs for instance are believed sometimes to "rise up" as lions. The belief is consistent with the theory of ancestral presence in animals, trees and artifacts dedicated to ancestors. (Fortes 1987: 136, about the Tallensi of Northern Ghana)

> God's existence is taken for granted by everybody. (Evans-Pritchard 1956: 9, about the Nuer of the Nile Valley)

That last sentence ends, as Clifford Geertz (1988: 58) remarked that all Evans-Pritchard's sentences end, with an implied "of course." That's the way it is. These people think that the gods are real, that they are present, and that they are powerful.

In fact, when anthropologists write this way, they often intend to convey that the people they study are so unquestioning that it would be a mistake even to describe them as "believing." That was Evans-Pritchard's point. He wrote that sentence to reject the very possibility that the Nuer would ever say something like "there is a God."

> That would be for Nuer a pointless remark.... There is ... no word in the Nuer language which could stand for "I believe." (Evans-Pritchard 1956: 9)

It is a claim echoed by anthropologist after anthropologist. Thus Christina Toren:

> We [anthropologists] may characterise as *belief* what our informants *know* and, in so doing, misrepresent them. If I am to correctly represent my Fijian informants, for example, I should say that they *know* the ancestors inhabit the places that were theirs. (Toren 2007: 307–8)

They do not "believe." They "know."

When anthropologists insist that the people they study know, rather than believe, that their gods are real, they are often making a claim about the foolish mistakes modern people make. They are often asserting that "believing in" is a Western or Christian thing, an argument made vigorously by Talal Asad (1993). Sometimes they are insisting that when anthropologists talk about the beliefs of other people, it is really a way to dismiss them. Eduardo Viveiros de Castro (e.g., 2011), Morten Pedersen (2011), and Martin Holbraad (2009) have written fiery texts about the ways that anthropologists have examined the belief commitments of people like those in Amazonia, Mongolia, and Cuba. They argue that most anthropological observers write as if they presume that such beliefs are wrong—and that view, they argue, is driven by deep-seated colonialist impulses or by a scientific imperialism. This is Viveiros de Castro (2011: 133): "Anthropologists must allow that 'visions' are not beliefs, nor consensual views, but rather worlds seen objectively; not world views, but worlds of vision."

I agree that there is something quite culturally specific about the way that people in the modern West think about what is real, both because of the Enlightenment heritage of their society and because of its Christian roots. I completely disagree that other people do not distinguish between the realness of humans, trees, and rocks and the realness of ghosts, gods, and spirits, and that they do not have to go to any effort to experience the latter as real. I think that the evidence suggests that all human groups distinguish what counts as natural from what is beyond the natural, even though they may draw the line in different ways and come to different conclusions at different times about what is on which side of the line. As Robert Bartlett points out in *The Natural and the Supernatural in the Middle Ages*, people can have unstable views about what is natural without rejecting the idea that some things are natural and other things come from a god. In fact, to me it seems somewhat insulting to assume that non-Western people don't think of objects like rocks and gods as being real in different ways, as if they had a less subtle ontology than we moderns. I suspect that all humans have flexible ontologies, and that they hold ideas about gods and spirits (on the one hand) and the everyday world (on the other) in different ways.

FLEXIBLE ONTOLOGIES

To understand the point, let us turn first to what philosophers and psychologists have taught us about human thought in recent years. Over the last four decades or so, it has become clear that humans use two different patterns of reasoning. The terms used to describe these two patterns vary: heuristic and analytic reasoning (Evans 1984); system one (intuition) and system two (deliberate reasoning) (Kahneman 2003); implicit and explicit beliefs (Boyer 2001); unreflective and reflective beliefs (Barrett 2004); and alief and belief (Gendler 2008). Each pair emphasizes somewhat different phenomena, but all point out that humans come to different conclusions when they think quickly, automatically, and intuitively as compared to when they think slowly, carefully, and deliberatively.

We call ideas produced by the first pattern of reasoning "intuitions," the beliefs people generate when they think "from the gut." Some intuitions seem more part of the package of being human. Even infants expect solid objects that bump into other solid objects to bounce back. They act more surprised if the objects seem to ooze into each other. We seem to have not only an "innate physics" but also an innate biology, an innate psychology, and even an innate mathematics (Spelke and Kinzler 2007). Other intuitions are based on acquired knowledge. When people are asked whether it is more likely that "a flood caused many people to die in California" or that "an earthquake caused a flood to cause many people to die in California," many pick the latter because they have learned that California is associated with earthquakes, not floods, even though logically the first is more likely than the second. When they are asked whether a young female Berkeley philosophy graduate became a bank-teller or a bank-teller and a feminist, they often pick the latter because they have learned that people at Berkeley are politically progressive, even though (statistically speaking) the latter is less likely than the former (the existence of something that is both "a and b" is less likely than of something that is only "a").

These examples are among the many illustrations generated by Daniel Kahneman and Amos Tversky in their remarkable research, summarized in Kahneman's (2003) Nobel acceptance speech. (Tversky died before the prize was awarded.) They use them to show that our quick judgments are shaped in specific ways: representativeness (earthquakes are more representative of California than floods, feminists are more representative of female Berkeley graduates than bank-tellers); salience (a vertical line and two vertical semicircles can look like a "13" in a line of numbers, but like a "B" in a line of letters); and framing effects (tell people that a program will save half the lives of a population, and they will like it more than a program that leads to the death of half the population). These are principles that help people make rapid decisions based on prior knowledge, and in many settings they help people save cognitive effort and likely help keep them safe.

By contrast, deliberative thinking is what we do when we come to what we call a rational decision, or when we write an analytical paper. At these times, we are aware of the steps in the argument. We think those steps through consciously, and we consider carefully whether they are supported by the evidence. Deliberative thinking may be fueled by intuitions, but when thinking deliberatively, people try to lay out the analytical elements clearly enough so that someone else is not confused. Deliberative thinking is hard, as anyone who has written a research paper can testify.

The models behind these two modes of thinking suggest that humans are constantly generating intuitions to help us solve all kinds of problems: where to sit on the train, whether there is anyone else in the house, whether we should trust the person we are talking to. More information will usually help us to overturn initial intuitions. If I hear a crash in the next room, I might initially worry that an intruder is there—but if I go into the room to investigate and see that the dog has knocked something down, my fear would give way to annoyance. We have intuitions about all sorts of things that we quickly decide are not true when we learn more—intuitions that we trust someone, or that the shirt on the rack on will look good on us, or that the dish we ordered will be tasty.

The great achievement of the field now called "the cognitive science of religion" has been to show that our evolved mental habits generate many intuitions that might support more reasoned, deliberative commitments to a supernatural presence. Pascal Boyer (2008) summarized several of these features for a paper in *Nature*.

First, he pointed out, humans are wildly anthropomorphic. Humans see agents everywhere—at least when thinking quickly. Humans see faces in the clouds and eyes on cars. When two geometric shapes move sequentially around a computer screen, people ascribe intentions to them. Second, humans are not only able to hold people in mind when they are absent, but they form enduring relationships with absent and even imagined others. Third, when humans are young, before they develop an understanding that humans have minds, they assume that what they know, everyone knows. The idea of an omniscient knower, then, is in some sense familiar to anyone who has been a child. Fourth, humans form groups in which they are sensitive to trust and to hard-to-fake signals of commitment. The willingness to assert claims for which there is no evidence but that entail costs (tithing, scarification, time) may facilitate the building of those groups. Fifth, humans are highly alert to danger. They seem to be acutely aware of the possibilities of predation and contamination. Our ancestors were probably more likely to survive if they treated unfamiliar noise as a signal that a predator might be present. Possibly as a result (although perhaps there are also other causes), we do see agents everywhere.

The intuitions that these mental habits produce likely do, indeed, make the apparently irrational idea of an invisible agent seem plausible. "When a reflective belief nicely matches what our nonconscious mental tools tell us through nonreflective beliefs," Justin Barrett (2004: 13) remarks, "the reflective beliefs just seem more reasonable." In fact, when people hold a deliberative commitment (God is everywhere always) that does not seem to make intuitive sense, you can interpret some of the work they do (seeking to find God's presence all the time) as an attempt to make these deliberative commitments feel more intuitive (Boyer 2013).

But the observation that people have different patterns of reasoning—system one and system two, Kahneman and Tversky called them, or thinking fast and slow, to borrow the title of Kahneman's (2011) famous book—should not only tell us that there is a difference between the plausibility of an idea and sustained commitment to that idea, but also remind us that belief is not one kind of thing. People have all sorts of ideas they call beliefs. They believe that the train will arrive at 10:12; that the coffee at Peet's is better than the coffee at Starbucks; that in the Harry Potter series Hermione should have fallen for Harry and not for Ron; that gravitational force draws all objects; that there's a carpet on the study floor; that there is no God but Allah and Muhammad is His prophet. These are beliefs with different kinds of ontological commitments: expectation, preference, pretend, scientific, factual, and religious. The mere existence of these differences should invite us to ask whether there might be something consistently different in the ways people hold different beliefs and that people are able to move flexibly among these ways with ease. In short, these differences should lead us to ask whether different kinds of beliefs might consistently be held with different ontological attitudes.

ONTOLOGICAL ATTITUDES

The philosopher Neil Van Leeuwen (2014) argues that religious beliefs and mundane beliefs are held with different "cognitive attitudes." That is, people evaluate these beliefs using different evidence, commit to them for different reasons, and draw different kinds of inferences from them. To be clear, there are no doubt many kinds of belief commitments held with many different kinds of cognitive attitudes: beliefs about fiction as opposed to beliefs about facts, beliefs about doing as opposed to beliefs about knowing, beliefs about matters that define one's identity as opposed to beliefs about the mundane world. But the argument that cognitive attitudes toward beliefs in spirits are different in kind from cognitive attitudes toward beliefs about the ordinary world has proved controversial (Boudry and Coyne 2016). I am persuaded by five of the arguments Van Leeuwen makes.

First, people use language differently when they talk about spirits, and in a way that suggests that they think about the realness of spirits and mundane objects differently. You do not say, "I believe that my dog is alive." The fact is so obvious that it is not worth stating. You simply talk in ways that presume the dog's aliveness. You say that she's adorable, or hungry, or in need of a walk. Van Leeuwen contrasts these two beliefs:

"Jennifer believes that Margaret Thatcher is alive."
"Sam believes that Jesus Christ is alive."

The first is a mundane assertion. If Jennifer held her belief about Margaret Thatcher after Thatcher died in April 2013, she'd just be wrong, and it likely would not take much effort to get her to admit it. Sam, however, asserts his belief against his own sharp awareness that there was a man called Jesus who died and was buried some two thousand years ago. His statement "Jesus Christ is alive" assumes the historical reality of the death—and then denies it. It is an epistemologically complicated commitment, and its complexity is present in the very structure of the sentence. If you told Sam that he had made a mistake, he would probably argue vigorously that you were wrong.

In fact, these two different kinds of belief commitments—one mundane, the other religious—are so distinct that we often use different verbs to identify them: "think" and "believe." We treat them as making distinct ontological claims. In a series of studies, Van Leeuwen and his colleagues (e.g., Heiphetz, Landers, and Van Leeuwen 2018) have found that people typically default to talking about factual claims with "think" (*Gustav thinks that his final paper is due on June 18*) and talking about religious claims with "believe" (*Lisa believes that burning incense at the temple can keep her family safe. Zane believes that Jesus changed water into wine*). In work that Van Leeuwen and I have done together (still in progress), we have found that people draw these distinctions not just in English and in the United States, but in other cultures and languages as well.

Second, religious beliefs become part of the identity of those who assert them, and humans evaluate challenges to identity-defining beliefs differently from challenges to mundane beliefs. Mundane beliefs adjust to the empirical details. If I believe that my dog is in the study but I find her in the kitchen, I adjust my beliefs. If I am Jewish and believe that to be a faithful Jew I should keep kosher—a belief that is important, then, to who I am—it will take much more effort for someone else to show me that I am wrong. People evaluate religious beliefs more in accordance with their sense of who they are and how they think the world should be.

In fact, when their beliefs are under stress, people at times even adjust the world to make sense of their religious commitments. Yoram Bilu (2013) has for years been studying the Messianic Lubavitcher Hasids who held that their rabbi Menachem Schneerson was the messiah and would never die. After he did die, many reported seeing and hearing him, just as the disciples saw and heard Jesus. And perhaps also like the disciples, it was only after his death that they began to proselytize in earnest, seeking to persuade others of the truth of a belief that had been so profoundly disconfirmed. The central claim of the classic *When Prophecy Fails* (a study, led by the psychologist Leon Festinger, of a Midwestern doomsday cult) is precisely that people evangelize because they fear that the belief to which they have committed themselves may not be true.

Third, religious beliefs and factual beliefs often play different roles in interpreting the same events. Malinowski (1954) pointed this out years ago. The Trobriand Islanders put amulets on the fields to ward off thieves, and they used magical incantations to protect their wooden canoes on the turbulent seas. But they also kept a sharp lookout for intruders, and they carved carefully, with all the practical knowledge at their command, to build seaworthy vessels that would not sink. They used magic to handle what we would call luck: the unexpected circumstance, the unpredictable event, an overlarge wave. More recently, Cristine Legare and her colleagues (2012) have demonstrated that natural and supernatural explanations are used pervasively across cultures to do different things: one to explain how, the other to explain why. We know from science that tumors arise because cells begin to divide in abnormal ways, but why this tumor, for this person, at this time? That is when people turn to supernatural explanations.

Fourth, supernatural beliefs are not "natural," as Robert McCauley (2013) puts it. At least, they are not part of the package of being a human child. Children do not believe the local cultural accounts of magic and spirits more readily than adults. In fact, in some ways children seem to be less committed to and less interested in these ideas than adults. This is what Margaret Mead (1930) saw in New Guinea. When Mead tried to talk to Manus children about magic and spirits, they gave her disinterested stares. It was the adults who spent hours discussing ghosts. Legare and her colleagues (2012) not only documented the coexistence of natural and supernatural explanations in many societies, but set out to understand whether natural explanations replaced supernatural explanations as people aged. They found that the reverse was more often true. It is the young kids who seem skeptical when researchers like Legare ask them about gods and ancestors, and the adults who seem firm and clear. Nor do religious commitments seem like a natural part of growing older, even though people are more likely to become religious as they age. In a secular society, people can grow to adulthood quite comfortably without any religion at all.

Fifth, scholars have shown that people don't always use rational, instrumental reasoning when they think about religious ideas. This is not to say that they can't reason about religion: the works of Augustine and Aquinas are testament to the human ability to think logically about things divine. But often people do not. The anthropologist Scott Atran and his colleagues (2014) have shown that faith commitments, which they call "sacred values," are often immune to the constant assessment of costs and benefits that govern other dimensions of human lives. Offer a Muslim woman money to take off her veil, and she may insist even more fiercely on its importance. Offer a Christian woman money in exchange for her wedding ring, along with a ring that looks just like her wedding ring but isn't (as Douglas Medin and his colleagues did [1999]), and most likely she will refuse. When people feel themselves to be completely fused with a group defined by its sacred values, they commit acts that most others would not. They become what Atran calls "devoted actors," who are unconditionally committed to their sacred values, and they are willing to die for them.

Beyond these five points, one can say that religious beliefs are always in effect secondary to what we know about the everyday natural world. The everyday world always matters. You must still stop at stoplights, study for exams, and feed the dog. Someone who prayed that their car would stop without braking would seem mad, not devout. Ditto for a student who prayed to turn in a paper without writing one or a dog-owner who prayed that the dog would get fed without filling up the dinner bowl. There is, indeed, a famous Islamic hadith about this. "Anas ibn Malik reported: A man said, 'O Messenger of Allah, should I tie my camel and trust in Allah, or should I leave her untied and trust in Allah?' The Messenger of Allah, peace and blessings upon him, said, 'Tie her and trust in Allah'" (Jami' at-Tirmidhi, hadith 2517). Focus on God, the hadith says, but do not forget to tie up your camel. The mundane every-day world is a given. In some sense, it is always prior.

Van Leeuwen (2014: 701) calls this "continual reality tracking." Children who play at giving their teddy bear a bath may wash Teddy with pretend soap and dry him with a pretend towel. They may give Teddy a play-dough cookie for his bedtime snack and mop up the pretend milk from the floor where he spilled it. They will behave as if all these pretend items were real. But if an adult takes a real bite out of that playdough cookie, this startles the child (Golomb and Kuersten 1996). The psycholo-gist Paul Harris (2000) uses this example to point out that make-believe never fully replaces the everyday world. The factual composition of the playdough is not food—and the child knows it. In the same way, pray-ing to solve an everyday problem—the dog is hungry, the paper is due on Monday—never fully replaces the need to act in the everyday world.

Of course, there are counterexamples. Snake-handling sects encour-age congregants to hold copperheads and swallow strychnine to dem-onstrate that, as Mark 16:18 suggests, they can pick up snakes and drink deadly poison without harm (Covington 1995). Christian Science en-courages congregants to refuse medical care on the grounds that it should be God alone who heals. In 1997, a cult called Heaven's Gate per-suaded thirty-nine people that if they downed barbiturates and vodka, they would leave behind their bodies to join a spaceship riding behind a comet's tail. Yet these counterexamples are relatively rare. Most people behave as if there are ordinary expectations about how the world works, and that special expectations associated with spirits become meaningful and relevant only at special times and in special ways (see Taves 2009b).

This is my puzzle: People may talk as if the gods are straightforwardly real, but they don't act that way—not in the Bible Belt, not in medieval

England, not in Fiji, and not among the Nuer. People behave as if making invisible others real enough to impact one's life in a positive way takes effort, as if one has to learn to think in certain way and—in consequence—to behave as if invisible others are not real in the way that ordinary objects are real. They seem to treat gods and spirits with different ontological attitudes than they do things of the everyday world.

DOUBTING THOMAS—AND TOMÁS, AND THOMASZ, AND TOMASSO

When I argue that people must work hard to keep their gods real, anthropologists often respond, yes, what you say is true for modern Christians in the secular United States, but it is not true of people in traditional societies that have never been secular. "Believing in" is something Christians and Westerners worry about, but not other people. For example, Aparecida Vilaça (2013: 362) once objected that American evangelicals might doubt, but not the Amazonian Wari': "questions of the kind posed by Luhrmann vis-à-vis her material only make sense within a cultural frame informed by a very specific notion of personhood." In other words, people only doubt that spirits are real in modern, secular, individualist societies. Yet Vilaça's own ethnography suggests that in some ways, the Wari' behave as if the spirits' existence depends upon the way people treat them—and that spirits are real for humans in a different way than the ordinary objects people can see.

First of all, the Wari' need to be shown the spirits. The arrival of spirits is theatrical and mimed.

One day in 2003 I asked the jaguar-shaman Orowam, whom I call grandfather, whether I could film a conversation with him about jaguars and their world. He sat on a wooden trunk close to his house and I positioned myself in front of him with my video camera on a tripod next to me. Several people sat around Orowam to hear him speak. After a long silence, Orowam began to look to his left and talk in a low voice, and immediately all of those on that side ran away, especially the children, shooed away by their parents. From the comments, I understood that the jaguars were present, arriving from that direction. Not knowing what to do, I remained seated looking towards Orowam, until he turned towards me and began to tell me what the jaguars were saying. They asked him who I was. He replied that I was his granddaughter. Again he looked to his left, listened and turned back to me, saying that they wanted to know what I would give as a present for filming. I answered. Turning to the jaguars, he repeated my response in a loud voice: "a shirt," she said. Both the dialogues were spoken in the Wari' language. The three of us (or more, since a group of jaguars was involved) talked like this for about fifteen minutes, after which the jaguars left. The others then drew near again, surrounding Orowam and remarking on what had happened. Nobody, as far as I could tell, doubted the presence of the jaguars. (Vilaça 2013: 361)

The Wari' may not be voicing doubt: but the shaman is certainly going to lengths to demonstrate the invisible spirit's presence. The shaman points with his eyes, speaks out loud in dialogue, and reports the invisible other's speech. It is a skilled, practiced performance. The Wari' need this kind of performance because spirits are not present to the senses in ordinary ways. Spirits are different in kind from ordinary objects, and the behavior of the Wari' expresses that.

Praying and Preying, Vilaça's 2016 book, shows that the Wari' do just as much active keeping-spirits-in-mind work as my evangelicals did for God. In the pre-Christian Wari' community, there were endless rules about relationships with animals, often presented via myth-like stories. Vilaça writes that people explain, "It was also essential for prey to be roasted and eaten quickly. Immortal, the animals would return to their houses after being eaten completely, and would even ignore the predation, telling their own relatives that the injuries to their body (caused by arrows) had come from getting scratched in the forest" (2016: 198–99). Doing these things of course is an act of pointing to the presence of spirits—look, I am roasting the meat quickly, because that is what the spirits want. The difference is that for US Christians, the drawing of attention happens through church, housegroups, Bible reading, and prayer. Among the Wari', it happens through shamans, who admonish children not to play in the river (because the river might house the spirits of dead Wari'), insist on specific behaviors at meals (like eating quickly), explain illness as spirit-related, and so forth. Vilaça writes, "In the diverse curing sessions that I saw during my initial field research, the shamans, usually working in pairs, would make long moralizing discourses to all those present, saying that people could not eat such and such an animal" (2016: 199). When Wari' no longer keep the food taboos, they say, the animal spirits disappear. Vilaça quotes a Wari' man: "The animals' doubles [their supernatural spirits] have vanished. . . . We are completely white" (2016: 243). In short, the Wari' talk as if spirits only become relevant, and may even only become real, when humans call them properly and treat them appropriately.

Even among the Wari', then, there is a sense that someone needs to be in the right frame of mind to enable the spirits to be present. The Wari' talk as if they need to pay attention and to behave as if the spirits are real in order to make them present in their lives. If people don't do that, the spirits disappear.

In fact people often behave as if gods and spirits are real only under certain conditions. That is what the anthropologist Rita Astuti saw when she went to do her fieldwork among the Vezo, a small Malagasy fishing community at the edge of the sea. The Vezo told her that after death, people become ancestors and communicate through dreams: "In dreams, the dead can be seen with their original body form, they can talk and be heard, they can move and be seen, they can touch and be felt" (Astuti 2007: 231). And yet the Vezo also clearly thought that the dead just die. Carrying a corpse, the Vezo laughed at Astuti when she wondered whether the dead woman would be warmer by the fire. Dressing the dead woman, someone remarked that she wouldn't need a bra because although her breasts were large, she "would have no chance to swing them around" where she was going (2007: 234). Everything survived, it seemed, but nothing did.

So what in fact *did* they believe? Astuti worked with Paul Harris to develop two death stories. In one, people were told that Rampy was a hardworking man who'd fallen ill with a fever and had been taken to the hospital; there, although the doctor gave him four injections, he died three days later of malaria. In the other, a man called Rapeto, with many children and grandchildren, died at home among them, and after his death they dreamed about him and built him an ancestral tomb. After hearing one of the two stories, subjects were asked what "still worked"?

They were asked about bodily functions (does his heart still beat? do his eyes work?) and mental ones (does he miss his children? does he know his wife's name?). Regardless of which story they heard, people said that most functions no longer worked, but that more of the mental ones did than the bodily ones. They also said that significantly more functions worked for Rapeto than for Rampy. That is, when people were reminded of their religious ideas, the dead man seemed less like a corpse and more like an ancestor. Astuti and Harris concluded that

> Vezo do not believe in the existence and power of the ancestors in the abstract, but they believe in them when their attention is on tombs that have to be built, on dreams that have to be interpreted, and on illnesses that have to be explained and resolved. In other contexts, death is represented as a total annihilation, and in these contexts it would be misleading to insist that Vezo believe in the existence of ancestral spirits. (2008: 734)

It is a striking claim: in ordinary contexts, reminded of ordinary events, the Vezo do not think and act as if they believe in spirits.

Indeed, the head of Astuti's adoptive family addressed the dead during a major ritual and ended his delivery with a joke: "It's over, and there is *not* going to be a reply!" (Astuti 2007: 241). People laughed, Astuti said, because as the ritual draws to a close, they "shift out of the frame of mind that has sustained the one-way conversation with the dead and they come to recognize the slight absurdity of what they are doing" (2007: 241). This is not a perspective in which religious commitment is a thing in the world, like a sofa in the living room, and either you have it or you don't. From this perspective, faith is an act of paying attention, and it is hard to sustain because in many ways faith flouts facts. *It's over, and there is not going to be a reply*.

In a later essay, Pascal Boyer makes the point in his characteristically clear way: "The world over, people do not (easily) believe in gods and spirits."

> Observing rituals in the flesh, so to speak, one is bound to derive the . . . impression, that beliefs are often an occasional and elusive consequence of ceremonies rather than their foundation. Indeed, if beliefs were as straightforward as Lévi-Strauss (and many others) assume, rituals would be quite strikingly inefficient. As my colleague Denis Vidal once put it,

if it takes a whole night of scripted ritualized behavior and 10,000 verses of opaque speech to cure a common cold, then calling all this "efficacité" seems a bit of a stretch. (2013: 350–51)

What rituals do is to remind people that gods and spirits matter. Rituals describe the gods, talk about the narrative in which the gods are embedded, get people to sing and pray and dance and enter states in which that which must be represented in their imagination (because the gods, of course, are invisible) can sometimes be experienced in the world.

> Initially, spirits may or may not be around. But after the whole night of ritual and the 10,000 verses, to some people at some junctures this conjectural representation becomes more vivid, more accessible, is associated with actual experience, is given some explanatory power—in other words is potentially turned into what we commonly call a belief. (2013: 351–52)

People need rituals because people do not in fact treat their religious beliefs—their conjectures, Boyer calls them—that a helpful god is real the same way they treat their beliefs that trees grow upward and coconuts fall down. They need to be reminded that spirits are present, and they need to act in order to get them to respond. This is particularly true for helpful gods and spirits. The idea that there is an invisible other who takes an active, loving interest in your life is in many ways preposterous and takes effort to maintain, even in a community that has never been secular. It takes intention and attention. It requires a frame of mind in which one remembers and anticipates as if gods and spirits matter.

KINDS OF REALNESS

To be clear, it does seem likely that people in different cultures think about realness in different sorts of ways. The anthropologist Jonathan Mair opens an essay with a wry observation that public debates about religion often seem to consist of people shouting at each other without any sense of what the other party is saying. The New Atheists (Richard Dawkins, Daniel Dennett, Sam Harris, Christopher Hitchens, and so forth) insist that what Christians say and do should be taken as evidence of what they think—and that what they think is simply wrong-headed. The Christians writing back against them (he mentions Karen Armstrong and Mark Vernon) retort that Christianity is not about propositions at all, but rather about truths that are more transcendent, symbolic, and nonliteral. "The result," Mair comments, "is a loud conversation at cross purposes" (2013: 449). That's because, he argues, they think about realness differently. The two sides don't hear each other properly because they live in different "cultures of belief."

In his thoughtful essay *Did the Greeks Believe in Their Myths?* the classicist Paul Veyne remarks that in classical antiquity belief-like assertions were social assertions that interlocutors did not take to refer to the everyday world in the same way that later Europeans would assume that they did. "The Greeks believe and do not believe their myths. They believe in them, but they use them and cease believing at the point where their interest in believing ends" (1988: 84). All humans, he writes, hold contradictory commitments. These different commitments are managed with what he calls different "truth programs": different sets of ideas, practices, and interests that belong together in some social world and are held with a particular attitude. "A Greek put the gods 'in heaven,' but he would have been astounded to see them in the sky. He would have been no less astounded if someone, using time in its literal sense, told him that Hephaestus had just remarried or that Athena had aged a great deal lately" (1988: 18).

I take Philippe Descola's ([2005] 2013) project to be an effort to give more comparative depth and specificity to these observations. He takes as his central pivot the way social worlds distinguish between what is of the human and what is not: culture and nature, which to Descola is the great divide. His point is that the line must be drawn by all people—but that they draw it in different ways. It was the Enlightenment that made nature nonagentic, objective, and thus free of human intention, and changed forever the ontological commitments of the West. Animist worlds imagined human-like intentions throughout the world, so that all objects had agency and were different merely in their appearances. A totemic world understood shared human-like agency only in humans and a limited number of nonhuman animals and objects with which these humans identified. And other worlds made complex mappings by analogy, all different from each other. When the naturalism of the post-

Enlightenment world in effect strips mind from nature, he argues, humans then feel the right to pillage the world around them. These are cultural differences in what is real, in what way, and for whom.

There are, in short, varied ways that people judge the relationship between things of the everyday world and what the faith frame treats as real, even if spirits and everyday things are always differently real. It seems likely that Western culture invites people to make a realness judgment categorically: real or not real. That is Descola's point. The naturalness of the post-Enlightenment world creates a material world that is real and is fundamentally different from the stuff of the mind. Ultimately, G. E. R. Lloyd (2018) remarks, this is our legacy from the Greeks. Other cultures may be more likely to invite people to make that judgment on a continuum: more or less real. And so Western cultures likely worry about realness in a different way than many other peoples. The evidence still suggests that invisible beings are understood as differently real from everyday objects everywhere. It is just that gods and spirits are likely differently real from everyday objects in different places in different ways.

AND THEN THE DEVIL

It also seems likely that it is more difficult to sustain faith in a loving god than in a demonic spirit. That may seem counterintuitive. Belief in a loving god should comfort, while a demon scarcely can. And yet fear may be harder to discount than love, and the love of a god may seem frankly implausible.

In many modern evangelical churches, sin and judgment have almost vanished. These churches usually present themselves as reaching out to the unchurched, and they offer to potential converts a god who never judges, never punishes, and always loves. "From love, with love, and for love" was the way the evangelical prayer group I joined described the way we should experience our relationship with God. So, too, the book that has sold more hardback copies in the United States than any other single text aside from the Bible, *The Purpose Driven Life*: "Because God is love, the most important lesson he wants you to learn on earth is how to love" (Warren 2002: 123). Many people find it hard to take that kind of joyful promise seriously. Warren's book is sold as a workbook, with lessons and practices at the end of every chapter. He assumes that most Christians give lip service to these concepts but find them difficult to believe for themselves.

Meanwhile, the fear of dangerous invisible others is difficult to suppress. As Boyer points out in *Religion Explained*, humans are sharply aware of danger. He argues that what Barrett (2004) later called a hyperactive-agency-detector (the striking human tendency to see agents everywhere) evolved out of the need to avoid predators. Something goes wrong—a crash, a rustle in the bushes, a dark and lonely road—and humans look for an agent that could harm them.

In a conference in Finland in 2016, I heard a panel in which four papers explored spirits in different villages. Jon Mitchell described a Neolithic temple on Malta that had recently become a site for Marian pilgrimage, and Helen Cornish described the visitors to a museum of witchcraft who wanted to feel the uncanny. In both cases, they found people who wanted to feel spirits yet often did not. Two more papers described spirits that no one—including the locals—wanted to believe might be there and yet none of them, including the anthropologists, could entirely discount. Alex Aisher spoke about work with an animist people in northern India, and Callum Pierce described work in a predominantly Tibetan Buddhist village. Both related, with poignant anxiety, just how hard it was to ignore the local mutterings about malignant spirits, even when the locals refused to say that the spirits were real. A capricious spirit who wreaks havoc with one's crops or boats feels more plausible than one who promises a perfect harvest. A judgmental god who punishes might seem more realistic—more in accord with the world as it is—than a god who promises eternal joy. Fear of the unknown and dangerous can be difficult to disavow.

I propose that there is a *continuum of plausibility* for invisible spirits. At one end, there are spiritual worlds dominated by nonomniscient, capricious spirits whom humans fear. At the other end, there are spiritual worlds dominated by loving, monotheistic gods who promise a justice sometimes at odds with the earthly experience of the faithful. They are the "big gods" Ara Norenzayan (2013) describes: omniscient, omnipotent, and just. As one moves along the continuum from the capricious spirits toward the big gods, belief in the invisible others requires more effort to sustain. That may in fact be the reason the big gods have the social effects that Norenzayan describes. These big gods arguably demand more overt signals of commitment that do many smaller gods—everyone has to go to church, fast on certain days, make specific pilgrimages. He argues that as societies adopt omniscient gods, people trust members of the group more readily—and that trust enables the growth of larger social worlds. That creates more overt testimony and, perhaps, more overt signals of trustworthiness. Someone who asserts a belief in Jesus also, in doing so, asserts a belief that wrongdoing will be known and punished.

Not all faiths are represented on this continuum, nor does the continuum presuppose a common way of thinking. Every faith has its own conception of the good life and a distinctive moral end toward which it aims. For each faith, that moral end is framed against a supernatural world of more or less active spiritual beings that are managed in various ways. Thai Buddhists, for example, reject the idea of an overarching god who sees all things, and yet they live in a world teeming with ghosts. They reach for the good life by representing human experience as a life of suffering. Yet across these faiths runs a common thread: that which we fear is more believable than that for which we yearn. The god who will curse you if you do not propitiate him is more difficult to ignore than the god who promises a golden world without end.

THE FAITH FRAME

These observations suggest that those who are religious behave as if they have a faith frame as well as an ordinary set of expectations about an everyday world: a mode of thinking in which gods and spirits really matter, and a mode of thinking about the ordinary world of rocks and dogs and what to buy at the store. I use the word "faith" here, because belief is a promiscuous word. "Belief" refers to any kind of claim, intuitive or deliberative, that there might be an invisible spirit. By "faith" I mean a sustained, intentional, deliberative commitment to the idea that there are invisible beings who are involved in human lives in helpful ways. To operate in the real, everyday world while maintaining the idea that there is an invisible other who takes an active, loving interest in your life, people of faith adopt a mode of thinking and interpreting, a set of expectations and memories, in which gods and spirits matter.

In this way of thinking and interpreting, people hold gods and spirits in their awareness as if those gods and spirits are present and engaged. When they do that, all kind of memories, understandings, expectations, and hopes become salient. They think about what those gods and spirits might want, how they might please those gods and spirits, where those beings might be and what they might be thinking, and so forth. And of course, thinking this way even when feeding the dog, driving to the market, or shrugging on a coat is a goal in many sacred books. In Islam one should be *taqwa*, conscious and cognizant of God, or *muraqabah*, aware that Allah is watching. The Hebrew Bible instructs people to set their mind and seek the Lord (1 Chronicles 22:19); the New Testament, to rejoice always and to pray without ceasing (1 Thessalonians 5:16). Perform every action, says the Bhagavad Gita (2:48), with your heart set on the Supreme Lord. It is a point out of Mary Douglas ([1966] 2002): faith is a shift in attention that reframes.

This, as I have been arguing, can be hard. People can function quite effectively in the world without thinking about gods and spirits, and often they do—even when they are ostensibly religious. It can take effort to wrench their attention toward gods and spirits and away from the demands of making breakfast for the kids and clearing the kitchen sink. In an all-night drumming ceremony, or in a church or temple, it can be easier to turn one's mind to gods and spirits. And once people do pay attention, of course, those gods and spirits can seem *more* real than the messy sink. But rituals do not last forever, and people often talk and act as if they need to cultivate the right way of paying attention to their gods and spirits—because otherwise it can feel as if gods and spirits are not real at all. The everyday expectations are always relevant—the messy sink is there, demanding action—but the faith frame is not always relevant.

The challenge, then, for those who want to be faithful is to think with the faith frame as much as they can, despite how easy it can be to get distracted or discouraged, despite the competition from and contradictions of the everyday. The best comparison for this task is play: an as-if frame in which someone acts according to the expectations of the play frame, while still remaining aware of the realities of the everyday world.

A SERIOUS PLAY

To choose to think with the faith frame is a decision to enter into another mode of thinking about reality that calls on the resources of the imagination to reorganize what is fundamentally real and that exists in tension with the ordinary expectations of everyday reality. This involves a shift in perspective similar to the shift in and out of imaginative play—except that the play claims are also serious claims about the world.

I am not the first to note this relationship between faith and play: many anthropological observers (among them Peter Stromberg, Don Handelman, Jean Briggs, Michael Puett, and indeed my own early work) have seen that the sacred has a play-like quality. The point about play is that it is distinct from nonplay: a "free activity," as the historian Johan Huizinga defined it in *Homo Ludens*, "standing quite consciously outside 'ordinary' life as being 'not serious,' but at the same time absorbing the player intensely and utterly" ([1938] 1971: 13). When dogs play, they crouch to signal the play and then bare their teeth ferociously—but they do not bite. When children play, they too often signal the play—"Let's play!"—and they can then become pirates on the high seas on the living room couch. The anthropologist Gregory Bateson ([1972] 2000) talked about this as a layering of interpretive frames. There is a "play-frame" and a "reality frame," and when we play, we act within the play frame. We bathe the teddy bear in invisible water, and we dry him off with a towel of air, and we are not confused when our hands do not get wet.

Faith is like that in many ways. It is, as Adam Seligman and his colleagues (2008) say about ritual, an as-if, subjunctive mode, superimposed upon the indicative everyday thereness of the messy sink. When people act within a faith frame, they engage an ontological attitude in which they act as if something were true—that there is an invisible person who loves them or judges them or is willing to protect them—and they seek to take it seriously despite their knowledge that this as-if sits uneasily with the world they see and know. They set out to be the people they would be if they truly took seriously the lessons of the Bible or the Qu'ran or the promises of ancestors. And yet they also live within the reality frame of the world as it is. They must pick up the dry-cleaning, organize lunch money, and, in the case of Astuti's Vezo, recognize that the dead are dead and, in the ordinary course of things, there will not be a reply. People of faith live, in effect, on two levels, just as the child washing the teddy bear lives on two levels, attending to two different ways of making sense of the world. They behave (as Van Leeuwen puts it) as if they map the world in two different ways. It is hard because there are a lot of ordinary things to take care of that draw attention away from the faith frame; it is hard because it is difficult to be that person who is always compassionate and responsible. It is not easy to remember that you are protected by a mighty god when you are driving home for dinner and there is an accident on the bridge *again*.

And so the purpose of this book is to explain how this play-like stance, this as-if commitment, this faith frame comes to feel like it is not play but real. Belief in a just, fair, and good world is not some kind of mistake, not a deluded misconception that observers need to explain, but the fundamental point of the faith commitment: belief *despite*. Faith is about being able to keep gods and spirits somehow vital even when the crops rot, the child dies, and the war ends in dust and blood. Faith is about holding certain commitments front and center in one's understanding of reality even when the empirical facts seem to contradict them or just demand attention in different ways. Faith is about having trust that the world is good, safe, and beautiful—a world in which justice is triumphant, enemies are thwarted, and you can thrill at the delicate beauty of the day. It is about seeing the world as it is and experiencing it—to some extent—as it should be. To do that, people need to superimpose their faith frame upon an everyday frame. They can do that more effectively when gods and spirits feel real to them. We now turn to the specific ways that people learn to pay attention so that they kindle that sense of realness, so that the play-like faith frame comes to seem more like the everyday and gods and spirits feel alive.

2

MAKING PARACOSMS

> The surest way to arouse and hold the attention of the reader is
> by being specific, definite, and concrete. The greatest writers—
> Homer, Dante, Shakespeare—are effective largely because they
> deal in particulars and report the details that matter. Their words
> call up pictures.
>
> —William Strunk Jr. and E. B. White, *The Elements of Style*

Gods are supposed to be people-like, but people cannot see them; gods
are supposed to respond, but prayers are often unanswered; gods, at least
big gods, are supposed to be fair arbiters of the universe, but justice in
this world below is sometimes miserably slight. These are emperor's-
new-clothes flaws. What helps to kindle the sense that invisible others
are real? To begin with, one needs a world in which they respond.

ONCE UPON A TIME

To begin with, good religions need good narratives. A good and effective religion—by which I mean a religion that enables its followers to sustain their faith frame, their way of thinking in which an invisible being
is real and relevant to their lives in some positive way—becomes like a
"paracosm" for those of faith. A paracosm is a private-but-shared
imagined world, typically created by children, like the pretend lands of
Angria and Gondal that the Brontë siblings dreamed up together. The
term also describes the world-making that, for example, besotted Tolkien
fans engage in with Middle-earth. When people are able to experience

their faith as vividly as Tolkien fans experience Middle-earth, their gods feel more present to them.

I was one of those Tolkien fans when I was young. I never learned Elvish, but I learned to pick out the songs on a guitar, and I read the books to ragged shreds. I had a formula about what to read when. I'd read the folksy first volume at any time but reserved the high-flown third volume for more special occasions, as if it were sacred. I imagined my way into that long journey hundreds of times, and long before the movies set the Shire in New Zealand, I knew the caves of Moria and the hill at Bag End. When I thought about my life, I did so with the story as its backdrop: a quest, a task, a hardship, an endurance. Only later did I wonder whether it grabbed me so much because I did not have a biblical world to draw upon in the same way.

What enabled Middle-earth to become so vivid for me and for so many others is Tolkien's precise detail: the perilousness of the high platforms in the elven forest of Lothlorien, the smell of the rabbit the hobbits cooked on the outskirts of Mordor in the pot Sam brought from home. The details make it possible for the reader to remake the world as his or her own. It seems paradoxical: that the writer who creates the most complete story enables readers to rework it most deeply. Yet it is true. As readers read and reread, their own history with this enchanted world can become as layered as their memory of middle school. That detailed memory makes what must be imagined seem more real. David Brooks (2012) once attributed the frenzied love so many feel for Bruce Springsteen to Springsteen's capacity to create a paracosm out of his New Jersey childhood, with its ugliness, its biker gangs, and its shopping mall parking lots. "If you build a passionate and highly localized moral landscape," he wrote, "people will come."

God is, indeed, in the details. James Wood (2008) delightfully calls detail the "thisness" of literature, borrowing the concept from the medieval theologian Duns Scotus. "Thisness" is the detail that "centers our attention with its concretion" (2008: 67). It is, he says, what makes the difference between ordinary life and literature. "Literature differs from life in that life is amorphously full of detail, and rarely directs us toward it, whereas literature teaches us to notice—to notice the way my mother, say, often wipes her lips just before kissing me; the drilling sound of a London cab when its diesel engine is flabbily idling; the way old leather jackets have white lines in them like the striations of fat in pieces of meat" (2008: 64). So, too, with religion. If religion is a narrative that shifts attention away from the ordinary, detail is the narrative mechanism that makes this shifting of attention possible.

A paracosm in this sense is a private-but-shared imagined world sufficiently rich in detail that people become engaged in the stories and can return to them again and again, exploring them from different angles, reliving different moments, recasting the scenes as if they were there, even adding new chapters to the story. Many paracosms are created by fiction, and it is the text that people share. When a religion becomes a paracosm, the religious institution provides the narratives, in rituals and sermons and tales told around the campfire. If a follower takes those stories and begins to live within them, they grip the private imagination so powerfully that—I will argue—they kindle the sense that they are true. The faith frame comes to seem salient, and gods and spirits feel more real.

MAKING NARRATIVE REAL

In a remarkable series of arguments, the classicist Sarah Iles Johnston (2015a, b, 2018) sets out to describe the narrative techniques that helped to prepare the Greeks to feel as if their gods were real. Myths, she points out, are stories told again and again, stories whose meanings come to depend on what those who hear them already know about the characters. At festivals to honor the gods, people performed myths and told stories about humans that embedded them within those myths—and yet those myths were not meant to cause the grain to grow or bring success to soldiers. They had no apparent magical efficacy. So why were they told? What purpose did they serve? They made gods real to people.

Johnston argues that in some ways just telling the myths made their content feel more real. She uses the technical term "kennings": phrases whose meaning depends upon the listener's knowledge of the myth. The ancient Greek poets and historians regularly used kennings. Johnston writes that kennings immersed the listener in a mythic world, even if only for a moment. "When Pindar says that a victor won a crown at 'Nisus's hill with its lovely glens,' (i.e., in Megara, which exists in the everyday world, but as belonging to Nisus, who perhaps did not) we perceive that victor, if only for a moment, against the backdrop of the remarkable story of Nisus and his fatal lock of purple hair" (2015b: 189). In doing so, she argues, the poet merged the mythic world with that of the everyday. That was in any event the structure of history as it was at the time: no strict division between the world of humans and the world of gods, no specific moment when the heroes of the past gave way to the ordinary mortals of the present. To talk of gods and humans together implied a relationship, a copresence, a sense of sameness. "A well-narrated Greek myth would leave [the] listeners feeling not that they were *repeating* paradigmatic actions of the gods and heroes . . . but rather that they were *living* amongst the gods and heroes, even if as lesser partners" (2015b: 190).

That is what narrative does, Johnston argues. It enables those who hear or read it to enter in part into a different way of experiencing the world by eliding the narrated world with the ordinary. A reader sees differently at the end of a powerful book. Those who sink into Annie Dillard's *Pilgrim at Tinker Creek* probably notice more movement in the natural world around them. Dillard's prose is full of bugs, birds, clouds, shadows—sycamore roots sucking watery sap, a Polythemus moth cocoon thumping wildly against the walls of a Mason jar ([1974] 2016: 108, 68). At the end of a good novel, when you stir back into the everyday, you feel yourself changed, not because you learned new ideas, but because you felt and thought as if you were there. At the end of a Harry Potter book, you feel what it is like for the wand in your hand to leap with power. When Gatsby says that Daisy was driving the car that killed another man's mistress, you feel the narrator's gasp of horror. It is perhaps the most mysterious and fundamental feature of what it is to be human: that we can respond to another person, real or imagined, as if we suffer their pain.

The new theorists of narrative fiction—Joshua Landy, Blakey Vermeule, Zusanna Sunshine—argue that the cognitive effect of literature is to train audiences in a capacity for what Landy (2012: 76) calls "detached credulity," a capacity for simultaneous belief in and skepticism of, a capacity to hold parallel commitments that he says is at the heart of enchantment and of the change that literature creates for those who engage with it.

The purpose of the Gospels, Landy points out, is not didactic. It is not to impart information about Jesus, the way a railway timetable or an encyclopedia imparts information. The purpose of the Gospels is to train listeners to experience Jesus as if he were there by suspending the awareness that the parables are only metaphors. As he puts it, "The true insider is supposed never to return to earth . . . never to crush the lyricism with paraphrase: he or she is supposed, like the Syrophoenician woman [who answered Jesus's metaphor with another metaphor, and became the only person in the Gospels to change his mind] to operate exclusively on the higher plane, to live among symbols, to glide easily from image to image" (2012: 57).

The success of the narrative, then, lives in making it possible for the listener to be captured by the realness of the metaphor without losing sight of its figurative nature. Good narrative uses a basic human capacity to—as Johnston (2015b: 201) explains—"open the mind and the heart to being transported by well-crafted and well-delivered narrations into a state where figures who are not part of the ordinary world seem real and where one's view of how the cosmos works is altered." It does so because the specificity of detail allows us to imagine the characters as if they were real, even when we know that they are not real, at least in an ordinary way.

There is excellent evidence that even explicitly fictional narratives change the reader's sense of what is true. In 1956, the sociologists Donald Horton and R. Richard Wohl coined the word "parasocial" to capture a remarkable phenomenon they observed as the new device called the television took root in so many homes. They saw that many people created intense relationships with the characters played on television. The watchers knew that the actor was simply playing a part, but they reacted as if the character were real. The same is true of novels. Johnston points out that when readers of Dickens's serialized novel *The Old Curiosity Shop* realized that the character Little Nell was about to die—that Dickens would write her death into the story—many wrote to him in dismay to see if they could make him stop. They obviously knew that the character was invented whole cloth out of the author's head, but they could not bear to lose her. When J. K. Rowling mused aloud before the end of the Harry Potter series about how she understood the impulse to kill off her main character—a character not only obviously created but not even plausibly real—it made international news. Johnston (2015b: 198) says, "We engage parasocially with fictional characters because their creators have made them so convincing that they prompt the same emotional and cognitive reactions in us as real people do."

The same is true of the gods. A relationship with a god or spirit is a parasocial relationship, like relationships with all invisible others. One cannot have an ordinary face-to-face relationship with invisible others; they have no faces. A god is not of course thought to be a fictional character by persons of faith. Nonetheless, the relationship is parasocial because its content occurs largely inside the person's head, using his or her imagination, and what must be imagined about the god emerges from the rich stories in which that god is embedded: the myth-like stories of a serene Hebrew God surveying His creation or (in a more irritable mood) throwing His miscreant humans out of Eden. It is because Christians know the story of Jesus so well that his passion brings tears again and again to their eyes.

Faith traditions also train their followers to experience their gods directly, in effect training them to have more immediate sensory evidence of the invisible other. But before they get there, followers must know their god through the stories about him or her. They must be able to imagine their god as person-like, and they can do that because of the way the god has been described in their sacred books, in their gatherings, and by other followers.

To be sure, the Abrahamic God is often also marked as special and set apart. Jews will not pronounce His name; Muslims will not represent Him. Pre–Vatican II Catholics conducted their most sacred religious rite in a language few present could understand. But those qualities alert those who listen to pay attention, and the space in which those rules hold true is adorned all the more richly. Those features say: this is a being of note.

Narrative details become more effective when organized in particular ways. Johnston (2015b) argues that there are two more specific features of the narrative context that help to explain the way Greek myths enabled the gods to seem more real, despite their apparent absence to the senses. The first is the role of *serialization*. When stories come out in chunks, readers become more engaged. *The Old Curiosity Shop*, *Middlemarch*, the Harry Potter series, and *The Game of Thrones* all came out in installments. Readers came to the end of one installment and knew there was more, and they wanted to discover that more. Would *Downton Abbey*'s Lady Mary marry Matthew Crawley? Millions tuned in for the Christmas special to find out. When Jack Miles wrote *God: A Biography* as an account of the way God learned and changed over time, he outraged some biblical scholars. Yet he captured something deep about the way the Bible is read: as a series of installments in which the story develops over time, and the behavior of the main characters and the events that mold them cannot be predicted from the start. "Greek mythic characters, like Dorothea Brooke, Little Nell, Nicholas Brody, Lady Mary Crawley, and other serialized characters, were served up to their audiences in small doses, a circumstance that (if the narrations were effective) inevitably whetted listeners' appetites to hear more about them and encouraged them to think about those characters—even to develop [rich relationships] with those characters—during the intervals in between" (Johnston 2015b: 206).

The second factor is *plurimediality*. As a story is told again and again, a character will be represented in different ways. The God of the Hebrew Bible is beneficent as a creator, irate in the garden, commanding in the desert, and voluptuously seductive in the Song of Songs. The God of Islam has ninety-nine different names. The repeated exposures not only remind their listeners of the existence of the character but also force listeners to develop their own representations. "When experiencing plurimedial characters, each of us must repeatedly choose, even if unconsciously, to engage more deeply with some instantiations than with others, and each of us therefore ends up creating our own composite character, no two of which are likely to be exactly the same" (Johnston 2015b: 207). That personalization affects us by making us more responsive to the story. We have more sense of ownership, more responsibility, a more vivid memory of the cognitive and emotional resources we have invested. When, after reading Virginia Woolf's *Mrs. Dalloway* in college, I reread the book again much later on a long summer's afternoon, I reworked Clarissa Dalloway not only with a more developed sense of who she was, how she lived, and what she thought, but also with my own changed sense of who I was as an adult who had made irrevocable choices—and her regrets felt more poignant.

This leads us to an important point. For the faith frame to become a paracosm, it must be not only detailed but *personally* vivid. People must not only read the Bible but also have their own private representations, their own inner landscapes. I remember an evening during my fieldwork with evangelical Christians in a Bible study group working its way through Judges, an obscure and tedious book. People read a passage about the Israelites fighting with the Midianites and talked about it as if it were something that had happened to them that afternoon at work with a colleague. That is what a paracosm is: a personal imaginative world, private, precise, and intimate.

I can hear the protesters now: no faith is personal, they say. Faith— as Durkheim observed—is our most powerful representation of our social world. There are no private language games. But Durkheim's deepest insight was that faith was *made* private: that religion transforms our inner world until even the way we perceive time and space has been altered. Faith may be the socialization of inner experience, but the faithful each still have their own private, inner worlds. That is the paradox of the paracosm: the more richly detailed the shared imaginative landscape, the more vividly individuals can rework it as their own. A kindled god is both deeply communal and utterly individual.

SETTING FAITH APART FROM FICTION

There are other basic features beyond good narratives that a faith must provide to enable the faith frame to become a paracosm. There must be *rules of engagement*: principles and practices that determine how a paracosm is constructed so that it can be shared; domains of knowledge and codes of behavior that determine who can enter this community and under what conditions. There must be known *signs of participation*: strategies for entering the paracosm and signaling to others that one is there, often via ways of insisting that the invisible other is felt to be real. There must also be *means of interaction* with that invisible other, the god, ways of knowing when the beings in the paracosm are responding and speaking back. The interaction with the invisible other is one of the central features that sets the special world of faith apart from fiction. No one expects Aragorn or Dumbledore to answer them. But people expect gods to respond. Gods act, and gods effect.

That is what makes them gods and not just pretend play. The paracosm must specify how they do so.

In spelling this out more precisely, I draw on my own wanderings in the religious landscape. I have now studied many faiths. I wrote my doctoral dissertation on middle-class people in London who called themselves witches, magicians, pagans, druids, and initiates of the Western mysteries—people often reared on Tolkien and Alan Garner and the stories of the Greek gods, who set out to make those stories spring to life for them. I spent years with charismatic evangelical Christians who sought an intimate and immediate relationship with a mighty God. Between those periods, as an apprenticeship in the study of American religion, my colleague Richard Madsen and I spent many, many hours with traditions that might be called the growing points of American religion: an evangelical church that grew out of the famous cradle of post-1960s charismatic Christian spirituality; a Catholic church explicitly founded as a Black Catholic church whose parish had become Hispanic; a shul for newly orthodox Jews who set out to reach pork-eating Jews and bring them back into the fold; an Anglo-Cuban Santeria group with middle-class whites who wanted something more visceral than the to-them dull traditions in which they were raised. As diverse as these faiths are, all of them have the features described here that enable their followers to construct, enter, and interact with their paracosms.

RULES OF ENGAGEMENT

We recognize rules of engagement often in the breach, in novelistic mishaps and poorly plotted scenes. A reader enters the world of a good novel and absorbs its assumptions without being distracted by whether they make sense. We simply accept the information that Hilary Mantel's Thomas Cromwell loved the modest Jane Seymour before the king did. It fits our knowledge that his king will betray him and what we have learned about Cromwell's basic decency. Of course he prefers her to the brash, unhappy Jane Rochford, wife to Anne Boleyn's brother George. We accept the ridiculous plots twists in P. G. Wodehouse's creations because ridiculousness is inherent to his plots. In a world where Bertie

Wooster exists, it seems perfectly reasonable that an adult man, scion of a noble house, should protect a silver cow creamer with an armed guard. But I remember reading Frances Hodgson Burnett's *The Secret Garden* and stopping at the scene at which an obliging robin pulls a lost key out of the ground to give it to a lonely girl. No, I thought. Robins don't do that, and anyway the key has been lost too many years for some bird to find it on a path. And for a while, at least, my skepticism broke the story's thread.

What do I mean by "rules of engagement"? First, I mean that there are special knowledge domains for these special worlds. A would-be modern warlock learns that he must develop competence with astrology, tarot cards, and books about the gods in the old European pantheons. A would-be Christian learns that she must read the Bible and know its stories. Second, I mean that there are special behaviors demanded of participants. We call them rituals. People who enter Santeria must learn how to summon gods and how to behave when the gods arrive. Those who become observant Jews must learn how to hold Shabbos, keep kosher, and maintain family purity. Rules of engagement spell out what a participant in the paracosm should know and do.

A good way to see these rules—the special knowledge, the special ritual behaviors—are in the books people write to introduce newcomers to their faith practices. The different faiths I have studied were quite distinct, but in every one there were books. My participants had books spilling out from shelves and piled up on the floor. They had books in piles and books on tables. Those books told them about their faith. They told them about their god or gods and how to understand them, what to pray, how to pray, how to worship them, and what to experience when they did. (There are, of course, faiths without books. They too have rules of engagement, as a cursory examination of any ethnography on shamanism will confirm.)

I no longer remember how I came across my first start-from-scratch book on magic, *Mastering Witchcraft: A Practical Guide for Witches, Warlocks, and Covens* by Paul Huson. It seemed so extraordinary to me that there was such a guide published by Putnam's in 1970. But so it was. The book has a set of remarkably concrete suggestions, ranging from the way to draw a magical circle to recipes for love magic to instructions for making images that defend one from attack. There is a list of initial supplies ("Charcoal blocks for the thurible. Preferably self-igniting, but the regular kind will do ... be sure to get them unperfumed, though" [Huson 1970: 59]). There are lists of herbs, runes and their meanings, basic working tools, spells, and invocations. ("On a Friday morn (8 a.m.) when the moon is waxing, dig the earth out of the footprint of the one you would have as a lover, and ..." [1970: 102–3]). There are introductions to astrology, tarot cards, rune lore, and the names and behaviors of the gods. In many ways, this enumeration of specific words and actions, charts and lists, is reminiscent of medieval grimoires. In other ways, *Mastering Witchcraft* includes more: the kinds of overarching frame-setting that the *Key of Solomon* does not. "The ability to indulge in a flight of fancy is of paramount importance to a witch, for it is through this dark glass that she in fact will cast her spells and set the world afire with her incantations" (1970: 22).

Special ritual behaviors are at their most explicit in Judaism, particularly in a form that has grown in recent years: baal teshuvah Judaism, the faith for the newly observant. Orthodox Judaism bristles with rules. The Torah, the holy text, is understood to contain 613 mitzvoth—commandments or blessings—that are God's instructions for the way a Jew should live. (These have been embellished and interpreted through many layers of Rabbinic discourse.) The purpose of the mitzvoth seems, at least on the surface, clear: obey, and you shall be blessed; disobey, and God will destroy you. An "observant Jew" is one who observes these mitzvoth, or at least attempts to observe them. (Some have been impossible to observe for years, since the destruction of the Second Temple.) Observance is understood to be a continuum. At one end, there is the devout Jew epitomized by the Hasidic Brooklyner, with his payot (side-locks) and his black hat, black coat, and white shirt—traditional dress of eighteenth-century Poland. This Jew lives in a community of his own kind, prays three times a day in a synagogue, keeps all the many holidays (not only Rosh Hashanah and Yom Kippur but also Sukkot, Simchat Torah, Purim, Shavuot, and Tish'a be-Av), and does not touch adult women other than his wife. He will not eat in a nonkosher restaurant, or in a nonkosher home. To pray, he wraps long black leather thongs around his right arm. The thongs come from a small leather box holding parchment inscriptions of the Torah. He must also place a similar box upon his head. These boxes and their thongs are known as tefillin.

He must wear at all times a fringed undergarment (tzitzit) and, when he prays, a prayer shawl (a tallit). He believes that having children is commanded by God, and he cherishes his family.

On the other side of the continuum is the pork-and-lobster-eating secular Jew, perhaps intermarried, perhaps childless, uninterested in the faith of his birth. A baal teshuvah shul hopes to take people from one end of the spectrum as far as they can go toward another. This is the dominant narrative, the basic story to which a new member of the congregation commits himself. Who is a Jew? A real Jew—a faithful Jew—is a person who follows God's mitzvoth more than he did the year before. These are the rules of engagement in the faith: the rituals that make one a Jew.

The baal teshuvah congregation I came to know in the late 1990s and in which I participated for about a year began in 1990, after a local couple, then in their late thirties, took a trip to Europe and realized that while they were Jewish, they knew almost nothing of what it meant to be Jewish. It is a not uncommon American dilemma. Many Jews in the generation that had known the Holocaust became less religious, drawn away from their faith by the twin pressures of their own disappointment in God and their desire to assimilate into a country skeptical of Judaism in the first place. Their children grew up with little awareness of their own faith traditions. The couple who founded the shul came back from Europe with a sense that they wanted the "real thing"—not the watered-down practices of a Reform congregation, nor even of a conservative one, but the faith of their grandparents. They wanted to pray the way their ancestors had prayed: as they had prayed, people told me, for generations without number.

Through an organization, the couple located a young orthodox rabbi. He began holding services for a handful of families in rented rooms. He was a compelling presence: a man of substance, both physically and intellectually, with intensity and directness. He ran his shul along orthodox lines. Men and women sat apart, the men up front and the women behind and raised above them, separated by a curtain (the *mechitza*). The women could see the rabbi, but the men could not see the women. Services were held entirely in Hebrew, except for the rabbi's commentary (his *derashah*) on the Torah portion of the week (the *parashah*) and announcements. The men swayed back and forth as they prayed, huddled together because the room became crowded, wearing skullcaps (*kippot*) and prayer shawls. The prayer books were dog-eared from use. The services were long. The Saturday morning service began at nine and ended well after noon. At the time that I visited the shul, there were nearly 250 families, and they were looking for a larger space.

The rabbi never threw anyone out. Most of the women would come to shul dressed appropriately for orthodox women, with skirts falling below their knees and shirtsleeves past their elbows. But few of the married women covered their heads with hats or scarves, and very few wore wigs, as the fully observant would do. Some came to the classes in leggings and T-shirts. Some of the men were dragged to services by determined women. I knew one man who read archaeological histories about Israel while the men about him prayed. "The rabbi," another young man told me, "works best when people aren't that religious. It gives him something to do. It makes him really happy when he has an impact."

The rabbi's job was to inspire these newcomers to become more observant, without driving them away. And so he taught. There was a morning Talmud class for men after the day's first prayer. There was a woman's class during the day on Tuesday, so that mothers who needed to be home with their children in the evening could nonetheless do some learning. There were other Talmud classes, and a Thursday evening discussion of the weekly Torah portion, and a Wednesday class on prophets. Monday evening was the ethics class, the "beginners' class," where the group read a text from the Mishnah called Pirkei Avot, the Wisdom of the Fathers, at a pace of about one paragraph each week. Much was taught in all these classes. There was, of course, teaching about the texts themselves. There were also historical stories, religious explanations, and accounts of the mitzvoth themselves: what an observant person is meant to do and say, and even think and feel. The central lesson, however, was that to be a Jew was to strive for full ritual observance, a goal many thought no one could reach.

What did these mitzvoth demand? For most people, the first step in becoming more observant was keeping the sabbath. To "keep Shabbos" meant above all not to work from Friday sundown to Saturday sundown—a broad definition that included not driving, not touching money, not turning on electricity, and not cooking. Instead, one was meant to spend that time with others of the religion. Some members of the congregation had "Shabbos homes," small apartments within walking distance to the shul to which they would move on Friday afternoon. Others would stay with friends within walking distance. Many drove: the local real estate was just too expensive for most to live locally. They did all try to eat within walking distance on Friday evening and Saturday. At the weekend there would be groups of congregants walking up and down the hills around the shul—down for services, up for meals. Everyone was supposed to have a place to go. "Do you have a place for lunch?" was one of the first questions I was asked.

The burden of the sabbath fell upon the women because they were in charge of the kitchen. And because the rules of kosher were intimidating, baalei teshuvah usually began to keep the sabbath first before they convinced themselves to keep kosher. In families where the husband was more committed to the return to observance than the wife, the tension could be severe. One woman recalled,

> It's very expensive. It cost about a thousand dollars. We had to buy lots of things. It was really hard. Still, I decided to see if we could make the house kosher while Jonathan was in Israel picking up Gabriel and traveling with him. For many years Jonathan had said, "I'd wish you'd make a kosher kitchen," and I would say, first of all, all the major work would be on me. And I'm not going to do it unless I can do it really right.

One of the main concepts in kashruth, or kosher, is separating meat from dairy. As Rabbinic tradition has interpreted Leviticus, this means that meat and dairy cannot be consumed together in the same meal (Exodus 23:19: "You shall not boil a young goat in its mother's milk"). Meat and dairy cannot share the same plates. A kosher home, then, must have two sets of plates, and perhaps two more for Passover. Those plates may not be washed at the same time in the same dishwasher, and they must not be heaped together in the same dirty sink. There must be two sets of cutlery and two sets of implements. A container that held leftover meatballs may not the next day hold cottage cheese. Something which is pareve, neither meat nor dairy, takes on those qualities when eaten with meat or dairy, so the tuna fish your child eats tonight with a glass of chocolate milk cannot become your lunch tomorrow with that leftover turkey wrap. Many who keep kosher have two kitchen counters, two refrigerators, two large cabinets for the different dishes, two dishwashers. Meanwhile, most food must have rabbinic oversight and is sometimes purchased in special shops.

To keep kosher fully meant that one could not eat with anyone other than congregants. Most people compromised, eating only vegetarian food in restaurants, using paper plates in the houses of non-Jewish friends. Keeping kosher seemed to be a dance: now more observant, now less, struggling to find what "felt right" without going mad. But there were social consequences. On Shabbos, the more observant would not eat in the houses of the less observant. Only the most observant could invite anyone from the congregation to join them. Here the woman speaks again:

> I could make a kosher kitchen and still eat out—but then I couldn't have anyone from the community in our house. The standard that we follow here, because it's such a diverse community [in terms of observance], is that the only people who are considered strictly kosher are people who are "shomer-shabbas" and who don't eat out—who don't eat vegetarian in a restaurant or in someone's [nonkosher] house. You have to make that really strict commitment in order to open your home to other people.

The "shomer-shabbas" become literally holier than thou.

The next step, after keeping kosher, was family purity. In an orthodox household, a woman becomes impure during her menses. Her husband may not touch her, or she him; she is not even supposed to hand him something directly. Nor is she supposed to sleep in the same bed at night. Even after the end of her period, she must wait seven days before the prohibitions end. Then, to make herself pure for her husband, she must immerse herself in the mikveh, a ritual bath, constructed to blend still and flowing waters as the ancient laws dictate. This too was a domain of conflict between spouses, although the woman seemed more likely to agitate for observance than the man. I heard less about the challenges of family purity than about the challenges of keeping kosher. The commandments seemed to tug at people in different ways. But certainly they tugged.

In tugging, they built a remarkable sense of community. To come to keeping kosher as a newcomer, without a mother who had done these things; to learn how to make dinner for ten two days ahead and serve it warm without cooking anything on the day—that takes, as they say, a village. To keep Shabbos demands that neither child nor adult touch a screen for an entire day and night, and that people spend hours with other members of the community.

The rules also turned everyday life into a technical crossword puzzle. No one knew them all. Everyone thought that there were other people with a better grasp. Typically, the rabbi printed the meaning and rules of the many festivals in the monthly bulletin. But people wanted more information. They wanted to know whether you could use hand cream on a particular day when the congregation was supposed to be mourning the loss of the First and Second Temples and no cosmetics were allowed. They knew that you were supposed to eat an egg with ash, but they wanted to know where to get the ash. In a discussion once about how to prepare for this festival, a young teacher explained that over the nine days there would be no music, no laundry, no new clothes, no perfume, indeed no hand cream for appearances, and an uncomfortable sleep on the night of the fast. (Her husband, she said, slept on the floor.) We talked about what you could eat and how to prepare it; a few days later, the teacher came up to me in embarrassment, said she'd told me the wrong thing about one of the meals, and corrected herself. The rabbi, meanwhile, gave a class in which he said that hesitation and unclarity had caused the destruction of the Temple.

But of course, it is not about the rules at all. When I asked the rabbi for a book to read, he directed me to Benjamin Blech's *Understanding Judaism* (1992)—a heavy text with a dull, dry, plain cover, like a university press monograph on early Armenian inscriptions, the truth as we know it. To be a good Jew, Blech explains, is to observe the Torah, and to observe it the way God gave it to Moses. You observe the mitzvoth, each and every one, because God gave them to you as an obligation. You cannot pick and choose. Blech cajoles, he explains, he insists that the mitzvoth are required. Then he says that they don't really need to be followed. He shares a parable from the Talmud: a pious fool is a man standing at the seashore who will not interrupt his service to help a drowning man.

These rules of engagement are the rituals that make one a Jew. They are what you do to belong. And because their primary purpose is to identify who can participate, in a sense the rituals don't matter at all. What matters is that there are shared understandings of what "people like us" do. Each person's decision about what to follow—and, to be frank, the evident fun and frustration I saw in the way people really did fret about where they'd find the ash to go with the egg—becomes his or her way of reimagining the world of his or her ancestors, deciding how to remake it personally, and constructing a paracosm that can be shared.

SIGNS OF PARTICIPATION

Once the special world is constructed, the person of faith must know not only that he or she is present within it, but that the invisible other is there too. There must be ways of talking and acting that assert that the invisible other is present. Such "signs of participation" include the ways people use words in a religious setting to assert that humans and spirits participate in a shared relationship.

Albert Lord ([1960] 2019) famously distinguished "formula" and "theme" as building blocks for the great stories told by singers of tales, the Homeric bards among them. Such singers, he found (building on arguments that his supervisor Milman Parry made but never published, because he died in mysterious circumstances at the age of thirty-three), did not memorize and precisely reproduce the thousands of lines of text found in the great epics. Instead, they composed anew each time in what Lord called the "oral-formulaic" tradition. They became familiar with large and small plots that could be elided or elaborated as the occasion demanded, and they learned to use common phrases associated with the tale. "Rosy-fingered dawn" is a formula, a phrase often evoked to describe the Iliadic morning; the tragedy of Achilles and the deception of the Trojan Horse are themes.

As people enter the life of the faith, they often adopt some version of these devices, these formulas and themes. There are specific phrases that assert their personal relationship with invisible others, and specific plot lines that they learn to adopt as their own model of how that relationship might go.

Horizon Christian Fellowship in southern California has the no-frills, ordinary-folks approach characteristic of the "new paradigm" Christian churches (Miller 1997), but it is as rife with formulas and themes as any Homeric epic. Like other such churches, Horizon has a rock band on Sunday morning, not a choir; the pastors have an informal, anti-intellectual style; many congregants meet in small home Bible fellowships during the week; they hold their large worship meetings in a gym; and they call themselves "Bible-based," by which they mean that the written Bible is literally true and the only decisive authority. They are also entrepreneurial, well organized, and extremely effective.

Horizon is an offshoot of perhaps the prototypical new paradigm church, Calvary Chapel, which began to grow in the mid-1960s by reaching out to the countercultural Jesus movement on southern California beaches, and now has well over a thousand "seeded" churches around the country. By the turn of the millennium, Horizon served about five thousand mostly white congregants at its main church campus. It had seven offshoot associated churches in San Diego and claimed eighty offshoots around the world. It ran a preschool, an elementary school, a junior high, a high school, a school of evangelism with a master's program in divinity and pastoral studies, outreach evangelism in this country and abroad, youth programs, summer camps, and constant concerts, "getaways," and social events. The specific and much-reiterated goal of this busy institution is to lead each worshipper to have a personal relationship with Jesus.

At Horizon, certain phrases reverberate through the manuals and other books, the church services, and the transcripts of our interviews. As newcomers became members of the community, these phrases became part of their speech patterns. New believers acquire what Harding (2000: 19) calls a "shared elementary language" of faith. These are words or phrases to describe their new life in Christ, themes that structure the logic of their new understanding, and a common plotline that describes the way they decided to join this way of life.

The most important phrase was "to walk with God." Sometimes a noun—"my walk"—and sometimes a verb—"to walk"—this phrase describes the daily experience of living your life as this kind of Christian at the side of God. "To walk with God" includes both learning to develop a relationship with God and managing the everyday challenges to faith: temptation, frustration, and disappointment. One woman—young, blond, the perfect Beach Boys girl—said about her housegroup: "It's really just interacting with them so that they can get to a different level of their walk with God." To "walk with God" describes the way one is with God. "Walking with God" also implies presence. A tall, slender man related, "To me, well, now that I am walking with the Lord, I know that, like, I feel that God talks to me all day long. . . . I just think God's with me all the time."

Another common phrase is the "word of God." The phrase denotes the written scriptures, but it connotes the loving, personal, and unique relationship congregants believe God has with each individual Christian through the text. The tall man said, "I went [to church] for several weeks in a row, and I heard the Bible and it was addressing me and speaking to me personally. . . . I was realizing that it is a love story, and it's written to me." This is a remarkable claim: that a book compiled near two millennia ago was at the same time written for each of us alone. "The Bible says," the man continued, "that the word of God is actually written on the tablets of your heart." What he meant, in short, is that he was not just reading a book—he was being present with God.

Then there are themes that organize the way that Christian life is understood and experienced in a place like Horizon. The best way to grasp these themes is through the sermons, such as this one captured in my notes from the service one morning in May.

Someone, somewhere, has to start a revolution. The people of this government, they've been to Harvard and Yale, they just passed a law saying that pornography can be shown on television at any time, because it's protected by the freedom of speech. But that's not what free speech is about. We all know that free speech is about having the freedom to criticize the government, not to allow rubbish on television. . . . Remember that we are the children of God. You ladies [and here the room got very silent], you are the daughters of God. . . . Lift your head out of the gutter. You are noble. . . . [When] you realize this, and you say to God, I'm here in a place full of body odor and bodies, a fleshly material place, and can You please help me, He will help you. Even when you want to pray so badly and you can't really get it out, it's okay because there's a spirit inside of you helping it to come out. And if you are praying and being with Jesus, the devil won't distract you. He'll say, she's got the helmet of righteousness on. She can't be reached. And he'll move on. Because his time is short. Short. And your time is infinite. So don't numb your feeling, don't dull yourself with alcohol and drugs. Feel good. Reach out. Start living. Smell every flower. Live like that, live with God. Be alive. He loves you.

In a sermon like this, the pastor is teaching how one should think about how to live in the world as a Christian: what it is to be a person (you need to be responsible; you are noble, a child of the mighty Lord); what the world is like (full of rubbish, full of people who have been to Harvard and Yale but can't see what's morally obvious, a place of bodies and odors); who God is (He's responsible, He's pure, He loves you); and why a Christian person needs God (to keep you pure, to give you armor for protection from the devil, to help you be fully alive). Interwoven with these general spiritual themes are some remarkably concrete politics. Also worth noting: a good Christian might "want to pray so badly and . . . can't really get it out." These Christians expect that prayer does not come easily and naturally. It is a skill that must be learned, as a relationship to God must also be learned. That is part of the logic of faith. The point is that they are features of a life lived with God.

While congregants learn specific phrases to depict their new religiosity and thematic plots to describe God's human world, they also learn a specific personal narrative—the conversion story—to depict their own entry into committed relationship with God. This narrative form stands out from other kinds of narratives like the sermon above. It is both more personal and more stereotyped.

This combination of the very personal and the stereotyped is hardly unique to evangelical Christians. Those who become shamans, for example, know the expectations of those chosen to be shamans: among the Bororo, for instance, the shaman-to-be must see a stump or anthill or stone move suddenly in the forest, must catch a game animal like a wild turkey, must dream of attempted seduction, and so forth. Yet those who become shamans experience these stereotyped events with great personal intensity. An anthropologist who worked with them remarks, "Their details and sequences are standardized almost to the point of collective representations, known by most adult non-shamans. Yet the shamans I knew best spoke of them with vivid sincerity, adding variations and personal reactions at once idiosyncratic and consistent with the general pattern" (Crocker 1985: 206). The same is true of conversion stories in Christian communities.

At Horizon, the standard conversion story people told was that they knew God, or knew about God, in an abstract way or as children. Then they took a wild ride through drugs, sex, alcohol, and depravity until they hit bottom, at which point they realized that their life was empty, unsatisfying, and unfulfilled. When they accepted Christ as real (often as a result of coming to a Bible-believing church on a whim), they were filled with love, acceptance, and forgiveness. A male congregant, who worked in construction for Horizon, told us that he grew up in a house without religion, although he knew the commandments and that "there was someone I was accountable to, and that was God." By the time he was thirteen, he realized that "it all amounted to emptiness." The sense of emptiness, he said, "really hit when I was thirty-eight." He tried drugs, then what he called "Buddhism, existentialism, one romance after another," but never apparently a Christian church. "I had tried everything and, because of drugs, lost everything. I lost my business, lost my place, lost my hope. Absolutely rock bottom." Homeless, he moved in with friends, and someone invited him to Horizon. When he went, he said, "I just knew it. Without a doubt." The great majority of those we interviewed formally gave some version of this story of self-destruction, despair, and redemption.

Should we trust these stories? If accurate, they are an alarming glimpse into the American (or at least, Californian) life. It is possible that some congregants at Horizon learn to stretch their little sins until they become an abyss of wickedness, the way Augustine took his theft of three pears as a paradigm of sin. It is also possible that a church like Horizon offers the structure to enable an addict to abandon his addiction, just as the fast-growing Pentecostal church offers women a tool with which to detach their men from drink. In any event, the message of the narrative is clear: I was lost, so deeply lost, so lost that no one could love me—and then God did, and I knew Him to be God, and He was with me, and everything changed.

At a Catholic church called Christ the King, the signs of participation were different. Christ the King presented itself as a Black Catholic church. Its mission statement, written many years ago and now posted on its website, declares, "We place special emphasis on Black Culture." It was founded in a poor African American part of San Diego, but by the 1990s many of the African American residents had moved out and the neighborhood had become increasingly Hispanic. By then, the church was running two quite different services: a Spanish-language service for those who lived locally, and an English-language service for African Americans who drove in from the suburbs as far as ten miles away to be in a service that celebrated African Americans, along with the middle-class whites who wanted an integrated worship service and a gospel choir. I remember sermons about giving back, and about how fast food was not good food and fast faith was the same. And I remember a service about a drive-by shooting in an African American neighborhood, and the pain and remorse and defeated sense of struggle over what to do.

When people narrated their faith at Christ the King, they did not talk about learning to walk and talk with God. They spoke about moments in which the truth of the tradition came to life in the world around them. Here an older congregant describes such a moment:

> I'd gotten up very early in the morning, before it was light, and I went up on this mountain. I had my food with me and I just sat on this rock. All of a sudden, the fog from the valley came in and completely surrounded and swirled around everything. As it started to fade out, the enormous boulder in front of me became an enormous lamb looking back at me. It came through my mind without thinking: the lamb of God, who takes away the sins of the world. It was as if the mass were being played out in my mind.

The people of Christ the King did not talk of God becoming real by their side, as did the people at Horizon. They spoke about the story itself becoming more alive for them. "When we enter the mass," the man continued, "we are reentering into that moment with the original bread and wine: we are reinstating it." Rather than God entering their story, they entered God's. "As we go along with it and identify with it, like any good play, *you* become the drama."

So while the narrative focus of the evangelical church circled around the single individual's moment of choosing God, the narrative focus in Christ the King circled around recognizing God in the human community. Here is a woman who had been with the church for many years: "Christ the King is a real anointed community. I've seen the Spirit move and I've seen the Spirit change people and I know how it has changed me." The core members of the church spent a lot of time together— "sometimes we have thirty-five to forty people here for breakfast"—and they opened their houses to each other. There were a lot of adopted kids—

"at least sixty percent of the church has at least one adopted kid," some-one claimed—and many seemed to have friends and relatives and down-on-their-luck, lost souls who would stay with them for months at a time. "My daughter had a little friend who had just had an argument with her father and her stepmother and they kicked her out and she had no place to go. She ended up staying with me for about six months." People spoke of this practice as part of African American culture, but they also took it to be part of the culture of the church: a faith commitment to welcome, accept, and make better: "We just want to get together."

This was a more political church than Horizon. To be clear, the ser-mons at Horizon were far more directly political than those at Christ the King: my notes wryly comment that at Horizon God seemed to be not only staunchly Republican but a member of the National Rifle As-sociation. But in interviews, it was the Christ the King congregants who spoke about their political action. When a young man lost his life in gang crossfire, these congregants held meetings in the neighborhood and went door to door to talk to people. They volunteered in soup kitchens and worked with the homeless. They made girls into "altar boys" and wel-comed a man who rolled up in a painted van and spoke, during Prayers for the People that November, of the turkeys who would give their lives for us. They insisted that parishioners, and not the priests, ran the parish. They fought with the bishop about sexuality and even about abortion. "I just disregard [Rome's] leadership," one man explained with a grin. They chastised the leadership assemblies for their whiteness. As a woman recalled, "I told [a gathering of priests] that I understood that they were among the finest minds in the world and I knew if they wanted to, they could put together a program to recruit African American males to the Jesuit community."

They described themselves as anticlerical and as rebellious. Person after person laid out a vision of social justice activism worthy of the great Dorothy Day. They reveled in the diversity of the church, in its ethnic, racial, and class differences, and they took their relationships across these traditional social divisions as what it was to be a person of faith. "How is God related to that sense of connection?" I asked one woman after she spoke excitedly about her personal connection to others in the congre-gation. "That *is* my experience of God. That *is* when I experience God. God is not there and I am here." When we turned the recorder off, she stopped to think. "I've been trying to figure out God for twenty years, and I finally said, 'Let me just *do* God.'"

If the rules of engagement, the rituals of belonging, are ways of recognizing the boundaries of the special world, the signs of participation are ways of recognizing that God is present with the human in the world. One is not only stepping into a sacred space—a kosher home, for instance, with all its requirements—but one must be able to know that the sacred spirit is present. That is the point, for the evangelicals, of the new language about walking with God, or of telling your conversion story. These stories demonstrate that God showed up. That is the point of Christ the King congregants who discover God in the community. Those stories say that God is there by one's side. The paracosm depends on defining which humans have chosen to enter in. The paracosm also depends on the signs that show that gods and spirits will participate and be there too.

MEANS OF INTERACTION

Finally, for the paracosm to be a faith, the invisible other must respond. That is what makes the faith experience different from fiction for those of faith. They know that they are not just pretending when the main character of the story begins to talk back in some way. In all these faith settings, people engage in quasi-fictional narratives in which the invisible other is not only described but also experienced as interacting.

At Christ the King, some of the women would pray together by phone every morning at 6 a.m. For thirty minutes, they spoke in turn to God, asking Him to intervene in particular ways, narrating their own lives as evidence that God had intervened in them. At the shul during one Passover, a young man, frustrated by the early stages of his career, went out for pepperoni pizza. Meat and milk are never eaten at the same meal and certainly never on the same foodstuff. But the young man was mad at God, and he wanted to make sure that God knew it. So he went out for pizza in the holy week to thumb his nose at the creator of the universe, on the principle that if you provoke Him, He will come. And while I really began to pay attention to the way people learned to recognize God responding when a young woman at Horizon told me that she had coffee with Him regularly, it was only after I'd moved to Chicago and started to go to services at the Vineyard that I began to map out how it worked.

The Vineyard Christian Fellowship, much like Horizon, is another example of the new Protestant churches that grew up after the 1960s. These churches wanted people to experience God as concretely and as vividly as the earliest Christian disciples experienced Jesus. They set out to teach them how.

At the Vineyard, God was understood to speak back in several ways. To begin with, he spoke through the Bible. When congregants remembered scripture or felt powerfully moved or affected by a particular passage as they read, they might infer that God spoke to them through that passage: that He led them to it in order to have them read it and respond to it. As one young woman explained,

> The Holy Spirit will bring [a verse] back to your mind. I'll just like remember a verse, I really think that's the Holy Spirit saying, out of all the stuff you've read, this is what you need to know right now.

God was also understood to speak through people and circumstances. Congregants would describe events that might seem to be coincidences, but they would say that God was speaking to them through these circumstances in order to communicate something to them: that He loved them or wanted them to make this decision or that one. Another young woman, headed abroad, remembered,

> I needed to get some ID pictures. . . . One afternoon I just felt like God said, you need to get up and go get those. . . . I was like, that's totally inefficient. . . . But I felt it was a step of faith to do this thing. So I did it— grumbling. Then on the way there and back I ran into three people I knew, and I felt that there was a kind of pattern, and that I was in the right place at the right time.

This interaction model is found in many conservative Christian churches. It is a model of interaction through which congregants learn to interpret their everyday lives in accordance with a sense that God is "leading" them.

Congregants at the Vineyard church also expected God to speak back to them by placing mental images or thoughts (sometimes called "impressions") in their minds or by making their body feel a certain way. Here an older woman recounts how she first began to recognize this:

Back when I first started praying, I didn't realize that this is how God would start showing me things and speaking to me. I would just get so into the Word, and these images would come to my mind.

One day I was putting my pants on [she laughed here] and somebody came to mind. I was like, "Lord, please be with the person." Then I was like, I'm putting my pants on and praying for someone! But that was just when I was inspired to pray for them.

Congregants expected to experience mental events that they identified as not being their own, but rather as having been generated by an external presence, God. This intensely participatory sense of God acting in one's mind is not found in all conservative Christian churches. It was also more difficult for some congregants to experience themselves as hearing God in this way. But people wanted to experience God like this. It was such a clear way for God to speak back.

There were semi-explicit and socially shared expectations within the Vineyard community about what kind of mental events could be recognized as God's response. When I asked congregants how they distinguished the thoughts and images that came from God from those that were their own, they usually listed common "tests": that the thought or image was different from what they had just been thinking about; that the thought or image was in keeping with God's character; that the interpretation "this is God" could be confirmed in some other way; and that the experience brought peace. Here is an example from someone who explained that he decided to move to Chicago to join this particular church:

I really just felt really clearly that God put [the Chicago] Vineyard into my head. I didn't know the church at all. . . . I was like, this is really weird but I couldn't shake it. The rest of the service I just prayed over it and God just confirmed it. There was this total peace.

It was because of that sense of peace, the unexpected surprise of the thought, and his sense that the thought was insistent that he knew that the thought had come from God.

These tests, or expectations, were commonly described as *discernment*. Discernment was an ambiguous, complex process. When a decision was consequential (for example, was God calling a young couple to move to Los Angeles and away from their families?), it was not uncommon for congregants to spend many weeks praying about the decision and asking other friends in the church to pray as well and to talk to them about their prayer experience. Congregants gossiped about people who said that they were following God's voice but (the gossipers thought) were really acting on their own wishes. They expected that people would make mistakes.

In fact, people explicitly understood this process of recognizing God in their minds as a skill they needed to learn by repeatedly carrying on inner voice "conversations" with God during prayer and being attentive to the mental events that could count as God's response. The many prayer manuals presumed that prayer was not an intuitive act. "An essential part of living the with-God life is learning how we are to communicate with God. . . . But being aware of how God is supporting us and communicating with us is not always easy. We must train ourselves to listen for God and to respond to him" (Foster 2006: xvii). Congregants also often said that when they were learning to hear God speak in their minds—to distinguish between their own thoughts and God's thoughts—at first it was baffling. "When I was starting to be a Christian," a college student recalled, "people would be like, so what's God saying to you? And I'm like, heck, *I* don't know."

Nevertheless, many said that after a while they had learned to recognize God's voice speaking to them the way they recognized a person's voice on the phone. "It's a different sort of voice. I mean, I know my own voice. If I thought of your voice, I would think of how your voice sounds, and if I think of my voice, I think of how it sounds, even if I'm not hearing anything. It's a different tone of voice." Or: "It's like recognizing someone—it's like, how do you recognize your mom?"

It was acknowledged in the church that each person would experience God in his or her own way and develop his or her own patterns of learning to recognize Him: some through warm tingling; others through goose bumps; still others through images, impressions, or scriptural phrases. "I get a lot of images," one person explained. Another said, "I rarely see images. When I pray for people, I get sensations that I can in turn translate into words. . . . Like more than seeing the bird, you feel the flight of the bird." Congregants insisted that one could learn to identify God. "It gets to a point you just *know* it's God's voice. It's very snappy and comes with constant prayer just nonstop."

While Jews and Christians work to establish communication with one god, in Santeria people speak to many spirits through their minds. They also quite literally embody the spirits, and they build physical altars for the spirits to visit, crowded with the artifacts of their particular relationship with that spirit. Santeria is deeply plurimedial.

Santeria is a syncretic faith, a blend of Yoruba spirit possession and Catholicism that emerged among West African slaves in the Caribbean and took such various forms as Voodoo, Candomble, Bahia, and, in Cuba, Santeria. It has a pantheon of "saints" or "orishas." Some are embodiments of the natural world, others are more like traditional Christian figures, and still others are reminiscent of the ancient European pagan gods. Among them are Yemaya, sexy and potent goddess of the sea; mischievous Elegua of the crossroads; and Obatala, magisterial in flowing white robes, master of the sky and of all the orishas. But that is not all. There are ancestral spirits. There are spirits sent by other spirits. There are spirits that just show up during rituals, never explain themselves, and never come back again.

People know that these spirits are present because they dream about them or find themselves distracted by them—like the congregants in the Vineyard, they have thoughts in their minds that were placed there by the gods. More directly, participants find that during the ritual drumming spirits sometimes take over their human bodies and make themselves known. A santero told me that getting possessed was like stepping into a closet. She wasn't really gone, but she also wasn't in the room.

The Santeria "house" I joined in San Diego was run out of a botanica in an edgy part of town. (Botanicas are shops that sell herbs, candles, and other gear needed for these spiritual practices.) The shop was narrow and deep. In the front, they sold the kind of prayer candles that Catholics use to evoke the help of the Virgin Mary, St. Jude, St. Bartholomew, and others, as well as herbs and incense. Farther in there were cabinets for altars, candle holders, bowls for water. It was not obvious that these were for Santeria practice. The very back was a mixture of storeroom and altar. People would disappear into the back for readings, consultations, and chats.

The *madrina*—the highest initiate, the person who initiated the others and served as a symbolic mother to the group—owned the shop. She was Cuban, and many of the people who came for the drummings were also Cuban. But perhaps half the initiates were middle-class white people. They were much like the people I had met when doing fieldwork in London with magical practitioners: software engineers, nurses, students, people unimpressed with the faith into which they had been born and looking for something with more punch.

Mike was one of them. We met in the local metaphysical bookstore, where I had gone to find out more about a local cult-like group. The clerk wrinkled her nose at the group I mentioned ("You look into their eyes and there's no one home") and took me to Mike, who was reading tarot cards in the back room, so I could learn about Santeria instead. He had once been a practicing pagan witch, but it wasn't quite the right fit. When witches met trouble, he said, "they surrounded the enemy with white light and threw marshmallows at him." One evening he had come out of a gay bar to find that someone had thrown a rock through his windshield, slashed his car's tires, and scrawled "go home faggot" on the side. He thought he knew who had done it, but the police, he said, did nothing. So he went to the botanica and got some herbs and instructions on how to use them to send a potent curse. Within months, the guy he held responsible had moved to San Francisco and been beaten up by some leather boys. That led Mike into Santeria, and things began to go well for him.

People told stories like this in Santeria. They talked about cauldrons with human skulls and bones from graveyards. They said that Santeria really worked, by which they meant that its rituals had real effects in the world. They often said that they sought initiation because they were the kind of person who always "saw" things—in dreams, in shadows, in daily life—and because there were things going wrong that needed fixing. They said that after they joined, so-and-so learned that "she was messing with the wrong person." The clerk who introduced me to Mike explained that her aunt had murdered someone. Her uncle had been imprisoned for a crime he had not committed, and her aunt had prayed intensely for those who had accused him to die. They did die, and her uncle was judged innocent and released. Stories like these fill my notes about Santeria.

Santeria is an initiatory faith. New initiates are taken under the protection of one or more of the orishas. Newcomers may find themselves possessed by their Aunt Mary, but soon after the initial possession, others begin to appear. Each further step of initiation—and there are many—comes with an intimate introduction to a spirit. The more powerful the human, the more advanced the initiation, the more contact with that spirit there is. Advanced initiates manifest the gods at ceremonies. This was a world rife with relationships with invisible others, and those relationships were intensely social. Ruy Blanes and Diana Espírito Santo (2013) found these relationships so present and so human in the communities they write about that they simply describe the spirits as agents, anthropological participants with their own intentions and memories.

In the San Diego Santeria house, all the santeros had altars—platforms crowded with photographs, drawings, flowers, dolls, toys, coffee cups, rum, candles, glasses of water, and things that they thought their spirit might like. And because there were many spirits, there were many altars. The madrina's house was so crammed with altars that half the floor space was gone. There were altars in the hallway, the entryway, the living room, the dining room, and, presumably, the bedroom. The kitchen had an altar over the refrigerator. Each was covered with stuff. These altars were the way people made their spirits physical and the way they communicated. The humans learned what their spirits liked in the *misas*, gatherings where people got possessed. Other people would identify the spirit possessing an individual and tell him or her what that spirit wanted. Once, when I went with the bookstore clerk to a misa, the madrina told her she needed a rosary on her altar because her spirit had been a nun.

Once that contact was established, the person would hear from the spirit in his or her mind, in dreams, and through events, very much the way the Christians at the Vineyard or Horizon learned to hear from God. In Santeria, people seemed to perform more rituals to maintain the contact, and compared to the Vineyard, there was just a lot more stuff. Every day, initiates were supposed to pray before their altars, change (or drink) the water, and brew fresh coffee. Every day, they were supposed to look for the presence of the spirits in their lives—the way the spirits helped them, played with them, and asked for their attention, all according to the spirit's personality and style. Elegua was a trickster, Mike explained to me. "Elegua will put down a banana peel for you to slip on. Then when you break your leg and they take you to the emergency room, he'll be there to stitch you up." Spirits liked attention. People not only interacted with them through their altars and in their dreams and daydreams, but they treated them like friends. One woman, a nurse, would take Elegua (in the form of some round stones glued together) for Sunday drives around her neighborhood. Literally: she would take the statue, put him in the front seat of her car, and chat with him as she drove around a neighborhood she thought he would like to see. Sometimes I would call someone to arrange an interview, and my participant would pause and turn to ask a spirit if it was okay. "I really do talk to them as friends," the madrina explained.

For the paracosm to work, it is not enough that humans and gods both enter in. They must also interact. How they should do so is not, on the surface, obvious, as the god is a thoroughly nonordinary being. The special world must therefore have expectations for what counts as a spirit's response and how the human can answer back. In the Christianity practiced at the Vineyard, people call these rules "discernment." They spell out the events in their minds and bodies that count as God's communication: a surprising reaction to reading the Bible, a seemingly coincidental encounter with people, or striking impressions, thoughts or nudges in the mind. In the Anglo-Cuban Santeria I knew in San Diego, people focused more on physical altars through which humans communicated with their spirits—the candles, the coffee, the special dolls they thought their spirit might like—and on the physical expression of the spirit in their bodies. Yet they also described hearing spirits in their minds, and they talked to their invisible others as if to friends.

By this point, the similarity of the faith frame to play should seem clearer. The faith frame is very much like a play frame—except it is a serious one. There is a special world defined by special rules. Only some people participate and share the same assumptions about what is real. They signal their participation by special actions—we call them rituals. They keep kosher, they go to church, they kneel five times a day to pray. They also make statements that insist that a god or spirit is present, and they learn ways to determine whether a god or spirit is interacting with them. Those rules only make sense to others within the frame. To a Christian, it probably seems bizarre to take a chunk of stone for a Sunday drive. To a santero, it likely seems foolish to assume that a spirit who oversees two billion people really takes time to tell someone where to go to church. To Muslims and Jews, different rituals about how to pray and what to eat define them as being involved in different enterprises. If you put on a tallit, you likely do not expect that Allah will hear your prayers.

The implication of this play metaphor is that the individual chooses to participate. There is a frame that defines the faith with its rules and assumptions. Someone must decide deliberately to enter in and engage. Here the skeptic might say: most people are born into a religion and have no choice. I respond: they do have a choice. It is possible to carry out the rituals mechanically, and even in a never-secular world, it is possible not to care.

At the Vineyard, someone once said to me, "I can choose to believe that this is from God or I can think that this is just from me, and the reality is that it could be either, and I know that. There is always a choice to believe what it is." If the challenge for those of faith is to take what must be imagined seriously (one must use the imagination to represent an invisible god), narrative mechanism and ritual performance can help them to do so. The vividly detailed world of a good story, the multiple representations of its main characters, the repeated practice of interacting with a character as if the character were in a relationship with you— all these help to make the faith frame feel more compelling. All can help to make it more personal, more meaningful, more anchored to the everyday present.

By calling the faith frame a paracosm, I want to draw the reader's attention to the ways in which faith can work like a private-but-shared imaginative world. There are features of these shared imaginative worlds that may make the paracosm feel more real: a way to show that one is participating in the community that shares it, a way to indicate that one experiences the central character in the paracosm as real, a way to experience that central character as interacting with one. All these features make invisible beings feel more vivid and alive. More real.

This real-making still involves choice. People who can enter the faith frame and experience it more vividly will find that it feels more real. They will find their inner lives socialized by others as they accept the rules of the game and remake them as their own. They will become different people as they work with the invisible other and strive to become the persons they are meant to be in relationship with that other. But for this to happen, those persons must have a commitment to enter in, to accept and follow the rules of the frame. They must agree to play.

3

TALENT AND TRAINING

> When something is new to us, we treat it as an experience. We
> feel that our senses are awake and clear. We are alive.
>
> —Jasper Johns, *Jasper Johns: A Retrospective*

There are features of narrative and practice that help people to feel that
the invisible other is real, and there are also personal characteristics that
make it more or less likely for an individual to experience those narratives vividly. Some people are more willing to blur the line between inner
mind and outer world, so that which must be inwardly imagined comes
to feel more autonomous, more agentic, more given from without. This
is a human capacity—an orientation—that can be both innate and
trained. I call the talent "absorption," and the training "inner sense cultivation." They are disciplines of the imagination, rather than of the
body, technologies of the mind. I believe that Lucien Lévy-Bruhl meant
to capture something like this orientation to mind and world with the
term "participation." Absorption and inner sense cultivation kindle the
realness of gods and spirits.

THE MYSTICAL MODE

Nearly a hundred years ago, when Europeans were intoxicated by reports
of newly colonized natives who worshipped strange gods with ancient
rites, when the new school of English anthropology laid out a ladder of
intellectual evolution as orderly as a London timetable, the Parisian philosopher Lucien Lévy-Bruhl spun a philosophical psychology that was
so radical, so preposterous in its claims, that few English thinkers took

it seriously. One who did—E. E. Evans-Pritchard—rejected the ideas so thoroughly that he never even mentioned the Parisian's name in the famous book he wrote to refute him, *Witchcraft, Oracles and Magic among the Azande*. For many scholars, even now, Lévy-Bruhl's name carries the whiff of something unseemly. This is a shame, because Lévy-Bruhl saw something: that what it is to be religious is to experience the world as responsive and alive.

In *How Natives Think*, Lévy-Bruhl argued that the distinctive feature of the "primitive" mind was that such people (nonliterate, non-Western, and living in small-scale societies) experienced themselves as participating in the external world and the external world as participating in their minds and bodies. Such a man might believe that his enemies would have power over him if they simply knew his name; he might believe that his dream was a visitation by a real and external spirit. Among the Koyukon Indians of north central Alaska,

> Traditional Koyukon people live in a world that watches, in a forest of eyes. A person moving through nature—however wild, remote, even desolate the place may be—is never truly alone. The surroundings are aware, sensate, personified. They feel. They can be offended. And they must, at every moment, be treated with proper respect. (Nelson 1983: 14)

Lévy-Bruhl called such an orientation "mystical," and he described it as governed by "the law of participation," in which objects are "both themselves and other than themselves" ([1926] 1979: 76). He also called it "prelogical": avoiding contradiction is not its main aim. The primary difference between traditional thought and our own, he argued, is that "our perception is directed toward the apprehension of an objective reality, and this reality alone" ([1926] 1979: 59). We (rational Frenchmen) aim above all to define reality as independent of subjective representation or response. They (the primitive) do not.

At the end of his life, in the posthumously published *Notebooks*, Lévy-Bruhl abandoned the claim that so-called primitive minds were fundamentally different from those of Europeans. He also abandoned the term "prelogical" ([1949] 1975: 99) and began to write of participation as common to all people, different modes of thought rather than different minds. He described "a mystical mentality which is more marked and more easily observable among 'primitive peoples' than in our own societies, but it is present in every human mind" ([1949] 1975: 100–101). Both affective and conceptual, the mystical mode of thought had those features that he had attributed to participation all along: independence from ordinary space and time (Jesus is still alive), logical contradictions (a man both is and is not the eagle that is the totem of his tribe), a shared identity between objects or beings and their features (like hair cuttings and the person from whom they came), and "the feeling of a contact, most often unforeseen, with a reality other than the reality given in the surrounding milieu" ([1949] 1975: 102). He thought that the mystical mode intermixed with everyday thought continually in our minds. For him, the puzzle became: "How does it happen that these 'mental habits' make themselves felt in certain circumstances and not in others?" ([1949] 1975: 100).

How indeed? Many people assume that training and talent are important in many areas of life: ballet, violin playing, tennis. It seems more awkward to talk about talent and training when it comes to knowing gods and spirits because doing so seems to suggest that the human, not the god, gives rise to the events. Talk of talent or training can seem to explain God away. Prophets in the Hebrew Bible explicitly vowed they had neither. The denial was the narrator's way of insisting that what prophets heard and saw was truly from God. "Then the word of the Lord came unto me," says Jeremiah, "saying, before I formed thee in the belly I knew thee; and before thou camest forth out of the womb I sanctified thee, and I ordained thee a prophet unto the nations. Then said I, Ah, Lord GOD! behold, I cannot speak: for I am a child" (Jeremiah 1:4–6).

And yet in some respects, hearing gods and spirits speak and having other vivid, unusual experiences might indeed be like becoming a skilled athlete. I have found that something like talent and training facilitates the felt realness of gods and spirits and the kinds of experiences people deem spiritual. I suggest here that there is a human capacity for *absorption*—a capacity to be immersed in the world of the senses, inner and outer—and those who have a talent for it and who train to develop it are more likely to experience invisible others as present. Those who have the proclivity are more likely to report sharper mental images and more unusual spiritual experiences. They are more likely to say that they experience a god as being present. Does this mean that these experiences explain gods and spirits away, as if the experience of a god were nothing more than a temperamental byproduct? I don't think so. But I think it does explain why some people who want to hear gods and spirits speak find that it just doesn't happen to them and why some people who might not intend to have such relationships may stumble upon these unusual experiences entirely by accident.

THE MAGIC TRAIN RIDE

I was sitting in a commuter train to London the first time I felt supernatural power rip through me. I was twenty-three, and I was one year into my graduate training in anthropology. I had decided to do my fieldwork among educated white Britons who practiced what they called magic. I thought of this as a clever twist on more traditional anthropological fieldwork about the strange ways of natives who clearly were not "us." I was on my way to meet some of them, and I had ridden my bike to the station with trepidation and excitement. Now in my seat, as the sheep-dotted countryside rolled by, I was reading a book written by Gareth Knight, a man they called an "adept," meaning someone deeply knowledgeable and powerful. (The book was *Experience of the Inner Worlds*.) The book's language was dense and abstract. My mind kept slipping as I struggled to grasp what he was talking about, and I wanted so badly to understand. The text spoke of the Holy Spirit and Tibetan masters and an ancient system of Judaic mysticism called Kabbalah. The author wrote that all these were so many names for forces that flowed from a higher spiritual reality into this one through the vehicle of the trained mind. And as I strained to imagine what it would be like to be that vehicle, I began to feel power in my veins—really to feel it, not to imagine it. I grew hot. I became completely alert, more awake than I usually am, and I felt so alive. It seemed that power coursed through me like water through a chute. I wanted to sing. And then wisps of smoke came out of my backpack, in which I had tossed my bicycle lights. I grabbed the lights and snapped them open. In one of them, the batteries were melting.

Looking back, I would now say that I have a proclivity for absorption, and that when someone with that proclivity is invited to have a spiritual experience, it is not unlikely that she will. At the time, however,

I was thoroughly taken aback. (I also never figured out what was going on with the batteries.)

As I spent more time in London, I saw that experiencing supernatural power involved deliberate training (Luhrmann, *Persuasions of the Witch's Craft*). In the world I had entered—a secrecy-shrouded London society whose members were computer programmers and speech therapists by day and initiates of the Western Mysteries by night—people apprenticed to learn what they considered to be basic skills to recognize, generate, and manipulate what they called magical forces. The exact purpose of the training varied from group to group, but all groups recognized the need for training, and all groups identified some people as more skilled than others, with a smaller group of people considered experts. Some groups even had formal classes. Before I could be initiated into the most elaborately hierarchical and secretive of magical groups, I was required to take a nine-month home-study course complete with a supervisor and monthly essays.

Lessons in these classes typically demanded that students learn specific kinds of knowledge (what magical power is, who the gods are, what their symbols are), and they generally asked students to personalize that knowledge, to see it as relevant to and embedded in their lives. Each course also demanded the acquisition of two skills of attention—meditation and visualization—and each course required that the student learn to quiet the mind and to focus on some internal experience (an image, a word, or the apparently empty mind itself). Here is an example from one of my early lessons, which I did, in some form, for fifteen minutes a day for nine months:

> You should perform a meditation building up an inner picture of a walled garden (initially make it foursquare with an expanse of empty lawn in its center). . . . After an initial centering and when the bubbling of your consciousness has to some extent quietened and abated, begin to seed the center point of your consciousness with inner pictures of the Garden using all the senses if you wish. Then withdraw a little inward and let these images become wrapped around your inner point of soul, then re-seed the inner picture if you need to. Allow a space for the forms to grow and develop as they will. (Adam McLean, Inner School of Hermetic Studies)

The idea behind this was that if you could learn to see mental images clearly, with borders, duration, and stability, those images could become the vehicle for supernatural power to enter the mundane world. To do this, people deliberately engaged all their inner senses in the exercise: their mind's eye, their mind's ear, their mind's nose, and so forth. I came to think of this as "inner sense cultivation."

What startled me, as a young ethnographer, was that this training worked. At least, it seemed to change the way I experienced mental images. After about a year of this kind of training, my mental imagery *did* seem to become clearer. I thought that my images had sharper borders, felt more solid, and lasted longer. I began to feel that my concentration states were deeper and more sharply distinct from the everyday. I got better at focusing during rituals. And I began to have more "anomalous experiences." By this, I mean events that are unusual in the everyday world: visions, voices, a sense of presence, out-of-body experiences. Early one morning I had a vision with a tang of sensory perception. I had been reading a novel about King Arthur's England written by this kind of magical practitioner (Marion Zimmer Bradley's *The Mists of Avalon*), really trying to imagine what the characters were experiencing. One morning I awoke to see some druids standing by my window. I shot up in bed when I saw them, and they vanished. But for a moment, I really saw them.

And I felt different in rituals, when we shut our eyes, sank into contemplative states, and visualized what the group leader told us to. At those times, when I was trying so hard to see with my mind's eye and to be completely relaxed but mentally alert, it seemed as if there was something altered about the way I experienced the world—something different in my sense of self, sense of time, sense of focus, and also in how I sensed in my mind: in the way I saw, heard, and felt in my imagination. What I imagined just felt more real, as if I could reach out and touch it with my hands This was not true for all ritual gatherings, but during some rituals the difference was striking. Of course, I was socially immersed in this world, and I was learning new ways to interpret my awareness and my experience. But it didn't feel to me that I was just acquiring knowledge and narrative. I felt that I was acquiring new skills, and that the skills could be taught and mastered. And as I acquired those skills, the world became drenched in meaning. Nothing happened by accident anymore. A phone call, the kind of fruit the greengrocer sold, a book I glanced at in a window—everything seemed connected to my thoughts, my visualizations, and my dreams.

This did not just happen to me. Other people in these groups talked about daydreams that had grown more intense and images that had become more vivid. They spoke about losing time, about dreams drenched in symbolism, about going on walks and encountering gods. They told stories about moments when they saw or heard or felt invisible beings, and moments when a dream felt real in the world. Sometimes they spoke of "journeying on the astral plane," experiencing themselves as flying over London, long before the Harry Potter movies showed wizards on their brooms.

They attributed their experiences to becoming skilled in magic. They all thought that training was important. They all thought it was hard and took work, and they all thought that it changed the way that they experienced their world and gave them power.

I, on the other hand, had come to these experiences differently. I had gone to graduate school because I was fascinated by the problem of mind—how humans think, what constrains our thought—and in particular the problem of apparently irrational thought—of how apparently reasonable, pragmatic people can embrace beliefs that skeptical observers simply don't accept. I took this to be a problem of interpretation, knowledge, or discourse. A man ties special stones on the horns of his oxen to make the fields they plough more fertile; the skeptical observer can't believe that the stones have any effect, and yet the man repeats the action year after year. What, anthropologists had asked, is he thinking? What ideas does he hold in his mind? So when I began, I was looking for the words people used, the narratives they spun, and the consequences of their interpretations for their choices and actions. Like Evans-Pritchard, I had assumed that to study magic was to study the way people organized knowledge: how they identified what counted as evidence for these forces, how they compared (or failed to compare) the "outcome" of rituals over time, and the metaphors and narratives they used that might lead them to think differently about magical forces than about an experimental procedure in a laboratory. I thought I would be telling a story about concepts—an account of the kinds of categories people acquired, how those categories were structured, and the sequence in which they were learned. I assumed, before I did the fieldwork, that people who believed in magic held different ideas about reality—different mental models—and that those ideas were what led them to think differently about cause and effect.

Instead, what I learned was that people who practiced magic experienced different phenomenal events as well as different ideas. By "phenomenal" here, I mean that their immediate experience became different; what they felt through their senses was not the same as it had been. It wasn't just something people said. People certainly acquired a set of mental models, but those models became meaningful because the person's world became different. People not only learned about Demeter and Hecate through books, but they met the gods in their dreams, visualized them in rituals, and searched for their presence. And as they did so, they began to experience odd events that they felt in their bodies and associated with the gods. Something was going on that was more complicated than simply learning to use words in different ways.

Yet it was not all about training. Practice did not explain my experience when I took that train into London, even taking into account my determined attempt to imagine my way into that author's world. In fact, people sometimes went looking for books on magic when they had experienced an out-of-the-blue event—an intense sense of invisible presence, for instance—that they felt they could not explain. At the same time, it was also clear that anomalous experiences were more common among those who practiced: those who did the exercises and rituals again and again. What I saw seemed more like an orientation to inner experience, which someone might have by temperament but could also develop through practice.

I learned that in the London world of modern magic, the following was commonsense:

If you wanted to do magic, you had to practice magic. If you wanted to feel power flow through you and to direct it toward a source, you had to do it again and again, and you had to train, preferably under a seasoned elder.

Some people were naturally better than others. Magicians spoke as if there were people who were naturally good at being psychic, and people who were naturally good at doing rituals. The psychics (they said) did not feel things in their body. They simply knew things and had insights that others did not. Those who were good at doing magic were able to have the distinct sense that power was present. They could feel it moving through them, and they felt as if they could direct it.

Those who practiced would get better. People routinely said that over time they experienced power more intensely. Those who practiced found that their mental images grew sharper, and they were more likely to report unusual phenomena: they felt the power, they heard the gods, they saw the spirits.

As I began to read more intensively, I started to realize that what magicians did in their training could be found in other spiritual practices around the world: in Buddhism, Islam, Christianity, Judaism, shamanism, even spirit possession. The capacities to visualize and to sink into trance-like states seemed to be learnable skills. I began to think that mastery of those skills was associated with intense spiritual experience and the sense that gods and spirits felt real.

PRACTICING GOD

Many years later, I saw more or less the same process in charismatic evangelical Christianity (Luhrmann, *When God Talks Back*). To be sure, these people thought about their experiences differently. When they felt a force moving through their bodies, they attributed it to the Holy Spirit. They did not talk about training. They talked about prayer, and while they certainly talked about needing to practice praying, they focused on what they took to be its practical outcomes and attributed those outcomes to God. And yet what these Christians did when they prayed was really quite similar to what the magicians did. Their prayers were not rote but more like active daydreams. One book even called them "God-dreams." People told me that when they prayed, they sat on God's lap or stood in God's throne room. They described talking back and forth with God in their minds. These are acts that use the inner senses to represent God in the mind.

And in many ways what they experienced was similar to what the magicians experienced, and they said remarkably similar things about talent and training. The Christians sometimes said that after they began to pray actively, they not only experienced God more vividly, but their inner world became sharper and felt more real, as if those features were side-effects of training. They knew that practice mattered. They thought that powerful experiences were more common in the lives of those who prayed actively. They also knew that predisposition mattered. They were clear that some people had a hard time hearing God, even when they prayed, and they knew that some people had experiences that came out of the blue.

Moreover, those observations had deep roots in the Christian tradition. In his first letter to the Corinthians, Paul points out that only some people are able to speak in the language-like utterances identified as "tongues." Others have different gifts (1 Corinthians 12:8–11). Paul also repeatedly exhorts people to pray and suggests that people are more likely to experience God if they do. In a famous passage (1 Thessalonians 5:16–20), he writes, "Pray without ceasing; in every thing give thanks: for this is the will of God in Christ Jesus concerning you. Quench not the Spirit. Despise not prophesyings." Here is Luke 11:9: "And I say unto you, Ask, and it shall be given you; seek, and ye shall find; knock, and it shall be opened unto you."

One might imagine that gifts are really preferences: I could sing in the choir, but I prefer to bake for the church supper. I could prophesy, but I'd prefer just to read the Bible. Yet these Christians did not talk as if they *preferred* to do one rather than another. Some explicitly and repeatedly told me that they deeply desired to hear God speak out loud to them and they could not. "Please pray that I will hear God speak with a booming voice," one man asked plaintively in his housegroup meeting. And another: "I don't have these superpowerful experiences that make me fall to my knees." At the same time, they thought that if you wanted to know God, you had to pray; that prayer was a skill that had to be taught and that it was hard; that some people were naturally better than others; and that those who were naturally good would improve further with training. The changes they described included sharper mental imagery, sharper mental focus, and more unusual phenomenal events.

Here some active pray-ers describe what they had learned:

What does God's voice sound like? It takes practice. There were times when I just sat back and I was like, okay guys, I don't hear anything. . . . [Then] I felt like I was starting to hear from Him more. A small voice sounds very vague but it's such a good description, kind of like the impression words make on a page. I realized that I was going at it the way you would practice throwing the ball, because I didn't know what else to do. . . . [Now] I feel it as well as—not hear it, but it feels like—it's not a physical thing but it feels like more than just in my head.

Another:

It's just like an infant learns how to put sentences together, and then to have a conversation with someone and not just like be talking the whole time or just listening the whole time—to learn how to speak and respond and listen, speak and listen and respond. Just to like be there and be focused. I'm seeing how people have moved from praying where their mind would wander off to learning to pray so that they can focus more and just pray. I've seen this in my own life too.

It sounds a lot like tennis, figure skating, and other sports. Some people are naturally better than others, but if you want to be good, you have to train. People who prayed actively said that their sensory world became richer, more alive.

Disciplining myself to pray . . . it was like just opening it up, opening up your perceptions and tuning them up in a different way so that even just walking down a street and looking at flowers took on new significance.

Another:

My senses are heightened when I'm feeling especially close [to God], when it's like a joyful, a really joyful time.

They described shifts in their mental experience. They said that their mental images became sharper.

[Over time, as I have continued to pray], my images continue to get more complex and more distinct.

Another:

I see images. I would say that I didn't until I came to [this kind of church].

They talked about developing better focus, about "going deeper," and of feeling that God became more present as they prayed. They also reported that they experienced more perception-like events that felt sensory but had no material cause.

> A: I was walking up the lake and down the lake and I was like, should I go home now? And He [God] is like, "Sit and listen."
> TML: Did you hear that outside your head or inside your head?
> A: That's hard to tell, but in this instance, it really felt like it was outside.
> TML: How many times do you think you've heard his voice outside your head?
> A: Two or three.

And another person:

> I remember praying for a job and I interviewed and I didn't know whether I was going to take it or not. Then when I was cleaning out my room, I heard a voice say, "That's not the one." And then I said, what? I looked around, and I'm like, maybe that's someone outside. Then I realized: I clearly heard God say, "That's not the one." I have no doubt in my mind that it was God.

I came to call these "sensory overrides": hallucination-like moments when someone hears a voice while alone, or sees something that isn't there, or feels, tastes, or smells something that is not materially present, as if the inner world overrode sensory perception. These moments were not common. But they happened.

Prayer experts spoke as if what they were learning to do was to take their inner sensory world more seriously; to treat their thoughts, images, and sensations as more meaningful; and deliberately to blur the line between what they might once have attributed to an internal cause and what they might now wish to attribute to an external one. That, after all, is the point of experiential evangelical spirituality: to experience God—an external invisible presence—interacting with one through phenomena one would ordinarily interpret as internal and self-generated. It seemed that as these congregants lovingly attended to their internal sensations, those sensations took on a life of their own and become more and more vivid until the congregants occasionally experienced some of them as if they were located in the external material world, so that they saw and heard and smelled and felt sensations in ways not caused by material things.

ABSORPTION: THE NATURE OF TALENT

What, then, makes some people "better than others" at magic and at prayer? One answer is that they have a proclivity for absorption.

The Tellegen Absorption Scale (Tellegen and Atkinson 1974) has thirty-four statements that the person filling out the scale marks as "true" or "false." (The scale does not measure religiosity per se; it has only one statement that could be construed as religious.) The sentences ask whether you can "see" the image of something when you are no longer looking at it, whether you sometimes experience things as if you were a child, whether you sometimes find that you have finished a task while your thoughts were elsewhere, whether different smells call up different colors, whether you often sense the presence of a person before seeing him or her, whether you can become oblivious to everything else when listening to music. There are statements about how one experiences nature and color and texture and smells, statements about poetry and the fascination of a voice.

When Auke Tellegen and his students first drafted the questionnaire, they were trying to develop a pen-and-paper measure of hypnotizability, a term that refers to how likely it is that someone will respond to hypnosis. Yet the way people answered the Absorption Scale correlates only modestly (if significantly) with the way they responded to the gold standard measure of hypnotizability, the "Stanford C." Tellegen and his coauthor Gilbert Atkinson concluded that absorption was a character trait, a disposition for having moments of total attention that somehow fully engage all of one's attentional capacities—perceptual, imaginative, conceptual, even the way one holds and moves one's body. "This kind of attentional functioning is believed to result in a heightened sense of the reality of the attentional object, imperviousness to distracting events, and an altered sense of reality in general, including an empathically altered sense of self" (1974: 268).

In other words, when you get absorbed in something, it seems more real to you, and you and your world seem different than before. From this perspective, absorption is the mental capacity common to trance, hypnosis, dissociation, and perhaps imagination itself. Later, Tellegen (1981) decided that the real distinction the scale pulled out was the difference between the instrumental and the experiential. By "instrumental," he meant the attitude of being pragmatic and effective, focused on what is realistic, making decisions, and pursuing goals. By "experiential," he meant being open, receptive, and in the moment. That, he thought, was the heart of absorption: the mode of the beach-walker gazing at the sunset, caught up in imagination or appreciation.

All this suggests that absorption is the capacity to focus in on the mind's object—what humans imagine or see around them—and to allow that focus to increase while diminishing one's attention to the myriad of everyday distractions that accompany the management of normal life. You let a daydream unfold, or you become absorbed in watching the purple finches at the birdfeeder, and your to-do list fades. The Absorption Scale seems to pick up the enjoyable dimension— imaginative involvement, the delight we take in letting a story or sensation carry us away.

In study after study, I have found that people who score highly in absorption are more likely to say that God speaks to them; that they experience God with the senses; that they have had intense spiritual experiences; that they have seen, heard, or felt God or ghosts or spirits; that the world of invisible others is viscerally real to them and feels alive.

In the first of these studies (Luhrmann, Nusbaum, and Thisted 2010), I sat down with twenty-eight people I had met through the Chicago church that I had been visiting for several years. They were all members of the church. Some were new; some were longtimers. All of them sought intimacy with God. First, I asked them to fill out the Absorption Scale, and then we spoke. I asked them all the same questions (for example, Do you speak to God freely throughout the day? Would you describe God as your best friend, or like an imaginary friend, except real?), but I also let them talk. I was struck that not everyone was able to know God as a person who spoke with him or her, even when he or she tried.

I compared the answers they gave to the Absorption Scale to the answers they gave to the questions I asked about their spiritual experiences. A person's absorption score was not related to the length of time he or she prayed on a daily basis. But the way a person answered the absorption questions was significantly related to the way he or she experienced prayer. The more absorption statements people marked as true, the more time seemed to change when they prayed, the more they had images and sensations during prayer, the more they were able to experience God as a person. You might think that my questions would lead people just to parrot back what the pastor and the books and the conferences said about God. Yet those with high absorption scores were much more likely to report that they experienced God as if God really were a person—someone they could talk to easily, who talked back, with whom one could laugh, at whom one could get angry. People with low absorption scores said that they couldn't. When I held the absorption score constant, the time spent in prayer turned out to be significantly related to how person-like God was for someone. It looked like there really was something like talent and something like training, and that both mattered to the way someone experienced God.

There was another interesting thing that the Absorption Scale predicted. If people answered "true" to at least half the items on the Absorption Scale, their chances of reporting that they had heard God's voice, seen the wing of an angel, or smelled, tasted or felt the touch of something supernatural was *six times* as high as for those who said "true" to less than half the statements. It turned out that slightly over a third of our participants reported one of these sensory overrides. Again, practice made a difference. If I held absorption constant in the analysis, the length of time someone prayed every day was significantly related to whether he or she reported seeing a vision or hearing a voice. That too was striking. These basic findings hold up in study after study.

Absorption does not explain religion, and far less does it explain it away. But understanding that some people may have developed their talent more than others may help us to understand why some people become gifted practitioners of their faith and others with the intention and desire to do so struggle and do not.

INNER SENSE CULTIVATION: THE WORK OF TRAINING

It turns out that deliberately cultivating the inner senses—the practice at the heart of evangelical prayer and modern magic—has more or less the same effect as absorption does. Inner sense cultivation is the deliberate, repeated use of inner visual representation and other inner sensory experience. Sometimes that deliberate cultivation is explicit, as in the specific visualization exercises of Tibetan or Mahāyāna Buddhism. As presented in one Mahāyāna text, "[The practice's] main subject is a special kind of visionary meditation in which the Yogin sees himself face to face with any Buddha of the present time" (Obeyesekere 2012: 83). Sometimes we need to infer the deliberate cultivation from the designs of deer or birds tattooed on Siberian mummies, from talk about ritual journeys to the sun on the backs of flying reindeer who turn into sacred cranes (Vitebsky 2005), or from the vividly imagined myths that become how someone learns to do the rite. When shamans journey between worlds in trance, they are naturally cultivating the inner senses, using their mental imagery (Noll 1985). The great Sufi traditions of Islam are evidently often a training of the inner senses (Corbin 1969a, b; Doostdar 2018), but the sheer difficulty of memorizing a text likely involves a similarly intense cultivation (Gade 2004). Jonathan Garb (2011) goes so far as to describe modern Kabbalah practices as "shamanic trance."

Many Christian texts say similar things about the cultivation of inner imagery and the experience of God. In a much-loved text called *The Practice of the Presence of God*, Brother Lawrence (1982: 42) writes, "Sometimes I imagine that I'm a piece of stone, waiting for the sculptor. When I give myself to God this way, He begins sculpting my soul into the perfect image of His beloved Son." St. John of the Cross not only describes prayer as an active use of the inner senses, but remarks that the practice leads the one who prays to perceive what is not perceptible to the outer senses:

> There may come, and there are wont to come, to spiritual persons representations of objects of a supernatural kind. With respect to sight, they are apt to picture figures and forms of persons belonging to the life to come—the forms of certain saints, and representations of angels, good and evil, and certain lights and brightnesses of an extraordinary kind. And with the ears they hear certain extraordinary words, sometimes spoken by these figures that they see, sometimes without seeing the person who speaks them. As to the sense of smell, they sometimes perceive the sweetest perfumes with all the senses, without knowing whence they proceed. (2010: 120)

Inner sense cultivation often involves three features: interaction, interweaving, and sensory enhancement. By "interaction," I mean that the practitioner interacts with what she or he imagines. The person who prays imagines Jesus and talks with him. The shaman imagines the spirit of the jaguar and has a dialogue with it. By "interweaving," I mean that these practices commonly interlace scripted prayers (like the "Our Father") with private, personal reflection. You think about the scripture, and then about yourself in relation to the scripture, and then about the scripture in relation to yourself. By "sensory enhancement," I mean that the practitioner uses many of his or her inner senses to engage with the story. In the Christian tradition, one of the most explicit examples is in the contemplation of hell from the *Spiritual Exercises* of Ignatius Loyola:

> I imagine that I see with my own eyes the length, breadth and depth of Hell. I beg God for what I want. Here I ask for an intimate sense of the punishment suffered by the damned, so that if my failures ever make me grow forgetful of the love of my eternal Lord, at least my fear of these punishments will keep me from falling into sin.
>
> First point: to see in imagination those enormous fires and the souls, as it were with bodies of fire.
>
> Second point: to hear in imagination the shrieks and groans and the blasphemous shouts against Christ our Lord and all the saints.
>
> Third point: to smell in imagination the fumes of sulphur and the stench of filth and corruptions.
>
> Fourth point: to taste in imagination all the bitterness of tears and melancholy and a gnawing conscience.
>
> Fifth point: to feel in imagination the heat of the flames that play on and burn the souls. (Loyola 1992: 114–15)

Ignatius wanted people to see, hear, feel, touch, and taste the scripture with their mind's senses. He wanted his participants to see the characters from the texts, to envision the details of how they stood, how they held their shoulders, where they rested their arms.

The practice of inner sense cultivation blurs the boundary between what is external and what is within. The mental muscles developed in prayer work on the boundary between thought and perception, between what is attributed to the mind—internal, self-generated, private, and hidden from view—and what exists in the world. The practice focuses attention on the words and images on one side of the boundary, and then treats those words and images as if they belonged on the other. It is this inner sense cultivation that seems to train the capacity that the Absorption Scale identifies.

Is it really absorption? Tellegen and his colleagues treat absorption as a psychological trait with high test-retest reliability. I have found high test-retest reliability in my own work with the scale. From this perspective, absorption is more like a feature than like a skill. Nonetheless, it seems clear that there is a relationship between what the scale identifies and the ability that practice trains. In this way, absorption and inner sense cultivation might have a relationship similar to hypnotizability and trance. Many scholars treat hypnotizability as a trait, but clinicians who use hypnosis in practice talk about trance as a skill that can be learned.

In 2007, I ran an experiment to learn more about practice. We brought in over one hundred Christians, most of them from churches like the Vineyard. Participants filled out a series of pen-and-paper scales, including the Absorption Scale. Then they sat in front of a computer and did tasks to see how they used mental imagery. Finally, we interviewed them, for at least an hour and often longer, about how they heard from God, how they prayed, and what other spiritual experiences they had.

When the interviews were done, the participants then picked up one of several identical brown packages sitting on a side table. Inside each package was an iPod. Some of those iPods were loaded with inner sense cultivation materials. They had four tracks of thirty minutes each, in which a biblical passage was read to background music, and then reread while inviting the listener to use all his or her senses to participate in the scene ("See the shepherd before you . . ."). The other iPods had twenty-four thirty-minute lectures on the Gospels. (There were also some iPods with pink noise and instructions about Centering Prayer, but those I discuss elsewhere.) The lectures were a scholar's account of the differences among the Gospels and how they are constructed as narratives. People were asked to play the iPod for thirty minutes a day, six days a week, for a month.

When our participants came back, we found that those who had done the inner sense cultivation practice had scores on the subjective measures of mental imagery vividness that were significantly higher, compared to their initial scores, than those who had listened to the lectures (Luhrmann, Nusbaum, and Thisted 2013). They said that their images had more detail. They were more likely to say that they had begun to experience God as like a person. They also reported more sensory overrides. These experiences were not, in general, very dramatic, and there weren't many of them, but they were meaningful and often moving. One participant, for example, had a powerful experience of God holding her hand. Another woman saw her beloved dead dog. Another had a session in which she closed her eyes to visualize the angel Gabriel and found that the angel's light was so bright that she opened her eyes because she thought someone had turned a lamp on in the room.

It is as if this intense inner attention makes the world of the mind more vivid, and the vividness leaks into the world. People with higher absorption scores reported more of these events before they started their discipline, and the inner sense cultivation affected how much they experienced during the month.

BLURRING THE BOUNDARY

At the heart of the religious impulse lies the capacity to imagine a world beyond the one we have before us. To do so requires a narrative, but it also requires the capacity to hold in abeyance the matter-of-fact expectation that the world of the senses is all there is. That is why absorption and inner sense cultivation are central to religion. Those who say "yes" to the absorption questions, and those who practice experiencing the narrative with their inner senses, are more likely to be and become comfortable with blurring the boundary between that which is within and that which is without, between an image held in the mind and an object that stands on its own in external space. An invisible spirit can be made more real by this sensory blurring—can be imagined and felt to be more than mere imagination. An old Christian tradition speaks of the "spiritual senses," the use of the senses to know God, who has no sensory presence (Dyrness 2004, 2008; Gavriyuk and Coakley 2011); in Islam, the term is al-'aql al-batin (Mittermaier 2010). Herewith Augustine in his *Confessions*:

> You called, you cried out, you shattered my deafness: you flashed, you shone, you scattered my blindness: you breathed perfume, and I drew in my breath and I pant for you: I tasted, and I am hungry and thirsty: you touched me, and I burned for your peace. (2001: 229)

The language reaches for the senses so vividly that what is seen, felt, and heard is not just sensorially imagined but somehow creates a feeling of something beyond the senses.

Absorption and inner sense cultivation facilitate what the ecological philosopher David Abram depicts as the entanglement of our senses with a world around us. The point for him is that entanglement means that we experience the world as responding: "The landscape as I directly experience it is hardly a determinate object; it is an ambiguous realm that responds to my emotions and calls forth feelings from me in turn" (1996: 33). Abram argues that in the modern world we have lost our primordial manner of sensory experience—that before the alphabet and the supermarket, we understood ourselves to live in a world that was alive and responsive, and that we attended to that world with senses alert in a way we can barely imagine today. He calls this magic: "the experience of existing in a world made up of multiple intelligences, the intuition that every form one perceives—from the swallow swooping overhead to a fly on a blade of grass, and indeed the blade of grass itself—is an *experiencing* form, an entity with its own predilections and sensations" (1996: 10). To him it is an intimate reciprocity: "as we touch the bark of a tree, we feel the tree touching us" (1996: 268).

What Lévy-Bruhl described with the word "participation"—and what I think the Absorption Scale picks up—is such a blurring of boundaries, so that a footprint can connect to a man's feelings and a tree can know what a woman was thinking. At the heart of participation is a responsive world, a sense that the world is alive, aware, intelligent, interested—that it contains, in short, invisible others. It may be that this is also what people mean when they talk of the spiritual senses: that sense of awareness of the aliveness pulsing through the earth, felt with the senses of the mind.

In recent years, we have begun to extend the items on the puzzling, fascinating, and powerful Absorption Scale. A group of us sat around the table with snacks, generating long lists of possible items, in part because we were curious, in part because the Absorption Scale is under copyright and we wanted to create an alternative. (Julia Cassaniti was particularly good at this.) We had a long list, and then had different people respond to those items and to those on the Absorption Scale. We built the "Sensory Delight Scale" out of the items that were most strongly related to the Absorption Scale. Like the Absorption Scale, the Sensory Delight Scale predicts unusual sensory experience and spiritual experience. Chances are that if you score highly on this scale (score the items false=0, true=1, and total them), you are someone who is more able, by temperament and choice, to have vivid experiences of gods and spirits.

Here is the Sensory Delight Scale:

When I'm listening to music, I like to imagine the sounds taking shape and moving in the air around me.

When I finish reading a really powerful book, I find that the ordinary world around me seems oddly unfamiliar.

Sometimes I feel like my body is weightless, as if I'm floating, even when my feet are firmly on the ground.

I like to watch the shapes and movements that sunlight makes reflecting off of water.

Sometimes the world seems intensely present to me.

I like to think that the trees in a forest are talking with each other.

I have had a distinct sense of a watchful presence.

Sometimes when I am at a concert, I find that the music has ended a few seconds ago and everyone is clapping before I notice.

The sounds of different languages seem to be connected to different colors in my mind.

Sometimes I feel like the air is full of little bubbles of light.

Sometimes I feel like I can sense the passage of time almost tangibly.

When I hear the waves lap against the shore, I sometimes think of how much those waves might know.

I find joy in little things, like a newly opened flower.

Exquisite pleasure sometimes floods my senses.

I can get lost watching a spider lower itself on a thread.

Sometimes I feel the arms of the universe embrace me.

When I dance, I like to feel that my body is simply responding to the music.

Thoughts can have different colors for me.

Absorption and inner sense cultivation kindle the felt realness of gods and spirits. The pleasure of being caught up in the inner or outer senses, an orientation toward mind and world that allows someone to focus in on the unseen and allows the everyday world to fade—these acts of attention change the way people come to experience gods and spirits in profound ways. Gods and spirits feel more present. They feel more real. And that allows the faith frame to become more anchored in their lives. When you can sing with the angels, it is harder to lose track of the gods.

4

HOW THE MIND MATTERS

> In the course of our discussion it will become evident that
> certain basic mental patterns exercise a varied control over men's
> minds and leave their imprint upon the manner in which man
> takes cognizance of himself.
>
> —Bruno Snell, *The Discovery of the Mind*

Faith is about the mind. It is about the ontological attitude people take toward what must be imagined—not because gods and spirits are necessarily imaginary, but because they cannot be known with the senses, and people of faith must allow those invisible others to feel alive to them. You must be able to look at a glorious forest, and see not just an ecosystem but intentions. You must be able to be moved by a sunset, and to think not only of the structure of light, but of a maker. You must allow yourself to move beyond the bare world and trust that there is more to the world than you see. That is the challenge of the faith frame: a commitment *despite*.

It is tempting to see what I have just said as a mere matter of belief. One might say, people believe that there is a maker because they hold the cognitive proposition that there is an extra thing in the world, which happens to be a god. But realness is a feeling, as well as a judgment. Matthew Ratcliffe writes of a "feeling of being," an existential emotion that ought, he suggests, really be on lists alongside sadness, anger, and happiness.

> [Existential feelings] form a recognisable group in virtue of two shared
> characteristics. First of all, they are not directed at specific objects or

situations but are background orientations through which experience as a whole is structured. Second, they are all *feelings*, in the sense that they are bodily states which influence one's awareness.... [T]hey constitute the basic structure of "being there," a "hold on things" that functions as a presupposed context for all intellectual and practical activity. (2005: 48)

This captures something deep—that there is a sense of "thereness" more akin to an emotion than to a belief. This is the quality of realness I mean when I say that gods and spirits must be made real. They must be made to feel as if they were there—not just known to be there abstractly, like the sky, but felt to be present, responsive, and engaged.

In this chapter, I want to show that this feeling of realness is facilitated not only by absorption (an experiential orientation toward inner and outer sensation) but by the way people imagine the relationship between inner and outer. When people hold what I will call a "citadel" model of mind, in which the mind is central to one's own identity but fundamentally disconnected from one's world—perhaps the dominant way people think about mind in Western settings—this can make it more difficult for them to experience gods and spirits as palpably present. The way they think about their mind affects the way gods and spirits are kindled for them.

To understand how that works, I need to explain the in-between.

THE IN-BETWEEN

Much of the phenomenal evidence for the presence of invisible others comes out of what I will call the "in-between": a domain that is felt to be neither in a person's own inner awareness nor in the everyday world. People will say that they heard God speak with a whisper inside their ear, that their dead spouse spoke from their abdomen, that the spirit spoke without words, that the voice was not in their mind but not in the world, either. When people talk about seeing things, they often say that they saw with their mind's eye but not in their mind. They gesture toward a space in front of their eyes, but say that they did not see with their eyes. They talk about experiencing God in a spot cut away from the ordinary world. They say things like this young man in Chicago did, at the moment of his conversion, lying on the floor during a weekend retreat:

I could hear people praying around me, but it felt like I was in a bubble and that everything outside of this bubble just did not exist. Like it was me and God in this one little tiny capsule and the rest of the world could go by it a billion miles per hour and I wouldn't care. Time stopped, and where I was felt absolutely weightless.

Here is a woman in northern California describing her turning point, when she wanted to shoot up with a needle and she thought no one else would know:

And then—He spoke. He said, "But I know," and it was—everything— heaven opened up, and I went—I always look up like I can see Him, but I couldn't see Him, but heaven opened up, and He spoke to me.

Here a woman in San Diego describes a moment in her small apartment just before she entered training as a santero:

I woke up in the middle of the night because I was hearing music, and I thought, "It's a stereo. I wish they'd turn it down." Then I start realizing it's just drumming going on—boom boom boom—and there's a rhythm to it. There's like singing starting to come. It starts getting louder and louder. And as I start to wake up and come out of my dream, I realize this is coming right outside my bedroom window. It is like there is band playing outside my bedroom window.

But there is nothing outside the window. It goes out to a back area that's just a brick wall. It was like the spirits were having a party or some-thing. [And then] I wake up this morning, I hear this soft voice in my right ear: "The orishas are with you."

Here is a young woman who was dating a medical student (also a Chris-tian) who seemed more involved with medicine than with her. They broke up, and she was devastated. Then God spoke to her:

I just felt this overwhelming sense of joy that came from God. And I knew it wasn't from myself. I felt like God actually was coming to me and just explaining more of His love for me, and it was just unconditional love that was different than the love that my parents gave me. . . . When I was feel-ing those experiences, the words just kind of flowed into my mind, and I didn't hear anything, but it was just more [than] my thoughts. It's like poetry actually. It was very beautiful. I just remember thinking that this was amazing.

These are quasi-sensory moments. People speak of seeing, hearing, and feeling, but they neither see, hear, nor feel in an ordinary way. They hear as if the sound is coming from inside their ears, not from the room outside. Sometimes they hear things at the edge of sleep. The seeing is not ordinary seeing. People often struggle to describe exactly what kind of experience it is. People sometimes say that the moment feels like it did not come from them—but they are not sure. Here is an American Christian reflecting on what he took to be God's voice:

> Yeah it's very clear, but sometimes have to say, am I just making—you know am I thinking this—is this God or cause I've misinterpreted things in the past and so I'm really kind of um, skeptical sometimes I kind of question it.

These moments are neither fully in the everyday nor fully in the mind.

Such in-between ambiguity is true of the experiences we call psychosis, as well. When we talk about people who struggle with intrusive sensory experiences that we call voices, most of them in fact are reporting moments that are more thought-like than sound-like. Even very articulate people struggle to put their experiences into words. As one woman, diagnosed with schizophrenia, recalled about her early experience,

> It becomes really, really difficult for me to distinguish (or explain the difference) between real voices, "hallucinated voices," thoughts in my own head, other people's thoughts, thoughts that might be circulating in the air, and then even the extent to which anything exists other than thoughts. Once everything starts to seem like a thought, then it's really difficult because voices are thoughts, but so are visuals. (Jones and Luhrmann 2015: 195)

This woman explains all these experiences as "voices," but what she means by the word is an event that seems more external, more "not-me" than an ordinary thought, and yet still different from ordinary sensation.

I do not mean to suggest that the experience of gods is like the experience of madness. It is more that madness and spirituality do their work in the same human space: in ambiguous moments that stand out from the everyday and demand that we make sense of them.

It is because of the ambiguity of these experiences that the way people think about their minds matters to the way they judge the nature of the event. One can be agnostic about the ultimate source of the event—about whether a god or spirit has actually spoken. The point I want to make here is that the way someone thinks about the domain of inner aware- ness that English speakers call the "mind" can affect how they judge, and thus how they experience, the event. Judgment, I will argue, can change the event. I have found that American evangelicals, compared to evan- gelicals elsewhere, experience God more internally and less sensorially, as if their God feels less real to them than to evangelicals in other cul- tures. I suggest that is because of the way they think about their minds.

THE MIND

Humans distinguish between mind-stuff and body-stuff, between inner awareness and an outer world. They may draw the line in different ways, they may make mistakes, but they are conscious—and to be conscious is to know a difference between awareness and the world. I will call this domain of awareness the mind, or mind-stuff, recognizing that the term "mind" is one that English speakers use to map this human terrain. Humans in different social worlds think about the relationship between mind-stuff and body-stuff in socially specific ways (see, e.g., Heelas and Lock 1981; Lillard 1998). They might imagine that emotions are more as- sociated with the body than with the mind. They may have different expectations about whether inner events can and should be shared or not, and what inner events can cause. Consider the questions one can ask about thought: Is thought a thing, a possession, as John Locke de- scribed the mind, or is it more like the Jedi's Force? Is it appropriate to speculate on what someone else intends—or is that rude or even impos- sible? Can impassioned silent prayer or an intense wash of anger affect the world directly, or is it just neuronal noise? These judgments are so intimate that people may not recognize that they are, in fact, judgments. But they are, and the way social worlds invite people to make them has real consequences for the way that those people understand what is real.

I call these "invitations" because social worlds rarely provide explicit models of the mind, the way there are explicit rules for, say, baseball games. Instead, I suspect that people come to think about mind stuff through inferences that they draw from what they see in the everyday world. If they see that those around them are afraid of witchcraft, they likely draw the inference that powerful feelings (anger, jealousy, and brooding resentment) can hurt other people directly. If they see that those around them treat psychics as weird and marginal, they likely draw the inference that people cannot really hear from the dead or predict the future—that such knowledge cannot enter the mind in mysterious ways from outside.

This matters because the implicit expectations people have about mind-stuff affect the way they experience the in-between, and thus the way they experience gods and spirits.

COMPARING APPLES TO APPLES (SORT OF)

I went to Accra, Ghana, and Chennai, India, to see whether American charismatic evangelicals were more likely to imagine hearing God as an inner phenomenon than charismatic evangelicals in other countries. Since 2004, I had conducted fieldwork in Chicago and on the San Francisco Peninsula in the Vineyard Christian Fellowship, churches where God is imagined as person-like and as someone who seeks a conversation with those who worship Him. Congregants talk of hearing God speak. This is meant to happen in the mind—that is, in inner, private experience. Congregants learn to pick out particular thoughts that they might otherwise have taken to be their own thoughts and to identify these thoughts as God's voice through a process of discernment. Certain thoughts are assumed to be better candidates for God's voice than others—thoughts that are spontaneous, thoughts that seem to express the kinds of things God might say. The people I knew in the Chicago and northern Californian churches were very clear that they had to *learn* to hear God speak. They were also very clear that they could be wrong— that one could pick out what one thought was God's voice, and it wasn't. One man said to me wryly, "Sometimes when we think it's the spirit moving, it's just our burrito from lunch." What struck me was not only that much of this process of hearing God involved attention to thoughts and inner experience—the stuff of what Americans would call the mind—but also how very American that understanding of this mind appeared to be.

European Americans are invited by their cultural heritage to imagine the mind as a private place, walled off from the world, a citadel in which thoughts are one's own and no one else has access to them. The mind is the source of what makes people who they are. Our identity comes from what we think and feel, rather than (for example) our family origin (e.g., C. Taylor 2007; Makari 2015). Just think of the enormous amount we spend on psychotherapy and our intense concerns with self-esteem. Middle-class Americans tend to assume that what they feel and think really matters. They also assume that thoughts and feelings are not materially real. The citadel dominates the town, but it is not part of the town. Educated Americans often assume that the brain, that pulpy, wrinkled, three-pound weight, is real. But the mind, they will say, is an epiphenomenon, a byproduct: immaterial, nonsubstantial, and invisible. Nor does the mind act directly on the world. If thought were material, we could call the thought imagined in this model "inert." That is, those who adopt this model imagine that thought affects the world only because it affects the thinker, the one who really acts. Thought does not leak from the mind to affect another human's body and make that person ill.

In a social world with a citadel model of the mind, what is real is what is materially present and independent of the observer. Here is *Merriam-Webster*'s definition of real: "having objective independent existence." And from *Macmillan*: "in the physical world; not just in someone's imagination." We talk of real causes, real evidence. Psychiatry achieved far more status as a form of medicine when it began to focus on brain disorders rather than on emotional conflict, because disorders of the brain seemed real in a way that disorders of the mind did not. A brain disorder was there in the world in a way that someone's thoughts and feelings simply were not. The historian and psychiatrist George Makari (2015: 475) describes the post-Enlightenment era as a time of the "mind eclipsed," when some thinkers could describe the mind as a puff of mysticism. The mind of course remained part of the cultural vocabulary, source of our capacity for free will, ethical action, and rational reflection. But Makari writes that as science emerged as a social force, the mind became imagined as even more limited and fallible, a source of illusion, error, and prejudice. G. E. R. Lloyd (2018) attributes the Western fascination with the real-unreal distinction to the fascination that distinction held for the ancient Greek world.

I saw these expectations/ideas at work in the American church. The charismatic evangelicals I knew were confused at first when they learned that God spoke to them in their minds. It took them some time to grasp the idea because it felt odd to them to have God breach the mind-world boundary—even though they knew from church that God would talk to them through their thoughts. Meanwhile, because they assumed that their feelings were so important, they used their prayer conversation to talk to God about their feelings. "It's just like talking to a therapist," one woman told me, "especially in the beginning when you're revealing things that are deep in your heart and deep in your soul, the things that have been pushed down and denied." And when they were learning to experience God as real, they used their imaginations deliberately. They imagined that God was present—but they were acutely aware that what they imagined (God's arm around their shoulders as they sat leaning back against the park bench) might not "really" be God.

Being struck, then, by the apparent Americanness of these ideas, I decided to compare similar churches in two different settings: Chennai, India, and Accra, Ghana. I decided to look at a similar church in Chennai because I'd been in and out of the city for years, working with a local institute on the voices people heard in schizophrenia. The ethnographic literature suggested that in Chennai there would be different cultural invitations toward thinking about thinking: that South Indians placed less social importance on their own thoughts and feeling than Americans—that they would neither define identity as so clearly based on a person's inner thoughts and feelings, nor feel so strong a need as urban middle-class Americans to understand and process their own emotions (Mines 1994).

The theme that runs through ethnographies of Chennai is interdependent relationships (Markus and Kitayama 1994). People imagine themselves as densely and complexly intertwined with others, and they are socialized to pay close attention to the feelings of others. What elders think about what the younger generation should be thinking—about schooling, about marriage, about what they eat and wear—may be socially more important than what those younger people were actually thinking, and juniors are expected to know what seniors are thinking and to respond empathically to them (Marrow 2019). Meanwhile, the great literature of the language represents acts of the imagination as "more than real" (Shulman 2012). This is a literature about the great deeds of skilled yogis, whose capacity to imagine with concentration and intensity generates power. India, Shulman writes, has thought more boldly about cultivating imagination than most human societies (2012: ix). In a short poem, a mid-fifteenth-century poet in Tirupati wrote, "God is what you have in your mind" (2012: 147).

I decided to add Ghana as another point of comparison because unlike India, which has a tiny proportion of charismatic Christians (although they are more concentrated in Chennai and elsewhere in South India than in the north), Ghana's charismatic Christians dominate the religious landscape. Around 70 percent of Ghanaians are Christian, most of them charismatic. The ethnographic literature also suggests that Ghanaians might think quite differently about mind and mental process than North Americans (Levine 1973; Reisman 1977; Horton 1993). To be clear: the literature does not suggest that Ghanaians and North Americans have different mental processes. But it suggests that Ghanaians imagine the mind as less private, less bounded, and more supernaturally potent than Americans do. Most Ghanaian words for thought and emotion are rooted in bodily experience. The psychologist Vivian Dzokoto (2010; Chentsova-Dutton and Dzokoto 2014) has shown that even Ghanaians who speak English fluently behave as if they are more concerned with and pay more attention to their bodies than to their inner worlds, compared to Americans. The anthropologist Kathryn Geurts (2002), who wrote an ethnography about the Anlo-Ewe people in southeastern Ghana, observed that they have a highly salient category of sensation (*seselamene*: feel-feel-at-flesh-inside) that Westerners just don't have, and the Western emphasis on mind-body dualism simply wasn't culturally relevant. Meanwhile, just as psychotherapy is greatly important to many in the United States, ideas about witchcraft—and in particular, the ability of one human being to harm another human being through the potency of their own thoughts (Geschiere 2013)—are quite important in Ghanaian culture. Even if a Ghanaian does not believe in witchcraft, he or she surely knows someone who does. That suggests that Ghanaians are more invested than Americans in the idea that mind-stuff is continuous with world-stuff rather than fundamentally different from it, that it is entangled with the spiritual forces that permeate the material world, and that thinking is an action in the world (Verren 2001; Dzokoto

2020; Dulin 2020 and forthcoming). The somatic and the supernatural, not introspected mind, are often what counts.

Thus there are different cultural invitations in these different settings, different available ways of drawing inferences about inner worlds: in the United States, that the mind is private, bounded, and supernaturally inert; in Chennai, that the mind involves a social process; in Accra, that the mind is supernaturally charged, more a bodily process, and evil thoughts can harm. I characterize these differences as self-oriented (United States), other-oriented (Chennai), and soma-and-spirit-oriented (Accra).

I then set out to compare. I sought out churches like the Vineyard: churches that were middle class and self-consciously modern, with English-language services, technological sophistication (amplifiers and PowerPoint), and the explicit theological expectation that God is intimately present as a supernatural presence, that God is a friend, and that He will talk back directly in the mind to those who seek to speak with Him. These are often described as "neo-Pentecostal" churches: Pentecostal churches adapted for the modern age.

Pentecostalism is sometimes described as a "hard" cultural form—a culture within a culture that spreads vigorously around the world in a surprisingly stable form (Robbins 2004b; Freston 2013; see also Eriksen 2018). Arjun Appadurai (1996) used the phrase to capture practices that seem to have links between meaning and practices that are hard to break, in contrast to soft forms, like friendship, which have different forms in different settings. The overt features of Pentecostalism—tongues, spiritual warfare, biblical literalism, and the direct immediacy of an encounter with God—make church practice clearly recognizable. In Accra and Chennai, these are colonial imports. They have been embraced with vigor.

CHENNAI

The air in India smells like nowhere else, a mixture of heat, dust, and spice. I have loved it since I stepped out of a plane for the first time in what was then called Bombay. Chennai is technically a smaller city, but the road in front of my hotel had eight lanes for traffic, not that cars and the autorickshaws paid much attention to the lines. Chennai is a city of around ten million. Of them, 8 percent are Christian.

In Chennai, my choice of a church was obvious. The New Life Assembly of God is a member of a Pentecostal denomination with tap roots in the United States and a historical tradition of social conservatism. Assemblies of God churches were founded in 1914 in Hot Springs, Arkansas, shortly after the Azusa Street revival in Los Angeles, when Pentecostalism suddenly landed on the national stage. Back then, men and women sat separately on Sunday mornings. They neither drank nor saw movies; earlier, they were sometimes told not to vote, because that would make them complicit in a fallen world. In early and mid-twentieth-century America, Assemblies of God churches were often described as rejecting modernity and its sinful temptations (Wacker 2003).

In recent decades, some of the once-traditional congregations have loosened up—both in the United States and around the world. They have become more casual, more technologically savvy, and more engaged with the modern world. Members vote, they dance, they often drink, and they no longer see politics as tainted. Many Assemblies of God churches are now indistinguishable from the new charismatic evangelical churches that emerged as their competition. That was true of the English-language service of the New Life Assembly of God in Chennai.

The church is home to thirty-five thousand congregants. Its English-language service meets on the top floor of a vast building and is led by the main pastor's son. When I was there in 2014, about four thousand people came to the various English-language services that met throughout the day on Sunday. Most of them were middle class.

Middle-class South Asians highly value bodily and mental control. They look down on the abandonment of young rural women who become possessed by spirits and roll on the temple grounds, their fists in the dirt, their eyes wild. When lower-caste Hindus convert to Christianity, women still become possessed by demons, and they embrace speaking in tongues as a bodily practice, swooning into near possession by God. As I climbed up the stairs toward the English-language services, past the Telegu service and the different Tamil services, it was like ascending a ladder of bodily restraint. In the English-language service, there were no writhing bodies. People stood calmly. They sang quietly, to songs very much like the ones I'd heard in California. When they spoke in tongues, they did not provide the wash of sound I had heard in Accra, but a gentle background hum. Yet the church clearly had the qualities of the new charismatic churches, and God was understood as a friend who would speak back in dialogue.

I arrived in Chennai in time for the 2014 New Year's Eve service, one of the biggest worship celebrations of the year. The service had moved to a room capable of accommodating all four thousand congregants; most of them seemed to be there, packed in around the walls. When the pastor came up on stage, he said, "We are standing in the presence of God as one family." It was the theme of the night. We sang songs of joy and love and acceptance, with lines like "You are good, and your love endures forever." We sang a song in which we insisted that God was our friend: "He is a friend of mine."

After twenty minutes or so, the pastor then formally welcomed God into our midst, an invitation I had heard every Sunday in the Vineyard, although less often in Accra. "Lord, we welcome you in this place. We trust in your name. We hold on to your name. Let's lift up our hands and surrender ourselves to God. God is here in our midst. Forget your past. God is a God who makes things new if you surrender. Lift up your hands as a sign."

The pastor then introduced the church, presumably because some who had come to this large celebration were new. He brought his large family up on stage. Then he brought up the pastoral team, mostly men and women in their twenties and thirties. (These were the people I would later interview.) He described the church's housegroups (there were eighty-four of them—a quarter to a third of the church seemed to attend one). He spoke of how many people helped out on Sunday morning (three hundred, in multiple services). And he said that because of all these people and because of what the congregation did, the scent of Jesus spread through the city as a sweet-smelling aroma. At this, people held up their hands and spoke in tongues. He prayed for families, and he prayed for love; he prayed that the evil one would be broken down by the Lord and that we would also experience a breakthrough from the Lord, who was absolutely good. Then he delivered a sermon on the acronym GROW: Grace, Relationship, Obedience, and Worship. "The single thing that counts is quality time with your family," he said. He spoke on the need to follow the word of God, to resist temptation, and that we should remember above all else that "no matter what happens, you are special to God." When we took communion, he asked us to hold our small cup of juice and bread until all had been served. Then he asked us to exchange our juice with someone else, and to drink what they had held in their hands. I remember thinking that this seemed a distinctly South Asian gesture, interdependence made holy.

Evil was more real here than it was in the churches I knew in the United States, although the sense of the demonic would be even more pronounced in Accra. A number of people told me stories about people who attacked them by leaving cursed lemons or a small sheet of copper on the premises. The stories were a piece with the idea that when people become Christians, their enemies increase—but that God would now fight for them. The pastor told me that the church had been attacked many times. "We have taken [cursed items] out of one stage near the choir underneath the place where the cameras are. We have taken [them] out of doormats. We have pulled [them] out of cars." People spoke about awaking in the middle of the night unable to move because of a demonic force in the room—a condition of the body often called sleep paralysis in the medical literature. In the American churches I knew, people spoke about evil and demonic presence, but demons did not seem terribly important, and few people described sleep paralysis as evil.

Still, the basic ideas about who God was and how God would interact were very much the same in Chennai and in the United States. God was a person. He was your best friend. You should talk to Him about everything, and He would give you what you needed because He loved you. As one woman explained, "I call him my Dad. Even when I pray, you would hear me say it's my daddy I pray to. . . . I love that, when my father puts me on his lap. That's an image I can't forget from my childhood." This God was deeply loving, deeply responsive. Here, too, God would come and go like a person. Like the Christians in the United States, these Chennai Christians felt God working through them, being with them, being by their side. They prayed with great intensity and they said that God would answer their prayers. Here is a Chennai congregant:

I was really praying. I was thinking, "Oh God, this person is in the ICU. Please God watch over him." And immediately I had this conviction to tell them, "Okay, don't worry. Your son will be alright." And the next week, the son was out of the ICU.

As in the American church, people said that God placed thoughts in their minds to transmit to others, and He placed thoughts in their minds for them. They used the same means of discernment to identify what God said in their minds and to distinguish that voice from their own thoughts. God's voice was spontaneous. "Suddenly words come to mind," one woman explained. "[His voice] will be louder [than my thoughts] and more clear." God's voice "popped." When I asked a young man whether God ever spoke into his mind, he said, "After I prayed, it was in my mind very clearly to read 2 Thessalonians 3:10. I had no idea what that meant. It just popped into my mind." God's voice brought peace and relief. "God's voice is always comforting," said another woman. And a man: "When He speaks, there is a complete peace in the heart." And as in the American church, there is a sense that one must test the inference that the voice in one's mind is God. "I would ask for confirmation," one person said. As in the United States, people spoke about learning to hear God more effectively, and with more confidence, over time.

ACCRA

I remember thinking, that first week I spent in Accra, that I envied my anthropological ancestors. I had done my doctoral work at Cambridge, back in the days when most of the great shaggy lions of the department had worked in Africa—most of them, in fact, in Ghana. Jack Goody, the chair, and his wife, Esther, had spent years in northern Ghana among the LoDagaa. Meyer Fortes had worked there with the Tallensi. Audrey Richards, with whom I had tea every month in the modern apartment building we happened both to live in at the end of town, had written her famous account of women's initiation rites from her work among the Bemba in Northern Rhodesia, now Zambia. The principal lessons I remember from the departmental course on fieldwork were to bring mosquito netting and tennis shoes and never to trust our fieldnotes to checked baggage. I thought of village Africa as a serene world of thatched hut villages where chickens scattered as you entered the family compound and the ocher earth dusted your shoes. My actual experience of Accra, Ghana's main city, was of a cacophonous, billboard-studded snarl of traffic. My anthropological seniors told stories about long stretches of time where nothing happened. I never had this experience in Accra.

There are a handful of churches that people recognize as the new charismatic churches in Accra. They are the big congregations in raw new buildings, with live Internet streaming and websites and CDs for sale so that you can listen to the sermons again and again. Their Ghanaian pastors travel all over the world speaking to massive conferences. Their faces appear on the large, colorful billboards that smile down on Accra traffic. As the sociologist Paul Gifford (2004: 23–24) describes them, "Everyone is aware of charismatic prayer centres, their all-night services ('All Nights'), their crusades, conventions and Bible schools, their new buildings (or the schools, cinemas and halls they rent), their car-bumper stickers and banners, and particularly the posters that everywhere announce an enormous range of forthcoming activities."

These churches grew from small fellowships that turned the dull drone of mainstream Christianity into something fun. In the old Pentecostal churches, pastors had read their sermons. People spoke in tongues, but they sat separately and dressed modestly so as not to be tempted by the flesh. In the new charismatic churches, people dressed casually (at least, as casually as middle-class Ghanaians dress), they sat together, and they clapped, danced, sang, and even cheered. They sought a God who loved them more than He judged them, a God who was present there in the service and who sent them supernatural power that coursed through their bodies and attacked the evils that beset them.

The ideas in these churches were nurtured by the American teachings of Kenneth Hagin and Oral Roberts that were widely read in Ghana in the 1980s, but the churches were African: planted by Africans, pastored by Africans, financially supported by Africans, and shaped by their pastors to speak to African realities. A leading Ghanaian scholar of these churches, Kwabena Asamoah-Gyadu, calls them Independent Indigenous Pentecostal churches (the locals, however, just call them "the charismatic churches"). Asamoah-Gyadu (2005) argues that they appeal so deeply precisely because unlike the mainstream churches, they focus explicitly on the invisible realm of benevolent and malevolent powers one finds in traditional African religion, a point Birgit Meyer (1999) also makes. "Worship in the traditional religious context," he writes, "is built around an ardent desire to communicate with and experience the felt presence of the supernatural" (Asamoah-Gyadu 2005: 31). The new charismatic churches in Accra make a commitment to the immediate presence of the divine, supernatural healing, deliverance from evil, and a spontaneous, passionate celebration of God.

The US churches also make that commitment, but I felt a more visceral quality in the sense of that power in Accra. In August 2013, I went to the final night of the International Central Gospel Church's (ICGC) Greater Works Conference. Over ten thousand people were there. More plastic chairs than I had ever seen stretched out like a pixilated field around the main building, two thousand on each side and thousands more in front, with overflow even into the parking lot, each area with its own large screen and a team of ushers so efficient that when someone left they filled the seat with another person standing on the sidelines. No doubt people came for the spectacle and for the party, even though all the music was worship music. "If you have never danced this year," the pastor promised, "you will dance tonight!" and a roar went up from the crowd.

They also came for the power: the supernatural force that would help them to combat malevolent evil and to achieve their goals. This was the "anointing" service. More than three hours into the evening, each person was given a small plastic vial of oil. At the apex moment of the evening, they held the vial up in the air to be blessed and charged so that they could take it home and use it like a potent talisman.

Just as in Chennai, the basic ideas of who God was and how God would communicate were similar to those in the churches I had worked with in the United States. I chose as my participants a class of pastoral students studying at a college associated with the church. I interviewed them in depth, along with their pastors, their teachers, and others who attended this church and similar churches. What they said about God was very close to the kinds of things people said in America and in India. God was a person, they said. He was your best friend. You could and should talk to Him about everything, and He would talk back because you had a personal relationship with Him and He cared. "Daddy Lord," one student called him. Another student said, "For me, I would say that God is many things, but first I will say that God is—I see God to be more like a best friend, yeah." The students described themselves as talking to God in daydream-like encounters they experienced in their minds, just as the American congregants had done.

How do you know that it is God who speaks through the words you hear in your mind, and not your own eager, selfish, inner voice? The congregants in Accra used the same language congregants used in Chicago and in the South Bay. They talked about learning to recognize God's voice through discernment, which they took as a skill they had to master that, once learned, would help them to hear more effectively. They spoke of becoming more spiritually "sensitive," and when they described how they identified God's voice, they used the same principles I heard from congregants elsewhere. They recognized God's voice because His words felt stronger or louder or more spontaneous than their own thoughts. "It comes so strong," one woman explained, and a man remarked, "I will not be thinking about anything, but all of a sudden in the course of praying then a thought just struck me to the mind." Just as people did in the United States and in India, they would check to see if what they thought God said accorded with scripture, and they too felt a sense of peace when He spoke.

And yet evil was real in these Accra charismatic churches in a way I never saw in their American counterparts, more even than in Chennai. Now, it is true that in the American churches in which I did research, people would say that demons existed. One cannot take the Bible to be true in all it affirms—a common evangelical commitment—and not take demons seriously. In the Gospels, Jesus spends much of his time getting rid of them. In Mark, the demons are about the only beings that know him for who he is. But in the American church I knew, demons just weren't particularly salient for most people. They did not come up—for the most part—on Sunday mornings, and—for the most part—people did not pray about demonic oppression.

That was not the case for the new charismatic churches in Accra. In these churches, prayer is warfare. People imagined a world riven by dark forces that swarmed around them, attacking their bodies, their families, and their means to earn a living. Prayer is also the means to love God, and the pastoral students told me about praying to God with love and weeping with their joy. Almost all the students also spoke about demons, about spiritual attack, and about prayer as the means to protect and shield and fight. They talked about aunts who tried to poison them, about their father's sister who did kill their father and confessed it at the funeral, and about the demons who choked them and sat on them and drank their blood.

In the American church, people loved C. S. Lewis's image of God as a mighty lion—not a tame lion, but one you could embrace and bury your face in his mane the way Lucy did with Aslan in *The Lion, the Witch and the Wardrobe*. The institute library in Ghana held no C. S. Lewis, and the only mention of a lion in my interviews was this young man's metaphor (1 Peter 5:8): "Your enemy—the devil, your adversary—is walking to and fro like a wounded lion looking for someone to devour."

Every church service I attended in Accra—from any of the new charismatic churches—focused its emotional crescendo on a counterattack to evil. One warm Friday evening, I found myself in an all-night prayer session at an ICGC church branch led by a man associated with a pastoral institute. All-night prayer had become wildly popular in the city, somewhat to the distress of those who objected to the late-night noise that rivals an American frat party. But the people who attend these sessions love them, because the long stretch of time allows them to pray more intensely than a mere two-hour Sunday morning church service permits. This Friday night, the focus of our prayers was a story in the Book of Acts. The Apostle Paul, arriving at an island on his journey to share the gospel, picked up some brushwood for a fire, and a startled viper within it leapt out and bit his hand. When the islanders saw the snake hanging from his hand, they thought that he would die. But Paul shook the viper off and lived. The pastor applied the scripture to our lives: "Say it out loud!" he shouted. "Every viper sticking to my hands, my marriage, my career, my destiny, I SHAKE IT OFF. I SHAKE IT OFF!" And the two hundred people around me jumped up and down and shook their hands with fury, hurling invisible and metaphorical vipers into the air.

Power here was a thing in the world, and its consequences were important. Church was about achieving practical ends. Material success was proof of spiritual authority. If the American congregants went to church to feel happier, and the Chennai congregants went to church to feel more connected, the Accra congregants went to church to be more effective in the world.

GOD SPEAKS DIFFERENTLY IN DIFFERENT PLACES: EXTERNAL PRESENCE

What startled me was how much more audibly God spoke in Accra and in Chennai. I had seen in the United States that people who were higher in absorption, or who prayed more actively, were more likely to report quasi-sensory moments in which they heard God speak in a way that that they thought they could hear with their ears. As a reminder, these events are quite different in kind from the voices heard by those with psychosis: rare, brief, and startling, but not distressing. In Chennai, people reported experiencing God talking more palpably, as if He spoke from outside their inner mind, than He did in the United States. They did so even more often in Accra.

That, at least, was what I thought, based just on informal conversation. After all, I had spent years listening to American charismatic Christians talk about God in Chicago and in the South Bay. When I arrived in Chennai and in Accra, I was struck by just how much less doubt people felt about whether God had spoken, and how much less God seemed to be located within the mind. (To be clear, they were also sure that if one did not pray and worship, one's sense of God would turn to mist.)

I decided to look at this systematically. We had interviewed thirty-four people from the Vineyard with a specific set of questions: how they prayed, whether God spoke with them, and if so, how, and what kinds of spiritual events they had experienced. I used that interview protocol to speak for over an hour with twenty committed Christians from the church in Chennai, and twenty from the church in Accra. As we had done in the United States, I lingered over the voice question. "Had they ever heard God speak out loud?" I asked in many ways: "Had they heard God speak with their ears?" "Was the voice outside their head?" "Did they turn their head to see who was speaking?" I recorded the interviews, coded their responses, and read them again and again. I saw differences I could not explain by their responses to the Absorption Scale, nor by the time they spent in prayer.

Of my American participants, 35 percent—about a third—said that they had heard God speak audibly in a way they could hear with their ears. They described these moments as casual and personal.

Riding in a car with a friend, [a voice] said, "You're playing with fire." And I turned around and like, where are you? . . . I felt like that was God, absolutely plain, flat out, whether it's the Spirit or His angels or however He wants to manage that one. That was definitely His.

The Americans made comments that indicated that they also thought that these experiences were odd. They said things like, "I don't know, they're just weird"; "I just assume I'm nuts"; "Hm, okay, that sounded odd." These participants felt a need to signal that someone could assume they were crazy, as well as a need to signal that they were not.

More people in Chennai (45 percent) reported that God had spoken in a way they could hear with their ears. They described God's voice as personal, soothing, and intimate.

P: So whenever I pray, I just feel like crying. I'll be continuously crying in God's presence and I feel like something is shaking me, something is shaking me and asking me—even when I'm crying, I'll be hearing that, "This is not you. This is not because of you," kind of words, and all that I'll be hearing, but at that time, I don't understand much because I was just coming to God.

TML: When you hear those words—when you describe that, "This is not because of you," is that audibly or was that in your mind?

P: That was audible.

The Chennai participants were more likely to say that God woke them up singing or soothed them in the middle of the night. One man said that God had played music for him to follow.

C: God taught me or maybe God played along, I'm not sure. But then there was a music that I didn't know myself. I think I should phrase it as "the heavenly music" that intervened inside my room. I played along with it.

TML: Did you hear it sort of outside?

C: Yeah, outside. With my ear. It was aloud. . . . I played it alone.

In Chennai, congregants seemed more comfortable than the Americans with these experiences. There was no talk of being crazy. They also seemed more able to identify explicitly events that were not in their mind, but which they did not experience sensorially in the world. That is, I inferred the in-between from what the Americans said about these experiences, but I heard them speak in a more puzzled way about the events. In Chennai, people seemed not only more at ease with in-between events but more able to describe the in-between quality. They spoke in ways that suggested what Jean Briggs (1998: 9) has called a "covert category": a concept that describes something, even though the concept is not specifically named. In Chennai, congregants described some experiences of God's voice as "not audibly, not in my mind, but in my inner"; "wide awake inside of me strong"; "not audible as you are talking, but it was a song in the mind"; and "in my spirit sense." I did not count these as audible events, but I was struck by them.

Even more people in Accra (55 percent) reported that they had heard God speak with their ears. Compared to the Americans and those in Chennai, participants in Accra were more likely to remember exhortations to action. Here is a young woman:

> L: That audible voice—even before I came to the Bible Institute I was contemplating as to whether I should come or not, or wait for a while, or—and I was laying down one evening. The voice was so clear. "You can do it."
>
> TML: And you heard it with your ears?
>
> L: Yes. "You can do it."

The Accra participants seemed much more comfortable with the idea that an invisible other's voice could have an auditory quality, and indeed more comfortable talking about hearing audible voices (in the absence of visible persons) in general. They seemed less interested in what Americans took to be that sharp line between inner and outer experience.

To be clear, in conversation, the Accra participants were well able to distinguish between a thought generated from inside the mind and an audible voice they heard from without. But that distinction was not as important to them as it was to the Americans, nor as troublesome, and it seemed that the Accra participants were at ease with letting the distinction slide and with experiences betwixt and between. They seemed less interested in naming the in-between. It was more that they seemed comfortable treating inner and outer as on a continuum. This was particularly clear in this account below, where I am interpreting this woman's hand gestures as well as her words as I speak:

TML: Have you ever heard God speak in a way that you can hear with
    your ears?

R: Yes. Many times, it's His word confirmed to me. Hear somebody say
    the word in my ears.

TML: Okay. How commonly does it feel like that's almost auditory? Or
    actually auditory? So you hear it with your ears?

R: As soon as I'm conscious of it.

TML: It stops?

R: As soon as I'm conscious. When I'm conscious that I am hearing God
    speak, I hear it.

TML: Oh, then it pops out and becomes more auditory?

R: Yes.

This woman is and is not making the distinction between hearing and
thinking. She asserts the distinction clearly in our discussion, then immediately blurs it. She wants to tell me that she has some kind of phenomenal experience when she prays that becomes auditory because she
knows the scripture, and her knowledge of the scripture makes the
prompting audible to her ears. In contrast, the Americans were often
hesitant to describe an event as auditory. It scared them.

I don't think that these different rates simply reflect different ways of
talking about God. I think that different ways of attending to experience
kindle God in different ways. Whether I spoke to people in in-depth,
probing conversations or had them complete various pen-and-paper
scales, the same patterns emerged. Congregants in Chennai spoke as if
they experienced God more viscerally than did those in the United
States—and congregants in Accra seemed to feel God even more palpably. Because I spent so much time with people and probed so carefully
about the felt quality of the experience of God, I am reasonably confident that these differences are phenomenologically real. They represent
different ways that God becomes present for people in different social
settings. That is what I mean by kindling: that people feel God differently, in specific ways, because of the specific ways that they attend to
their own experience.

Here is some more evidence. We gave Christian college students in
three settings pen-and-paper questionnaires. Students in Accra were
much more likely to say that they had experienced such a voice than in

the United States; Chennai was somewhat of an intermediate case. One question was, *Have you ever heard a voice when alone?* Of those in the United States, 44 percent said "yes" to this question, compared to 56 percent in Chennai, and a full 90 percent in Accra. There was a similar pattern in answers to a question on whether one had ever heard God speak outside one's head. Nor am I the only person to have seen this pattern, at least with respect to Ghana. John Dulin (2020) writes that "many Ghanaians might be habitually indifferent to typical western distinctions between mind and non-mind." He too found that charismatic Christians in Ghana reported—and seemed to experience—that God spoke with an auditory quality more often than charismatic Christians in the United States.

GOD SPEAKS DIFFERENTLY IN DIFFERENT PLACES: THE VEHICLE

It wasn't just God's quasi-audible voice, however. People in different places also described God as communicating with them in different ways. In general, Americans emphasized that God spoke in their mind; those in Chennai, through people; and those in Accra, through scripture, through a book they often held in their hands.

In all three churches in the South Bay, Chennai, and Accra, God was understood to speak back in several ways.

He spoke through the Bible. When congregants read scripture and felt powerfully moved or affected by a particular passage, they might infer that God spoke to them through that passage: that He led them to it in order to have them read it and respond to it.

God was also understood to speak through people and circumstances. Congregants would describe events that might seem to be coincidences, but they would say that God was speaking to them through these circumstances in order to communicate something to them: that He loved them, or He wanted them to make this decision or that one.

And God would speak back by placing mental images or thoughts in their minds. These were mental events that they identified as not being their own, but rather as having been generated by an external presence, God.

I thought there were real differences in the way people spoke about how God communicated, but those differences were more about emphasis—some kinds of stories were longer, or richer, or more meaningful. I am not using objective measurements here, but interpreting with an ethnographer's sensibility. I feel more confident about these judgments because I asked a young theologian, Paul Blankenship, to read the interviews alongside me. He too saw these differences, and did so independently. He was struck by the inwardness of the American accounts, where God seemed more like a friend. In Chennai, he pointed out, God seemed more like a father, and people were more likely to experience God in their human father and through other people. In the interviews from Accra, he saw authority and power and a God who acted in the world. His summary notes from May 2014 say that in the United States, God feels emotionally hurt when His humans don't pay attention to Him. In Chennai, he wrote, God withdraws; if you are not responsive, you cannot find Him. In Accra, on the other hand, God punishes those who neglect Him. Paul remembered two stories about men who shared similar names. In the first, the American came to the church after a breakup. He felt that no one in the room loved him. Then he heard God say, "But I love you." God became real to him, in short, through a private experience when his human relationships were in disarray. In the second, a man in Chennai converted when he, too, felt destitute, but he converted because he felt that the people in church really loved him. God became real to him through people.

It seemed to me that the Americans were more likely to describe an internal back-and-forth. They were more playful in interpreting what God had said to them, and were more likely to place what God had said in a semifictional frame. Here are three examples from South Bay congregants:

You know, you hear this thing about the onion where people say, "Oh yeah, well you're like an onion, and God peels back the layers," and I hate that analogy. [Laughter] I just think it's the stupidest thing I ever heard, and so one day I was driving to church, and I just said, "Okay, so what's up with this onion thing? I don't like the whole onion thing. It just seems stupid." I felt I didn't hear the audible voice, but I felt God just say, "You don't reveal yourself to me. I reveal myself to you," and I was like, "Really?"

"I'm the onion," He said. "I'm the onion." I was like, "Wow, that's kinda cool because it totally twisted it completely around."

Another:

And it was like, straight to the point, "Dude, you need to—you got—this is the only way."

Another:

I mean I think I sat there for like half an hour and just went back and forth and said, "Is that really you, God?" and He's like, "Yeah, of course it's me," blah blah blah.

The onion. Blah blah blah. This God chats.

For these Americans, God does command—"You are to stand up" or "Believe!"—but more often, He comments. He describes. He thinks. One woman explained, "He will give me insights into, 'You should go talk to that person.' Or, 'they're really in trouble, offer this type of advice.'" And the experience itself is often marked as mental. "It's something that I experience as a thought and it usually goes into words." Another example:

I feel like those conversations that I carry on in my head sometimes— that feels very like the part of me that is connected with God and that has the wisdom that I need—[that part] is able to articulate that to me in those conversations.

When these Americans spoke about God, they often cast their experience of God as interior.

At the same time—and this was striking—these Americans very often marked the appearance of God's voice in their minds as odd: "This is crazy, but I'm getting an image of . . ." Or: "You don't need to call the white coats for me." "It blew my mind." "You know, 'Those people are tripping.'" In other words, the US participants emphasized both that God spoke to them in their minds and that this experience was strange for them. They described God as speaking in ways that demanded the playful use of the imagination (God chats, God is personal, God says "blah blah blah"), and at the same time, they made it clear that this in-the-mind experience violated their sense of what a healthy mind should be (bounded and private). They felt that they had to signal that they knew someone could interpret this experience as crazy, and yet they were not crazy. I never heard this concern in Accra or in Chennai.

In Chennai, people seemed to experience God most vividly through human relationships, and human relationships were treated as entry points into the experience of God. When a young man explained to me how he chose to convert to Christianity, he did not talk about Christianity as a logical explanation, and he did not describe a road-to-Damascus spiritual awakening. He talked about people. "I slowly, okay, then I understood how God is actually showing his love to me through these people, and that's when I went to God. . . . That is the main thing that actually attracted me." When another man told a story about God speaking to him, the point of the story was the way he could touch the lives of others. "God said, 'Take your guitar and play along.' Then after singing two songs, I'm definitely sure I touched many lives because I am a very reserved type when it comes to onstage, but then I got off the stage, then I have to walk through people." There was even a poster in the pastor's office: "Relationships are more important than rules."

When I asked one newly married man how he knew that God was speaking, what he said was characteristic of the way many in Chennai responded.

> Last Christmas—this Christmas, that was the first Christmas after my marriage, my wife wants me to get something good, something for her. She wants a mobile. I was praying—I was asking God, "God, is it wise enough to get all these things?" And immediately God put a thought in me . . . so I was telling my wife, "Yeah, see, God is telling me like this. Already we have got enough, so why do we spend the money for the same thing? Rather we just wait for it." [Still] we were about to—so we were all like searching for what's the good mobile so we can get it for her Christmas. . . . And one of our friends—he is a great man. He has one new mobile coming end of January. So, we just wait for [the one he has now]. It'll be a nice one. So, I thought, "Okay, thank you, God, for giving me this advice," because God also speaks to us through some people.

This man neither directly quotes what God has said (as my US participants often did), nor ends with an affirmation of God's realness, as the US participants also often did. What he really wanted to emphasize was how following God had enhanced his relationship to other humans. "So exactly the amount we could spend on the mobile, we were able to spend for someone else. One of my friends, she [had her mortgage due]. She called up, 'Can you help me out?' She was not having enough money, so she was asking for help. So, we were just saving it for the mobile, and we were able to give it to her."

When the Chennai congregants spoke about their prayer, they repeatedly emphasized hearing from God through people (rather than in their minds). That is, they certainly spoke about hearing God speak in their minds, but their stories about hearing God through people were often longer, richer, and more emotional. God was represented as a parental relationship (being upset with God, one woman explained, was like being upset with your parents), and God was most often experienced through human relationships. "Life is about relationships," the pastor explained. "It's all about relationship, and this relationship is vertical with God, and it transcends horizontally with other human beings."

In Accra, God was different. People reported back-and-forth interactions, but for the most part these were not presented as dialogue. People described what God was saying, but usually they did not quote Him. Often, they spoke as if God communicated without words. They felt Him through their bodies. For example, a man said, "I basically pray by conversing with God as if we are friends, we are close pals. You know, I tell Him what's on my mind and heart." Yet that man then explained that he was the one doing the talking, and that God responded by giving him a physical feeling. "It is a sense or feeling that I get in my heart on a particular subject." Often, these interactions were mediated through the Bible.

So, I was lying on my bed, and then I started talking to Him. It's awesome. . . . I can talk to God like I'm talking to you, and as you are responding, even though I don't hear your voice, it comes. . . . I'll ask a question, and then He'll point me to a scripture I've not thought about.

These exchanges were not playful. I asked another man,

So, when you told me about praying to God, you told me then about praying about serious things, very serious and important things. With a friend you just kind of hang out and have a good time. Do you do that with God, too?

He responded:

> No, I mean business with God. It's business with God. So now I need to
> be serious with God. So, I don't go to God with stories, specifics, yes.

Someone else, discussing her interactions with God, rather huffily explained that she did not "play" with God.

In Accra, these interactions with God are presented above all as moral exhortations. They are about the struggle to achieve right behavior.

> You read the Bible and God says that, in Peter, add to your faith, knowledge, virtue. So, then I'm thinking that, "Maybe I don't have this virtue, I don't have that virtue, I don't have this virtue." . . . And I'm always talking to Him about that. My challenges. "God help me to be good." And if I flaunt His laws, I'll go to Him and—well, I've never really talked about it. But like when I flaunt His laws I go to Him and talk to Him. "Forgive me. Help me be good. Help me, show me what to do." It forms the greater part of my prayer.

In Accra, prayers are also about power. "I've had the knowledge that once I accept Jesus Christ as my Lord and Savior, I'm powerful. I have an inherent power . . . that can be used." In Accra, people spoke about a God who seemed to be more externally present than He was for the Americans and even for those in Chennai—more like a power they felt through their bodies than a pretend friend they imagined talking to in their minds.

All these congregants, in all three countries, were good people of faith who shared more or less the same theology in more or less similar churches. Yet they experienced God differently. (Table 1 summarizes these differences.) The self-oriented Americans, whose culture invites them to imagine their inner experience as very important as a means of self-understanding, emphasized God speaking inside their minds more than through scripture and people. They were more likely to remember His voice speaking as an imaginary-but-real companion—someone they experienced as not in the world but in their minds. What I heard from the Americans was a sharp, clear sense of the mind as a separated, interior place. Thoughts were private; imagination was good; voices even in the mind were a sign that you were crazy, so you needed to indicate to your audience that you knew they might think that ("that was odd")—

Table 1. God in the South Bay, Chennai, and Accra

US Vineyard	Self-oriented	Anchored in the mind	35% hear God quasi-audibly
		Richly imagined back-and-forth	
		Often playful	
		Voice marked as odd ["I'm not crazy"]	
Chennai NLAG	Other-oriented	Anchored in people	45% hear God quasi-audibly
		Relational	
		God caretaking, like a parent	
Accra ICGC	Soma-and-spirit-oriented	Anchored in the Bible	55% hear God quasi-audibly
		Moral exhortations	
		Rarely playful, less pretend	
		God an external presence	

and you needed to signal that you were not. Even in this religious setting, people had to learn to experience an internal voice as not being a violation of the private mind, and it was clear that in interacting with God, mental experience was what counted. This was not true of the Accra and Chennai participants.

In other-oriented Chennai, where the social world invites people to attend to the thoughts and feelings of others, my participants were more likely to experience God in the actions of others and to remember His voice in the context of relationships with humans. They did not describe His speech as being dialogical and playful the way the Americans did, though they did so more often than those in Accra. They had a sense that vengeful thoughts could affect the world through witchcraft, but this was not highly salient to them, and those thoughts had to be mediated through objects (lemons, copper).

In soma-and-spirit-oriented Accra, where the social world invites one to worry that negative thoughts can cause harm, where mental events are otherwise not given the same level of cultural salience as in the United States, and where the cultural emphasis is on actions and bodies, congregants emphasized moral action. They did not present elaborate, playful interior dialogues. They did not, in general, provide narrative accounts of God's speech inside their minds. They presented instead an intense awareness of spiritual authority and power, and they were sharply aware that they needed God because the malevolent thoughts of others (human and supernatural) could hurt them directly.

In some basic sense, it seems that God is kindled as more-in-the-world for congregants in Chennai and in particular in Accra than for congregants in the United States. The way His presence is recognized, felt, sought for, and understood is shaped by different ways of understanding and attending to awareness. All three groups of congregants had to work to sustain their sense of God's realness. All of them were praying and going to church and worshipping, and all of them agreed that if you stopped doing that, God would feel less real to you. In all these churches, God spoke through the Bible and through people and in the mind. In all these churches, God was also represented as speaking out loud to ordinary humans—after all, God spoke out loud to Abraham, Moses, Ezekiel, and John of Patmos, and evangelical prayer manuals are filled with vivid, auditory examples of God communicating in words the ear can hear. Yet because of the way that congregants thought about their minds, God feels real for them in different ways. In Chennai, He felt more real through people. In Accra, He felt more real in the experience of the body, in the felt power of the Holy Spirit. For the Americans, their experience of God was a little less palpable. For them, God seemed to feel less external and more mental. Or, to use the *Macmillan* dictionary definition, a little less real.

5

EVIDENCE FOR THE WAY GODS AND SPIRITS RESPOND

Individuality is founded in feeling; and the recesses of feeling, the darker, blinder strata of character, are the only places in the world in which we catch real fact in the making.

—William James, *The Varieties of Religious Experience*

I sat down on a flat rock ledge and started to do my deep breathing from Aikido. I was hoping it would take the edge off.... Somehow, I managed to get so centered that I detached from myself.... At that point, a crystal-clear voice comes cutting through all of this chaos and disintegration and says, "You know surrender is in order." ... There was a flash of white light.... There was an ever so brief revelation into the underlying unity of things.... It was a tremendous shock to my system to suddenly realize that Someone was running the universe, and running it with exquisite control, awareness, sophistication, and utter fairness.... I looked out at some sandpipers that were running around on the beach. I remember feeling so incredibly close to them.... At that point the voice came again. It was a crystal-clear voice. It once again cut through all the chaos in my mind and said, "It's time for you to walk in the water." ... As soon as the bottoms of my feet touched the water, a feeling of love, energy, and radiance coursed through my entire body.... Tears of joy came to my eyes, and at that moment it became pretty clear to me that there really was a God.

—Man, in his forties, on how he found orthodox Judaism

Very few people have full-fledged mystical experiences, these bathed-in-fire moments of utter awesomeness and a sense of intense union with sandpipers. In my experience, however, almost all people of faith have *some* kind of experience of the nonordinary, and many have a moment that stands out as extraordinary. These events matter because they are this-world evidence that the world of the faith frame is real. (To be clear, I am saying here that they count as evidence for people of faith. Skeptics are likely to interpret these events as brain accidents.) Otherwise, their best evidence for the realness of gods and spirits is testimony—what other people say about the world. Paul Harris (2012) tells us that testimony is the source of much of what children learn about their world—not experiment or rational analysis, although they too play a role (Gopnik 1996). Testimony is powerful, but it is also fragile. Harris writes,

> Children also come to entertain various culturally specific ideas about where human beings have come from and where they are going. They take these ideas on trust, not on the basis of rational scrutiny. Indeed, rather than seeking coherence, they sometimes accept ideas that are fundamentally incompatible with one another. The endpoint of cognitive development is not objectivity and equilibrium. It is a mix of the natural and supernatural, of truth and fantasy, of faith and uncertainty. (2012: 7)

Harris and his colleagues have found that everywhere in the world they have looked—in Boston, Massachusetts (Harris et al. 2006); in a Catholic school in central Spain (Guerrero, Enesco, and Harris 2010); in a Tseltal-speaking Mayan community in Mexico (Harris et al. 2007)—children are less confident about the realness of gods and spirits than about the realness of chickens and squirrels and even germs and oxygen, invisible entities with scientific status. He thinks that these differences come about because of the ways adults talk about these different kinds of objects, because of what he calls "children's keen antennae for a social consensus" (Harris and Corriveau 2014: 29). In other words, he finds that children aren't entirely confident that gods and spirits are real.

That is why spiritual experience matters and why personal experiences of the divine and supernatural are the most consequential effects of kindling: that someone feels the touch of the god's hand, knows that the spirit has spoken, has a moment of transcendental joy. These moments can feel like proof that the invisible other is present and has responded. We need the concept of the faith frame to capture differences in realness between things of the spirit and things of the everyday; we need the concept of kindling to describe the way things of the spirit come to feel more real.

In this chapter, I want to explore in more detail the way kindling works by looking at the way spiritual experiences become shaped, habituated, and fluent for those who have them. I have argued that the way people tell stories about gods and spirits, the way they practice engaging with them, the way they think about the domain between mind and world in which evidence for gods and spirits often appears, the personal orientation they bring to their faith—all these things make a difference in whether gods and spirits come to feel real to them in an intimate way. Here I want to show more precisely how these practices of attention shape the most basic evidence people have that gods and spirits respond. It will be a more technical argument, and I will use more technical evidence in making the point—but bear with me. I hope to demonstrate that spiritual presence events develop in specific patterns.

This is the opposite of what William James argued. In his magisterial *Varieties of Religious Experience*, James wanted people to see the mystical experience as the core spiritual event, so beyond the ordinary that it was impossible to describe with mere words, and yet so uniform that everyone who had one experienced it more or less the same way. A mystical experience made you feel as if the universe had cracked open to reveal that you were one with it all. And, James went on to explain, you were right. Religions clothed this basic insight about unity with theological chitchat—"overbeliefs" ([1902] 1999: 511), which were not what really mattered. This way of thinking about spiritual experience has been so compelling that people have called it the "perennial philosophy," the term popularized by Aldous Huxley's (1945) book of that name. The perennial philosophy is that there is a highest common factor of all religions that delivers to us true knowledge of the divine.

It's an appealing idea, but it does not capture the way people experience gods and spirits, at least most of the time. (To be fair, James knew this perfectly well.) Gods and spirits communicate and make themselves known in ways that are quite particular. These ways become more particular over time. The human begins to recognize the experience as a response, to look for the response again, and may come to have the response more often, the way friends and lovers learn to talk with each other and then grow more familiar with each other's ways.

For example, if people take their goosebumps to indicate that the Holy Spirit has come to them, they are more likely to pay attention to goosebumps and to remember their goosebumps than people for whom goosebumps have no particular meaning. They might arrange to put themselves in the settings where they would have goosebumps more often. Those who take their own goosebumps as the sign that the Holy Spirit is near, who know that they have goosebumps when listening to worship music, and who want to get to know the Holy Spirit more deeply, might well seek out worship music more often than others, and so experience goosebumps more often.

I want to suggest something further still: that goosebumps become not only the way a particular body responds to a particular stimulus, but that they become part of an expected response that indicates the presence of gods and spirits to them, so that someone comes to feel goosebumps not only with worship music, but at other music-free moments when the Holy Spirit (as they understand this) is present. I propose here that goosebumps (and other experiences) may be kindled in specific bodies as part of a learned response to what can be taken, in some social worlds, as the presence of gods and spirits. These events will become more fluent for an individual in that social world: they will happen more often and more easily. And so attention and expectation will change the nature of spiritual events. I am going to call this process "spiritual kindling," a specific instance of the more general process of the way kindling, through small acts of attention, shapes a person's unique experience of gods and spirits.

SPIRITUAL KINDLING

The concept of kindling first appeared in the medical literature in the 1960s, when neurologists observed that rats (and other animals) that were repeatedly stimulated with electricity appeared to become progressively sensitized, so that over time, they needed less stimulation for seizures to occur. In epilepsy, the body's response to the initial stimulation seems to predispose its response to later stimulation, as if the first seizures left kindling behind to build another blaze. Over time, the response becomes habituated, and a smaller spark can set the fire burning. Since then, the word "kindling" has been used to describe the body's apparent learning in substance abuse, multiple chemical sensitivity, long-term memory, physiological psychology, bipolar disorder, and major depression. Kindling in major depression was first recognized by the great psychiatrist Emil Kraepelin (1921), who observed that to the extent that demoralizing events—a job loss, a breakup, a bad relationship—play a role in a first episode of depression, they play a less important role in later episodes. The person who first becomes depressed after he loses his mother may find that he next becomes depressed because the spring was wet. Yet the nature of the blaze may vary. In epilepsy, seizures beget seizures, and the duration and intensity of those seizures increase over time. A second or third depression is not always worse than the first. The point of the kindling concept is that a body's response involves learning.

I use the kindling concept to talk about spiritual presence because the evidence suggests that people in different social and religious settings not only attribute different kinds of events to a supernatural source, but that the act of attribution changes the experience of the event, and of future events as well. A skeptic might say, are you not simply suggesting that the shape of spiritual presence changes in different social settings? Of course I am. I am also suggesting more—that local culture, as well as individual practices and individual differences, shapes the bodily experience of spirit and presence, and those experiences accumulate and change the nature of the experience over time. It is a complex process because the events are varied and because different bodies have different proclivities and vulnerabilities. Moreover, the cultural expectations in different faiths interact with the cultural expectations of different social settings. Nevertheless, I will argue that as a result of these different cultural expectations, certain patterns of experience become more habituated and more fluent for members of that social group.

There are two moving pieces here: events in the body, and the labels that the social world gives to these. The religious studies scholar Ann Taves (2009b, 2016; Taves and Asprem 2016) describes these as "building blocks" and "event cognitions." By "building blocks," she means that there are certain kinds of bodily events that strike people as special, and that these are often incorporated into accounts of gods and spirits. At times, she gives a very broad account of what building blocks can be: "all the cognitive, psychological and biological processes that guide human interaction with the environment (natural, built, and social) from perception and affect to memorization, categorization, and strategizing" (Taves and Asprem 2020: 5). In practice, she gives special attention to unusual or anomalous events and processes—visions, voices, dissociation, hypnosis, and so forth. Unusual or anomalous experiences often strike people as special, and thus they are good candidates to be evidence of special beings.

Of course, exactly what counts as an "anomalous event" is hard to specify. David Hufford (1995) called anomalous events "core experiences": experiences that can occur seemingly independently of a person's beliefs, knowledge, or intention, and which form distinct classes with stable patterns. Everywhere in the world, some people report that they have heard a voice when alone, or seen something that others cannot, or felt a presence that was invisible to others. For that matter, everywhere in the world people experience goosebumps, feel sometimes strangely hot or cool, light or heavy, and so forth. Some of these experiences are pretty common, like goosebumps. Some are more rare, like feeling that your soul has left your body and has floated away on the air. When people use the term "anomalous," they are typically referring to the less common ones. David Hufford's (1982) main example is sleep paralysis, in which people wake from sleep to find that they literally cannot move; they often feel a weight on their chest and the sense that there is another (usually malevolent) being in the room. As he points out, sleep science understands these experiences as an REM cycle dysfunction— in effect, a specific pattern of dreaming while awake. Hufford first began to study these events as a folkloric motif of the Old Hag. Once *The Terror That Comes in the Night* was published, people would write to him or buttonhole him when he gave talks. They had never heard anyone else talk about the phenomenon he described—but they recognized it from their own experience.

By "event cognition," Taves (2016) means the categories through which people identify the event. She argues that in order to have an experience, humans must—to some extent—have a preexisting representation, a model, of what they experience. "What we refer to colloquially as 'experiences' are simply personally experienced events that are particularly salient" (Taves and Asprem 2016: 4). She does not mean that events in the body (like sleep paralysis) have to have a local cultural name to be experienced. Experiences of sleep paralysis can be surprising and can indeed happen to those who do not have a term like "the Old Hag" to describe what happened to them. After all, experiences deemed religious often become so precisely because they stand out in unexpected ways. Instead, Taves suggests humans identify events with "bottom up" inputs from bodies and environment, "top down" predictions from shared understandings, and ongoing framing and reframing of moments as they become narrated to self and to others.

With building blocks and event cognition in mind, one might imagine the following as a field guide to the kinds of events that, to use Taves's (2009b) phrasing, people often deem spiritual (I spelled this out in an article with Julia Cassaniti in 2014).

First: There are phenomena that have names, but that do not have specific bodily anchors. An example might be the way God speaks through the Bible for charismatic evangelical Christians. In such churches, people learn to recognize when God speaks through His word, but different individuals often report different specific signs that indicate that He spoke to them—this person feels goosebumps, that person feels sleepy, another feels more alert. People learn that they are supposed to recognize when He speaks, and then they have to decide what counts, for them, as evidence that He did so.

Second: There are events we could call "bodily affordances." Here the term "affordance" (Gibson 1986) means that there are events of the body (crying, goosebumps, feeling warmth) that are available to be interpreted as religious but are only identified as religious in those social settings when they afford, or make available, an interpretation that makes sense in a specific religious tradition. For example, everyone cries. But only in settings when strong emotion makes sense as an experience of divinity will crying be deemed religious and be treated as evidence of supernatural presence. These bodily affordances deemed religious may or may not have names (e.g., "a Holy Spirit experience").

Third: There are anomalous events. These are specific patterns of events—Hufford's core experiences—often (but not always) identified as caused by things otherworldly, which are outside the range of everyday experience. They often have similar phenomenological patterns in different settings. Examples include hallucinations or sensory overrides, déjà vu, mystical experiences, out-of-body experiences, near-death experiences, and sleep paralysis. They may or may not carry culturally specific labels.

These, of course, are heuristic distinctions. There are no purely bodily events, nor purely disembodied cultural ideas. There are epicycles upon epicycles of complexity. Local social worlds sometimes have specific names for events ("slain in the spirit," for instance, when someone's knees collapse—in building-blocks language, they experience muscle cataplexy—and that person falls to the floor). But local social worlds also have general orientations—for example, toward kinaesthesia or toward dissociation. These general orientations are not event-like, and those people may not have specific labels for specific experiences. For example, as we saw, Ghanaians seem to have more of an orientation toward the bodily and kinesthetic than Americans do. Some Ghanaian peoples have specific terms to describe kinds of bodily experiences (like *seselamene*, among the Ewe), but they may not have a general term for this more body-attentive mode of awareness.

Then too, specific names may refer to a broader or narrower range of phenomena than the ones we typically associate with them. For example, in early modern England, the words "succubus" and "incubus" were used to describe demons that had sex with humans. Many observers think that these concepts were used to make sense of sleep paralysis. In an example from the 1692 Salem witch trial of Bridget Bishop, Richard Coman claimed that "the curtains at the foot of the bed opened, where [he] did see her and [she] presently came and lay upon his breast or body and so oppressed him that he could not speak nor stir, no, not so much as to awake his wife, although he endeavored much so to do it" (Adler 2011: 49). And yet the concepts of succubus and incubus could also be used to describe other sorts of phenomena, like sexual dreams or nocturnal emissions (Thomas 1971: 477). Peter Guarnaccia points out that one finds this sort of messiness in the term "ataques de nervios" in Mexico and other parts of Latin America. There is a specific meaning associated with the phrase (loss of control), which seems to imply that the words capture dissociative phenomena. Yet Guarnaccia and his colleagues (1993, 1996, 2010) found that the phrase was also used to describe many other forms of distress, which they identified with psychiatric terms like depression, anxiety disorders, and psychosis.

Moreover, there is much we do not yet know about the nature of anomalous experience. It might be the case that sleep paralysis usually co-occurs with hallucinated presence in the United States—but not, say, in Brazil.

The problems with categorizing anomalous experience and other events often deemed spiritual may turn out to be like the problems with categorizing psychiatric experience. In the 1970s, psychiatrists separated mental illness into distinct categories with the idea that these categories carved out distinct diseases—specific lesions or genetic deficiencies. And it is true that the prototypical examples of those categories—like bipolar disorder, schizophrenia, and generalized anxiety disorder—do seem quite different from each other. Yet after several decades of scientific research, few scientists are confident that there are reliable boundaries between the categories. Many psychiatric scientists have concluded that the apparent categories are less categorical and more dimensional, more like syndromes than diseases. That is, schizophrenia may be less like a thing and more like the behavioral outcome of a myriad of different causes and pathways—more like becoming a teacher and less like being right-handed. The core experiences often deemed spiritual may turn out to be similar. There is much we do not yet know.

With that complexity in mind, it seems unwise to pin too much on the search for "natural kinds" (Kripke 1980)—nature carved cleanly at its joints. Instead, we might look for characteristics that form themselves into patterns, family resemblances in which members all share some characteristics but there is no one characteristic that all members share. We can then look at the way in which those patterns emerge: at what one might call a "pathway," a specific way in which the person has experienced the event that he or she identifies as supernatural. (The medical definition of "pathway" is a network of interconnecting neurons along which a nerve impulse travels—a pattern of events in the body.) Here, following and developing Cassaniti and Luhrmann (2014), is an account of that process—the theory of spiritual kindling:

1. When a social world gives significance to a particular sensation, the threshold for identifying that sensation decreases. If

goosebumps and chilliness are signs of the Holy Spirit, one will notice them more in social worlds where they are meaningful than in social worlds where they are not.

2. If that sensation is a complex bodily event like sleep paralysis (or even a simple event like goosebumps), the frequency of the event will be constrained by an individual's vulnerability to these experiences.

3. The less an experience is tied to a specific complex pattern of phenomenology, the more directly its frequency will reflect cultural interest in it.

4. When a pathway is established for an individual, that individual is more likely to have that experience and related experiences in the future. The response becomes habituated and fluent for him or her.

Most generally, any spiritual experience will reflect both bodily vulnerability (from the body's genetic inheritance and the body's history) and cultural expectation. Their interaction creates specific patterns of events that become more habituated and fluent over time. The process of kindling changes the events.

To be clear, the most general mechanism at work here is the effect of prior expectation. Expectations are at the core of many foundational theories of cognition. For example, in Bayesian reasoning a person's understanding of a new event is taken to be firmly grounded in his or her prior beliefs about the likelihood of various possible events. These days, neuroscientists describe the role of expectation as "predictive coding." The brain is more likely to sense and experience what it expects to sense and experience (Friston 2010). Yet expectation is not everything. I am motivated here by my observation that any given community can have relatively homogenous ideas about the supernatural and more or less shared expectations—and still individuals within that community can have quite different experiences of the supernatural. My goal here is to add some specificity by exploring the ways expectation, practice, and bodily process interact. I want to point out that different kinds of events are affected by expectation in different ways. If some phenomenon doesn't require a specific bodily event, expectation is everything. But expectation shifts the dial less for ordinary bodily events like crying, and even less so for extraordinary events like sleep paralysis.

This theory has specific implications. In a Christian social world that recognizes the presence of God through any kind of emotional or bodily response to scripture, everyone should report that he or she has heard God speak though the Bible because what counts as evidence is so loosely defined. In the evangelical church I studied, people said that they knew God was speaking to them through the Bible when a passage "grabbed at their heart," "would not let them go," or "stuck in their mind." God was understood to be communicating when, as one congregant put it, "a verse just jumps out at me." It seemed to me that people could pay attention to any kind of powerful bodily or emotional feeling and identify it as the cause of those words—peace, intense joy, sudden sleepiness. Here is one congregant:

> All of a sudden, I was in the Book of Isaiah. . . . I felt that the Spirit was leading me. . . . I started reading about what the chosen fast was, which was to break the bonds of wickedness. And something about it made me think about my family members and how I wanted to pray for my family members. Like that was the answer for me. I really felt that God brought me to that Scripture and that this is where I need to be. . . . It was just such an amazing thing. It was like two o'clock in the morning, and I remember reading it wide awake, and as soon as I read that it was a relief, and then I felt really sleepy. It was comforting. And so that's an example of how I think God speaks to me through the Word.

The theory of spiritual kindling predicts that almost all members of this congregation would be able to say that God has spoken to them through the Bible—and that what counts as evidence may be different for each of them. At the same time, the theory also predicts that if there is a named event in a different tradition with little meaning for these congregants (like "rosary visions") and without a phenomenological core, these evangelical congregants won't experience it.

The theory of spiritual kindling also predicts that people for whom ordinary bodily events (like crying, feeling warmth, goosebumps) have supernatural meaning will often experience these events as spiritual. Not all members of the community will say that they have had those events because not all bodies experience those phenomena equally easily. Some people cry more easily than others. For those who do (cry, feel warmth, have goosebumps, etc.) and who also interpret that event as spiritual, the theory would expect that those ordinary bodily events might happen more often. Meanwhile, there will be people not in the community who will experience those ordinary bodily events but will not identify them as signs of supernatural presence. Because not all bodies experience them, though, these ordinary bodily events should be less frequent than named events that can be identified through a very broad range of bodily phenomenology, like hearing God speak through the Bible.

The theory of spiritual kindling expects that because rare events with specific bodily patterns, like sleep paralysis, are more narrowly available to some bodies than to others, not all religious participants will experience them, even in settings where such an event might be meaningful. The theory also suggests that these events might become more common in communities that regard them as evidence of the supernatural but not as common as, say, hearing God through scripture or experiencing God through ordinary bodily experiences like crying.

Absorption (as we have seen) likely also plays a role in whether people experience anomalous events, whether or not those events have supernatural meaning in their social world. So does inner sense cultivation. Absorption is also likely not the only proclivity that facilitates these events; nor is inner sense cultivation the only practice to do so. We are at the very beginning of understanding the ways in which people come to have, to remember, and to report experiences they identify as supernatural.

In other words, the theory of spiritual kindling predicts that the frequency of events deemed spiritual is shaped by culture. The more some phenomenological event (crying, goosebumps, out-of-body experiences, sleep paralysis, etc.) is valued within a faith community, the more it will occur. Yet the increased frequency will be an increase from baseline, constrained by the capacity of the body. It seems unlikely that even great cultural salience would lead every member of a community to experience sleep paralysis; it seems equally unlikely that even great cultural aversion would prevent every member of a community from experiencing sleep paralysis. Building blocks and event cognitions influence each other—but neither has the final say.

COMPARATIVE PHENOMENOLOGY

How does one establish that there is an object to study when so much of human experience is shaped by local knowledge? One needs a method.

The term "phenomenology" refers to the philosophical study of the way people experience their worlds. Phenomenologists zero in on trying to describe precisely the way someone sees, hears, and feels an apple (to use a famous example) without presupposing knowledge of apples in general. There have been, broadly speaking, two dominant schools. One has its roots in a European tradition with thinkers who sought to understand human experience in general. This phenomenological movement grounds itself in the work of Edmund Husserl and his followers: Martin Heidegger, Maurice Merleau-Ponty, Jean-Paul Sartre, and, more recently, Emmanuel Levinas. Because these scholars set out to distance their analysis from everyday categories of understanding, they invented a language of description that can seem impenetrably dense. There are now a number of anthropologists—among them Thomas Csordas, Robert Desjarlais, and Jason Throop—who have drawn their inspiration from this school, although they have not always used its complex phraseology. The other school owes its origin to these Continental philosophers but grounds itself in the study of remarkable experience, largely psychiatric and religious, and the assumption that conscious phenomena can be more or less systematically described. This is the domain of Karl Jaspers and William James, with modern descendants like Joseph Parnass, Louis Sass, and William Alston. This second tradition tends to use ordinary language to describe extraordinary experiences and has a distinctly more comparative bent, attempting to use phenomenological methods to sort out religious events from nonreligious events and illness from health. What I call the method of comparative phenomenology is rooted in this second school.

By "comparative phenomenology," I mean an approach to interviewing that homes in on felt experience with the aim of understanding that experience more deeply by exploring the event through comparison to other experiences in order to elicit more phenomenological detail. The method takes a phenomenon-focused, experience-near approach. That is, the goal is to understand the specific details of the event as individuals felt it in the moment—from their perspective, as the event unfolded. At the same time, the interviewer asks for more detail, based on his or her knowledge of other possibly related events. Comparative phenomenology interviewing is akin to clinical interviewing, although it does not presume pathology. Someone comes to talk to a clinician to complain about back pain. It is the clinician's task to have in mind a host of possible causes—along with the possibility that this back pain is explained by none of them, that it is novel. And so the clinician asks follow-up questions about the pain that draw from his or her knowledge of these causes but are open to other interpretations. The clinician asks where it hurts, how it hurts, whether it hurts when the person turns this way or that, and so forth. This knowledgeable but open-ended approach is particularly important when studying religious experience because reports of religious experience are often laden with theology. Just as someone at a lecture might tell a friend more about the content of the lecture than about the timbre of the speaker's voice, people who experience the presence of God often want to say more about their views of who God is than about what they actually experienced that led them to think that God was speaking. Comparative phenomenology assumes that there may be dimensions of an experience that people don't always bother to describe, and that careful interviewing and what Amira Mittermaier (2010: 10) calls "attentive listening" can teach us more about what people experienced at the time.

This is how the method works. When people say that they have sensed the presence of a divine spirit, the comparative phenomenologist wants to know where, precisely, the spirit was located and what, precisely, they felt that caused them to think that the spirit was there. The comparative phenomenologist is more likely to ask whether God stood behind the right shoulder or the left than to ask about the end of days. The method looks for phenomenological details to ask about in anthropological, historical, folkloric, psychological, and psychiatric literature that may not be part of the participant's local narratives about such events. For example, folklore studies tell us that in sleep paralysis people often experience another presence in the room; clinical studies tell us that some people who have voice-like events also hear those voices talking to each other; ethnographies report that the dead are sometimes present even when their corpses are stiff. By asking about all those details and more, the comparative phenomenologist can discover more about what people experienced than perhaps they felt that they needed to explain.

For instance, when someone uses the method of comparative phenomenology to ask about the voice-like events reported widely in the literature, he or she would ask the basic question as neutrally as possible: "Have you ever heard a voice when alone?" If the participant says "yes," the comparative phenomenologist is less interested in finding out how the person understands what happened (for example, who spoke, although surely those questions also come up) and more interested in the experiential details. He or she might ask, "Did you turn your head to see who was speaking? Did you hear it with your ears? Did it feel like it spoke from inside your head, or outside, or from in between? How far away would you say that it was? Did the voice have a timbre?" While I have described this as similar to clinical interviewing, it is often more phenomenologically detailed than many clinical interviews; these days, clinicians often do not have the time to talk with patients in depth. Psychiatrists are often more interested in whether the person heard a voice than in what the voice felt like to that person—they are focused on whether what they call a "symptom" occurred. Scholars of religion are most often concerned with the person's views about the god who might have spoken. Many historians and anthropologists are interested primarily in meaning and interpretation. Comparative phenomenologists are first and foremost interested in how the person experienced the event. Knowing about other possibly related phenomena can help to make their questions more precise.

In fact, comparative phenomenology interviewing can uncover details that elude even the existing scientific literature. Here is an example: the scientific literature speaks easily about the experience of those with psychotic disorders (like schizophrenia) who hear "voices," so many readers have assumed that all voices are audible. But when you talk to people with psychosis about the experience of their voices in phenomenological detail, you learn that most of them report events that are more thought-like than voice-like. In careful work with people who met criteria for psychosis in three countries, I found that despite the standard scientific narratives, many psychotic "voices" are experienced as occurring between the mind and the world—neither fully an interior thought nor an exterior voice (Jones and Luhrmann 2015).

If the subject says "no" to the initial question about hearing a voice when alone, the good comparative phenomenologist will circle back to that question in other ways. I myself have had interview participants reject the concept of a voice heard when alone—to them, that sounds like being crazy—but then later talk about hearing God speak in a way they could hear with their ears. The narratives people tell themselves about their experience have a complex relationship to what they experience. No interview or experiment can ever completely tease apart phenomenological experience and interpretation, though some researchers do seek to find "pristine" experience (Hurlburt 2011). But a phenomenological interview does better than most methods because it does not presuppose the nature of the object—and yet its questions draw from different disciplinary descriptions of related objects. Comparative phenomenologists should be simultaneously deeply well-read and determinedly open-minded.

The method of comparative phenomenology also asks about the features of the event that lead those who experience it to identify it as an event. If a participant reports that he or she has heard God's voice, the comparative phenomenologist asks, "How did you know?" The comparative phenomenologist might ask, "I'd like you to think back on a conversation you had earlier today. How was that experience like or unlike the experience you are reporting here?" These are questions that ask about the act of recognition—the explicit or implicit markers that the participant uses to recognize the event. Sometime the participant will say "yes" to the basic question but reject the phenomenological markers the interviewer might have assumed he or she was describing, as in this example from a pastor in Chennai, India:

PASTOR J: The second step was—I was clearly hearing the voice of God saying that—this question was put into my ears very clearly. God—

TML: Did you hear it with your ears? Or—?

PASTOR J: Yes. Yes. With my ears.

TML: Oh. Audibly.

PASTOR J: Audibly, I heard it. I heard this question: "Do you want to be in a job, working for a company? Or do you want to be my servant feeding my sheep? Or do you want to be a pastor working with the church?"

TML: That's amazing. So did you like turn your head to look to see who was speaking? Or did you know it was God?

PASTOR J: No. No. No. What I mean by audible is not a sound that is coming from outside. I could clearly *know in my spirit sense* this question coming through my mind—that I'm hearing a clear stated question that's coming to my mind.

This exchange teaches us two things. Pastor J does not appear to be reporting an auditory experience—even though he has been insisting that it was. What he says also teaches us something about the phenomenology of the object itself. It teaches us that in his social world there seems to be this category of a domain that is not in the world (the voice is not sensory) but also not in the mind, a domain that he calls the "spirit sense."

Comparative phenomenology is the means by which anthropologists might make constructive contributions to some of the puzzles about building blocks. If careful interviewing about anomalous experiences—including around details identified in the scientific literature but not included in the local cultural narrative around such experiences—finds different phenomenological patterns in different cultural worlds, we might then have a strong hypothesis that these experiences have been caused by a collection of factors rather than by a single specific factor.

With this method explained, I now want to turn back to the theory of spiritual kindling. My goal is to show that the act of attribution changes the experience of the events—that local culture, as well as individual practice and individual differences, shapes the bodily experience of spirit, and that those experiences accumulate and change the nature of the event over time. As a result of these different cultural expectations, certain patterns of experience become more habituated and more fluent for members of that social group. I will share two studies (the one on hearing God in the previous chapter is a third). Numbers are reported in the notes. I am hoping that words and numbers will work together to persuade the reader that the idea of kindling has something to it.

Table 2. Spiritual Presence Events among Thai Buddhists and
US Charismatic Evangelicals

	Thai Buddhist	US evangelical
Demonic encounters	20%	70%
Sudden muscle weakness	25%	39%
Electric rush of power	15%	52%
Overwhelming emotion	10%	64%
Sleep paralysis	58%	33%

STUDY 1: WHEN NEITHER THE LOCAL CHURCH CULTURE NOR THE GENERAL CULTURE IS SHARED

In 2011, Julia Cassaniti and I compared the responses of around twenty Thai Buddhists in Chiang Mai and somewhat over thirty US evangelicals on the San Francisco Peninsula to questions about spiritual experience. We found that American Christians and Thai Buddhists reported voice-like events at the same rates, but that the Americans were more likely than the Thai Buddhists to report sudden muscle weakness (being "slain in the spirit"), adrenaline rushes (Holy Spirit moments), and overwhelming emotion as spiritual experiences, and they were more likely to report everyday encounters with demons. But the Thai Buddhists were more likely to report sleep paralysis (Cassaniti and Luhrmann 2014). In short, American charismatic Christianity seemed to kindle certain kinds of ordinary experiences that were not experienced in Thailand, and Thai Buddhism seemed to kindle experiences of sleep paralysis that did not occur in the United States. In table 2, I show the percentage of people whom the interviewer considered to be having the experience described.

We thought that there are several broad reasons for these differences, following the main points from the first part of this chapter. First, if your experience has a specific name in the local religion, it is more likely to be reported. Sudden muscle weakness ("slain in the spirit") and adrenaline rushes ("the Holy Spirit experience") and "demons" are specific, named events for many evangelical Christians, and the American evangelicals reported them more often than the Thai Buddhists.

Second, the different religions value different kinds of experiences. The goal for a Thai Buddhist is to feel untethered from the cycle of suffering. One seeks *upādāna*, detachment. Cassaniti found that in speaking about spiritual experience, her Thai subjects were more likely to use an idiom of "weight." A lightness, almost buoyancy, is reported to occur in moments of positive spiritual attainment, but slight pressure on the skin is understood to represent negative, sometimes ghostly energy. By contrast, charismatic evangelical spirituality is all about connecting to a human-like God who thinks and responds. God is an agent, an actor; He is not under a human's control. Excited, aroused, uncontrolled experiences become signs of that divine being because those who have them feel like someone else is in control.

Third, there are pervasive differences in the way people value experiences more generally in these two cultures, although here distinguishing between the local culture and the religion is hard, because the cultures have been so shaped by their respective religions. While American Christians value intense, robust, and memorable moments of physiological arousal as an experience of God, it is also true that Americans in general value aroused, excited feelings; Asians are more likely to prefer calm. In a charming example, a study comparing Taiwanese bestselling children's picture books with their American counterparts, Jeanne Tsai found that the smiles drawn in the Asian books were significantly less excited (Tsai et al. 2007; Tsai 2007).

Our findings about sleep paralysis were most intriguing. One might think that since sleep paralysis can be described as a clearly biological event associated with sleep cycles, it should be reported at the same rate everywhere. In fact, Asians generally report it far more often than Americans (as Adler [2011] points out). Almost two-thirds of our Thai participants reported it. Most described sleep paralysis with a term, *Phi Am*, the name of a spirit who causes it, and talked about it at some length. Clearly the event was important to them in a way that the other events we asked about were not. But even so, not all the Thai reported sleep paralysis. Meanwhile, even though sleep paralysis is not particularly meaningful in US charismatic culture, about a third of our American participants reported sleep paralysis. In general, they did not name it, did not associate it with a supernatural presence, and did not give it much significance.

For instance, here are two American examples:

Yeah. But I think I was just overtired. It was pretty recent. No, no. I think I just overdid it and I got home from the gym one day and I was like—you know, and I was like, I cannot move. [Laughter] So it wasn't anything spiritual. It was kind of trippy though. Cause I couldn't move.

Another:

Yeah. Like it was really, really heavy. Well, once or twice in a lifetime. I didn't know [if it was a spiritual experience]. I just didn't know. I thought, "This is interesting" and I prayed about it so I could move.

And two Thai examples:

I was taking a nap . . . um . . . or maybe in the middle of the night, you know, I was like I was kind of awake but I cannot move my body . . . and I was kind of hearing the voice, the voice was laughing, she was a woman . . . like it was not like very clear laughing or anything, she was a woman and she was kind of, she sat on my shoulder and she was just laughing and I was so mad at her. I was like go away and then like she just kept laughing and then I prayed for my Buddha and God [Ganesh] and then she's gone. And just then I felt my body again. Maybe some kind of spirit like tried to tease me or something . . . maybe like some spirit came and tried to tell me that I should go to the temple and make merit or something. . . . It's a Buddhist thing, you know, when you experience some spiritual energy in some certain way. . . . They might come and tell me that it's the time to make merit and go to the temple and do something for them.

Another:

I have sometimes, if we call that the dream—it's not like that, though, not a dream, it was like Phi Am. I can't move. But I saw it, but I cannot talk, I cannot call anybody. There was one time, there was one person who died at the school. And then he came to the house. He came to tell me that his things were over there, that thing is over here. When I was sleeping, sleep but not sleep. And then I was like, "ah . . . that person is dead already, and why did he come to see me" I think like that. I think about why he came to me. I tried to get up and talk to him, but I cannot go. I cannot talk, cannot move, but my eyes see it . . . because I saw him come to me. I saw him stand over there and telling me what is over there, what is over here. I wanted to say something, but I really could not.

Anomalous experiences in these different countries are not kindled in the same way. Sleep paralysis is interpreted differently in each setting and seems to be more common for the Thai.

STUDY 2: WHEN PEOPLE ARE IN THE SAME CHURCH AND IN THE SAME PLACE

In 2007, I decided to ask charismatic Christians in the United States a set of systematic questions about the way they experienced God. I wrote out an interview about whether and how God spoke to them (through scripture, circumstances, or in the mind), about how they felt God in their bodies, and about a "spiritual inventory," if you will—about voices, visions, divine or demonic presences, sleep paralysis, out-of-body events, and mystical experiences—along with other questions. Then I had a research assistant, Christina Drymon, interview about 130 of them. We then went on to assign them randomly to different spiritual practices, after which we brought them in and interviewed them again. I have published elsewhere what we learned from assigning them to different practices (Luhrmann 2012). Here I describe, in a list of five points, what we saw about the kindling of spiritual experience from the interviews themselves (again, with technical details in the notes).

First: Events that are named but that have no particular bodily markers are most common; events that depend on bodily affordances are next common; and anomalous events are least common, and are not always identified as spiritual when they occur.

Among these participants, almost everyone agreed that he or she had heard from God in *some* way. Almost all these congregants said that God spoke to them through scripture, when a verse seems to leap off the page and grab its reader, in whatever way being grabbed feels like to them.

They almost all said that God definitely speaks through circumstances, as when someone goes for a walk and unexpectedly runs into a friend who says something specifically relevant to the issue that he or she has been praying about.

But far fewer reported the overwhelming emotion of crying as a spiritual experience, or the sense of being shot through with an electrical bolt that they associated with the Holy Spirit, or the sudden muscle weakness that they associated with being "slain in the spirit." Events like sleep paralysis, mystical experiences, and out-of-body events were even less common, even when we were coding generously. And even when someone reported one of these anomalous events, the event wasn't always described as spiritual.

Second: Proclivity mattered.

Those subjects who scored higher in absorption were more likely to report that God spoke to them clearly in their thoughts, through mental images, through feelings and sensations; and that He even spoke to them in ways that they could hear with their ears and gave them visions they could see with their eyes. They were also more likely to report any of a number of varied spiritual events: for instance, mystical-like experiences, out-of-body experiences, and sleep paralysis.

Third: These events are habituated for the group. Local social expectations shape the kinds of events people experience.

Only some of the items we asked about on our spiritual inventory are important to Christians: voices and visions (think Samuel [1 Samuel 3] and those shepherds in the fields at night [Luke 2]); mystical experiences ([Saul, Acts 9]); and the presence of God. They are likely most important for those Christians who are in churches that highly value spiritual presence (as charismatic churches do). For the specific spiritual presence events for which we have some epidemiological data for our participants (voices, visions, mystical experiences, out-of-body events, and sleep paralysis), the events important to Christians occur at a rate well above the US national average. Seventeen of the 126 participants who answered our questions about mystical experiences reported events that we judged, from their descriptions, to meet more or less the criteria William James laid out (passivity: the mystical experience feels completely outside one's will; noesis: the experiencer has an intense sense of knowing something new; transience: the event lasts a brief time; ineffability: although people write volumes, they have a strong sense that they can never put the event into words). Rates for the general population are usually much lower. Here are two examples from our participants:

> We were at the Presbyterian church on the twenty-fifth in San Mateo for worship service and our friend was music director or associate pastor—I think it was music director, and they had, as a church, made little poly film–type stars. It was a plastic kind of material, but it would sparkle. And they had cut them out and they had rented a machine that goes up high and strung fish line and attached these stars all over the sanctuary. And the choir sang, and they had a special dance with banners, and it was the most profoundly moving worship experience that I ever had in my whole life. Everything was different. Those stars moved. There was intense presence. A feeling of pressure of some sort in the room, a weightiness, if you will, like making your whole body tingle. It was just absolutely profoundly wonderful, so love and light will work. It definitely was the presence of God and the movement of the Holy Spirit as I'd never seen the Holy Spirit move like that.

Another:

> I had a moment of complete union with God where—I was not even aware of myself at all. I was not even there anymore and it was just—we all are just in one spirit. We were all in the room worshiping—but we were all one and there was no difference between us. It was just all one and it was all consuming, captivating, fulfilled, utter bliss, all joy, no tears, just beauty beyond anything you could ever know on earth. And it just—so I don't know. I had this experience just for, I don't know how long it was. It seems like a long time, but was only just probably a couple seconds. But it seemed like for that moment, it was like, "Oh, wow." But it wasn't me. I wasn't even there.

About half of our participants had seen some kind of vision; about half said that they had heard some kind of voice. Again, that is higher than the rates for hallucination-like events collected from the general population in similar ways—in the Census of Hallucinations and then the later NIH Epidemiological Catchment Area Survey, the rate

Table 3. Spiritual Presence Events in the General Population and at the Vineyard

	US general population (Various researchers)	US charismatic Christians (Spiritual Disciplines Project)
Voices and/or visions	10–15%	60%
Mystical experiences	1% or less	17%
Out-of-body events	10%	13%
Sleep paralysis	25–30%	27%

is roughly 5 to 15 percent of the general population. But people reported out-of-body events, which are not seen as desirable for a Christian congregation and which for the most part were not interpreted as spiritual by these American Christians, at close to the national rate. The same was true of sleep paralysis, again not marked as desirable nor generally experienced as spiritually salient by these American Christians. To be clear, these numbers are a little hard to compare, as they were collected by different methods and by different people (see the notes). They do suggest a consistent pattern, however: that if a spiritual presence event is highly valued within a social world, more people will experience it (see table 3).

Fourth: These events become habituated for individuals, and often an initial experience is more powerful than those that come after.

It is a cliché in the evangelical world that the first time God speaks, He needs to go to an effort to catch your attention, and that later events are compelling but less surprising. The Spiritual Disciplines Project was not developed to capture this kind of pattern with statistics, but comments that support it run through my ethnographic notes. As one man, a local college student, explained to me, "It's like the first day I got this whole cake, and then from now you get to have little servings of it from time to time again, but sometimes it's bigger and sometimes it's smaller." Another man, a medical resident at a different university, told me of a vivid moment in which God grabbed hold of his heart, and told him that He loved him and would always be with him. "In subsequent events, I have been more left with the sense that I can choose to believe this is from God or I can think this is just from me, and the reality is that it could be either, and I know that. But about that one, there was never any question. Everything else, there is a question. Not that."

The evidence also tells us that those who experienced significant spiritual events before we randomized them to different spiritual practices were more likely to report that they had had similar events during their month of practice. Kindling in this setting may lead to more common but less startling spiritual experience.

Finally: Anomalous events are associated with each other. If someone has had one, he or she is more likely to have another.

I did not see strong evidence that different spiritual experiences were sharply different from each other—that people who hear God speak in a way they can hear with their ears were fundamentally different from those who experience God's presence or those who have what seems to be an out-of-body event. Instead, I saw that people who experienced one of these unusual events were more likely to report another one. Those who reported out-of-body events were more likely to report voices and visions, more likely to say they'd had a mystical experience, more likely to report sleep paralysis. For that matter, they were more likely to report near-death experiences and events in which they felt some other force—like the Holy Spirit—had taken over their bodies. This did not seem to be just a consequence of saying "yes" more often, because they gave many phenomenological details.

Some kinds of events did seem more separate from the others. Sleep paralysis seemed to be a little less connected to the other events. I had the sense that someone who hears voices is likely to have visions, a sense of presence, and other sensory and somewhat sensory events, while sleep paralysis seems to be somewhat more connected to a different array of bodily capacities. The practice of speaking in tongues stood out even more as being a cultural practice within a church rather than a spontaneous event that happened to some people and not so much to others. I can believe that those who have had many unusual spiritual presence events also speak in tongues more readily—but I have never come across anyone who spoke in tongues spontaneously and was confused by how to make sense of the moment. In my experience, people only speak in tongues if they encounter the cultural invitation to do so (although different kinds of people, with different kinds of proclivities, may perhaps speak in tongues differently).

I have come to think that there are general patterns of reactivity that are distributed differently among individuals, and that in social settings or settings in which particular events are meaningful, those who are more reactive are more likely to have these events, to remember these events, and to develop an expectation of having similar events in the future, all of which will make those events more likely for them. People are undoubtedly reactive in different ways—this body more likely to have a vision, that body more likely to feel presence, the other one more likely to awake unable to move. But I was struck that the events of the spiritual inventory, in short, do not seem to behave like a true taxonomy. They behave as if they are related, cousins rather than strangers on the street. In short, as I said before, they seem more like the way scientists these days think about psychiatric experience. Modern psychiatric scientists seem to imagine depression, schizophrenia, anorexia, and so forth as less like animals and more like colors. Sure, blue is different from green, but the natural world mostly gives us continua of shades.

LEARNING TO PAY ATTENTION IN NEW WAYS

My point is that people of faith often come to have what they take to be direct evidence that gods and spirits are present—and that their evidence is specific and particular to their own manner of faith. That evidence depends on the ways people learn to pay attention to the everyday experience of their senses and to the in-between, the domain between mind and world. It depends on whether people get caught up in their inner worlds (absorption), and on whether they judge ambiguous events to be of their external senses (and so originating outside of them) or of their inner senses (and so originating in their minds). In 2012, I called this an "attentional learning" theory of religion (Luhrmann and Morgain 2012). By that I meant that the sense of realness rests in part on learning, that this learning involves practices of attention, and that the practices changed what people experienced. The way we learn to pay attention not only changes what we notice, but how we experience what we notice. It is not just that people pay attention differently. Instead, what I see is that their attentional patterns can alter something as basic as their perceptual experience. "Kindling" is a more specific account of how attentional learning unfolds for people.

The kinds of events people deem spiritual are kindled: the body learns to experience these events, and the experience changes the events so that they become more fluent and habituated over time. These events are important because they provide firsthand evidence that the claims of the faith frame are valid. The events offer what seems like bodily evidence— the most basic evidence we have of the world—that talk about the invisible other is more than mere talk. In the process, the events change the experience of the body. The man who has heard the spirit speaking is more likely to feel its breath, shudder at its power, be moved to tears by its love. Evidence begets evidence. The person of faith not only works to make a god real but comes to be a body in which that evidence is felt in a certain way, and likely more easily. Thus the secular and faithful may find that their most basic experience of the world drifts apart.

6

WHY PRAYER WORKS

Prayer [is] only attention in its pure form.
—Simone Weil, *Gravity and Grace*

How, exactly, does all this real-making change those who do it? The last three chapters have been accounts of kindling: the proclivity, the practice, the understandings of mind and the vivid experiences that help to facilitate the feeling that gods and spirits are real. But the feeling of realness is not quite the same as a belief. As Matthew Ratcliffe (2005) points out with such eloquence, the feeling of realness is more like an emotion or a sensation. Belief is an idea. I began this book by arguing that humans seem to think differently about invisible others and everyday objects, that they are felt to be differently real, and that to sustain a commitment to gods and spirits as beings that matter, people need to develop a mode of thinking—I have called this a faith frame—in which gods and spirits are present, relevant, and responsive. They need to go to some effort to keep that way of thinking meaningful as they make sense of their world. I compared the faith frame to serious play. One chooses to behave as if gods and spirits matter—despite the ways that the world seems to contradict their existence.

So there are, then, two different analytic objects: the way one thinks in relationship to gods and spirits (described as the faith frame), and the felt realness of gods and spirits (generated by kindling). They are not the same, but neither are they independent. One is a manner of holding something in mind and attending to it as real. At one point I called this an "ontological attitude." The other is something one experiences. Both are a kind of real-making. Both require effort. Now I want to turn to the way this effort changes people. In this chapter, I look at the most obvious place in which maintaining a faith frame has effects, which is prayer—the act of deliberately turning one's attention toward a god or spirit and speaking to it. How does prayer change the one who prays?

WHY PEOPLE PRAY

Prayers often include a request—for good health, for a just world, for a red bicycle—and secular observers often assume that the request is the point. They assume that the request is what the prayer is about, and that the request is possible because of a reciprocity between the worshipped and the worshipper. We give prayers to the gods, and they give life to us. We give pigs to the ancestors just as we give birthday gifts to our friends, just as bracelets are given in return for necklaces around the great kula ring, just as the texture of all human groups is created through small, repeated reciprocities of grain-threshing and dinner parties. This was Robertson Smith's ([1889] 1956: 27) argument: that sacrifice—"the central problem of ancient religion"—was a communal meal in which human and god created bonds of obligation. Again and again, the Psalms tell us that prayer and worship are a form of reciprocity: we speak, and God replies; we worship and sacrifice, and He gives us rewards. "Surely goodness and mercy shall follow me all the days of my life and I will dwell in the house of the Lord forever" (Psalm 23:6).

Yet sometimes someone who prays for an egg seems to get a scorpion. Sometimes the parking space does not materialize. The college admissions email begins, "We regret to inform you." The golf ball misses the hole. The tumor grows. It is not hard for a secular person to view prayer as a practice of monumental foolhardiness in the face of facts—in short, as a mistake. But those who pray usually continue to pray, even when the prayer seems to fail. Job (30:20) says, "I cry out to you, God, but you do not answer; I stand up, but you merely look at me." Failure sluices through the Psalms like water. "Lord, why do You cast off my soul? *Why* do You hide Your face from me?" (Psalm 88:13–14). Many Psalms adore and exalt God. "I will sing of the steadfast love of the Lord, forever" (Psalm 89:1). Many despair. "My God, my God," the psalmist cries. "Why have you forsaken me?" (Psalm 22:1). (Jesus utters this phrase on the cross: Matthew 27:46.) It would be hard to claim that the people of Israel did not notice that their prayers did not always achieve their goals. Still they prayed.

We cannot truly understand prayer if we insist that it is founded on a mistake: that people pray because they think that gods deliver the outcomes for which they pray, and that they are wrong. It is as Durkheim said of religion—no human institution can survive if it rests upon a lie without which it could not exist. It makes no sense to treat humans as fools who fundamentally never notice that the prayer exchange is asymmetrical, or that a request goes unfulfilled. Of course there is confirmation bias. Of course people remember the prayers that seem to be answered and ask what they must have done to disappoint God when they are not. But confirmation bias is not enough to explain the remarkable resilience of the human habit of prayer.

If we want to understand why people pray, we should instead begin with the observation that prayer is often rich in feeling. (Here, and throughout this chapter, I will focus on engaged prayer, not rote prayer, though some of what I say will apply to rote prayer as well.) This is an old observation in anthropology. Bronislaw Malinowski wrote *Magic, Science and Religion* because he was annoyed by the presumption that "we" had science and "they" (preliterate, primitive, backward peoples) had magic. "As the Melanesians are reputed, however, to be specially magic-ridden, they will furnish an acid test of the existence of empirical and rational knowledge among savages living in the age of polished stone" (1954: 27). He thought that his Melanesians were both empirical and rational. In their fields, they fixed their fences, sowed their seed, dealt with their insects, and worked on their plots with considerable diligence and ingenuity. Their navigation system was so sophisticated that decades later cognitive scientists would make their careers explaining how it worked. Malinowski argued that magic and religion dealt with everything else—with what could not be controlled, mastered, and managed—and that when you find what humans cannot control, you find intense feeling. "Man, engaged in a series of practical activities, comes to a gap; the hunter is disappointed by his quarry, the sailor misses propitious winds, the canoe builder has to deal with some material of which he is never certain that it will stand the strain, or the healthy person suddenly feels his strength failing" (1954: 79). Prayer and ritual ex-

pressed that intense feeling, and the expression—and transformation—
of the feeling was the point. Mary Douglas put it this way:

> Of course Dinka hope that their rites will suspend the natural course of
> events. Of course they hope that rain rituals will cause rain, healing rit-
> uals avert death, harvest rituals produce crops. But instrumental effi-
> cacy is not the only kind of efficacy to be derived from their symbolic
> action. The other kind is achieved in the action itself, in the assertions it
> makes and the experience which bears its imprinting. ([1966] 2002: 84)

The practice becomes its own outcome, Douglas thought, because expressing a sense of how things should be helps someone live with the
world as it is. As Kierkegaard saw so clearly, prayer may not change God,
but it changes the person who prays ([1847] 1948: 44–45). But how does
that work?

I have come to think about prayer as a metacognitive practice, by
which I mean that it is a practice of thinking about thinking. Those who
pray commit to the faith frame, and in so doing, they step back from
their everyday way of thinking to examine their thoughts, as if seeing
from a god or spirit's point of view. They look back on their thoughts as
if from outside and ask whether those thoughts are in accord with a
world in which gods and spirits matter. It is this metacognitive dimension of the practice that changes people and helps them to deal with the
disappointments and the difficulties of their lives. Once you focus in on
what prayer actually demands of the one who is praying, you can see that
emotion management is a consequence of the metacognitive features of
ordinary, everyday practice—whether the person praying has emotion
management as his or her goal or not. Prayer changes people because
prayer alters the way people attend to their own mental processes.

PRAYER AS METACOGNITION

The central act of praying is paying attention to inner experience—to
thoughts, images, and the awareness of one's body—and treating those
sensations as important in themselves rather than as distractions from
the real business of living. That is what makes prayer a metacognitive
activity: it is a cognitive action (broadly conceived) that takes the

cognition of the actor as its focus. Metacognition is thinking about thinking, training attention on the act of thinking as it happens. When people pray, they attend to the way they pay attention. They think about what they are thinking. They respond to their emotions. And often they try to change the way they think, feel, and attend so that those mental acts are in line with the way they would rather be—with the world as it should be, understood within a faith frame, as if gods and spirits matter. In expressing gratitude, they alter what they remember of the day: not the irritating comment but the warm smile, not the cold morning but the lovely afternoon, not the office quarrel but the smooth, dappled sunlight on the trees. So prayer is in part a memory practice: the practice reworks what those who pray call to mind. But prayer is also an exercise in anticipating the future. When people ask a god for change, they reach for a world to come that is better than the world in which they find themselves, and they ask themselves to imagine that better world and who they would be within it. Local cultural ideas of course shape the content of what the person praying for wants—a calm, smiling surface or an excited grin, detachment from a vale of tears or identification with a god in agony. But the point remains that prayer practice is above all things a reflection on reflection: an attempt to sculpt, shape, reframe, reword, and remaster thoughts and feelings so that those thoughts and feelings become different from, and better than, what they were.

A god—or a spirit who listens—is not necessary for all of the meta-cognitive effects of prayer. Some of these effects are also associated with mindfulness, a practice in which one pauses and attends in the moment and without judgment. Mindfulness in effect creates an outsider's perspective on the mind but puts the subject, rather than a god, in the outside observer's role. The goal of mindfulness is to be present and aware, and to detach from thoughts that draw us away from the present moment. Many mindfulness practices begin with the breath: with the intake and the outflow, with a gentle, rhythmic breathing meant to fill the whole awareness of the one who practices. Sometimes people direct their attention throughout the body, first noticing the sensations in the forehead, the scalp, the neck, the shoulders, then in particular noticing and letting go of tension. Every time thoughts intrude, the practitioner seeks to let them drift off, without hostility, arousal, or response. This is, of course, a thinking about thinking, and its goal is to detach the thinker from the arousal of the thought. Here is one version of the basic practice:

1. *Set aside some time.* You don't need a meditation cushion or bench, or any sort of special equipment to access your mindfulness skills—but you do need to set aside some time and space.
2. *Observe the present moment as it is.* The aim of mindfulness is not quieting the mind, or attempting to achieve a state of eternal calm. The goal is simple: we're aiming to pay attention to the present moment, without judgment. Easier said than done, we know.
3. *Let your judgments roll by.* When we notice judgments arise during our practice, we can make a mental note of them, and let them pass.
4. *Return to observing the present moment as it is.* Our minds often get carried away in thought. That's why mindfulness is the practice of returning, again and again, to the present moment.
5. *Be kind to your wandering mind.* Don't judge yourself for whatever thoughts crop up; just practice recognizing when your mind has wandered off, and gently bring it back.

That's the practice. It's often been said that it's very simple, but it's not necessarily easy. The work is to just keep doing it. Results will accrue.[1]

The extensive scientific research on mindfulness finds that the practice reduces stress and promotes well-being. At least part of the value of the practice arises out of its metacognitive training to disattend to thoughts, so that thoughts feel less intrusive, less disturbing. The rage feels overblown, the despair excessive, the yearning outsized. Those who practice learn to take their inner impulses less seriously.

Most prayer looks on the surface quite different from mindfulness. Prayers have words and concepts, usually structured as requests spoken to someone who hears. But prayer is also an act of slowing down, of taking thoughts to another thinker (a god or spirit) with the result that the one who prays does not react directly but slows down to observe.

Niloofar Haeri (forthcoming) illustrates this slowing down in her rich account of prayer among women in Tehran. The prayers commanded by Allah are namaz: obligatory ritual prayer performed five times daily

---

[1] "Getting Started with Mindfulness," *Mindful*, accessed June 23, 2019, https://www.mindful.org/meditation/mindfulness-getting-started/.

with prescribed movement. The words of namaz are scripted formulas, with intentions interwoven with Qur'anic verses. *Du'a* are informal prayers cast as direct conversations with God. In du'a, people thank God for snow on the mountains and plead with Him to end war in Syria and Yemen. They talk about death and difficult decisions and moments of desolation. They talk to God about matters as trivial as why a particular bird sings every morning outside the window. They take time to reflect upon the passage of the day.

In such prayers, particularly when the prayer session is long and the person who prays finds that the flood of inner words has slowed, there are sudden, unexpected moments of joy. Here is Maryam, who was almost seventy when she spoke with Haeri:

> In du'a, sometimes you get this feeling of joy—you realize that your whole being has just been taken over by love and you can give this love too. This is a great feeling. You think of the whole universe, the whole world, and that there is only God. This moment is very important. This is not a moment where you want anything from God. This love actually comes into existence in silence and not in speaking.
>
> Now at this time you feel that love, that kindness, that rain of mercy, that rain of love and your heart swells up and you think there is no one else [but God] and in reality there isn't.

In my own interviews with evangelicals, I found that people sometimes described a special moment when they suddenly grasped, as if in a new and meaningful way, that God loved them. Often, they cried. These were poignant moments, intensely felt, intensely joyful—and then the moment was gone. Still, the memory of that joy really mattered to them.

Such moments—and others—shift the sense of hurt and anxiety. One prays and something changes. Here is Maryam again:

> I was doing namaz recently and suddenly this *haalat* [state] came about which was great. I was standing there facing the House of God [in my mind's eye], and then it was as though space became light blue around me. It was so pleasant and I felt drenched in kindness, in the soft cloud of kindness. Of course these visions were just in my imagination. They didn't have a reality to them, there was nothing and yet that feeling transpired, that good feeling came about.

Such dramatic moments are rare. Still, in many prayers there are small moments that matter. As Maryam explains,

> These thoughts come with doing du'a. Are they du'a? In reality probably not, *but they come hand in hand*. They lead me to tell myself: Don't complain, it is what it is. This is the moment you live in, it is like this, don't ruin this moment, this day. To accept my state of needlessness that is what [I should be able] to do. I must be thankful and that is the best thing [I can] do.

Maryam feels differently after she voices her anxieties in the act of prayer. She also knows that the thoughts and images that emerge in prayer have a complex realness to them, as my evangelicals also knew. That is, it is not always clear to the person who prays whether or not such thoughts and images come from God or reflect the world. Yet they change the emotional state of the person who prays.

How does that work? In part, the answer is that hurt and distress, whether significant or trivial, are soothed by the slowing down itself. The practice, however, does more. Consider first what we might call the "overt" features of prayer. Anne Lamott (2012) charmingly names these "help, thanks, wow." A common evangelical acronym adds "sorry" in "ACTS": adoration, confession, thanks, and supplication—practices one certainly finds in faiths that are not Christian. Being grateful, asking, and confessing have metacognitive effects of their own, before we even consider whether there is anyone to hear them and be adored. We turn to these now.

GRATITUDE

The most explicit, overt feature of monotheistic faiths is that the one God is good. This assertion can also be understood as a statement that no matter what has happened that day, no matter what the sorrow or the loss, the world is a good one, and the person who prays is grateful for the goodness. "The Lord gave, and the Lord hath taken away; blessed be the name of the Lord" (Job 1:21). Judaism requires those who have lost loved ones to stand in public and recite the Mourner's Kaddish: "May His great Name grow exalted and sanctified in the world that He created as He willed." A man who has lost his father must daily say aloud before others that the God who has in some fundamental sense caused his pain is good. It is the most obvious feature of prayer: that those who pray describe their small griefs and larger struggles and then direct their attention to the ways in which their world is nonetheless good. One Christian explained to me that she walked out into the frozen grimy landscape of midwinter Chicago—"it was like icy rain and gray and cold and it was sleety"—and remembered how she prayed: "God, I praise you that it was just not snowing and it's not accumulating and the streets aren't icy." Giving thanks, expressing gratitude, and asserting that the one who made the world is good: those acts require one to look at troubles and insist to oneself that they contain blessings.

The themes of many Buddhist chants are similar. Here are some Buddhist chants one might pick up in any Thai temple, as the anthropologist Felicity Aulino remarks (personal communication). People recite these in the temple and in private religious practice.

> All beings subject to suffering
> Birth, aging, illness, and death
> May they be happy and free from enmity
> May they be happy and stop exploiting each other
> May they be happy and free from physical and mental sufferings
> May they live happily and free from all sufferings and dangers
> [and then the chant is repeated for oneself]

They are framed as requests, but they acknowledge that one can be happy and free from suffering, despite the human condition. To be sure, many forms of Buddhism do not assert that the world is good or that God is good. The world is instead represented as suffering. But the cognitive action is the same: to shift attention away from what is distressing and toward what is not distressing. Even some of the seemingly harsher practices (a meditation on one's own death) may have the effect of encouraging one to reframe one's current life: to live in it, to accept it.

The cognitive restructuring that is the basic mechanism of gratitude prayer is also the goal of cognitive behavioral therapy. Aaron Beck (1976), arguably the person most responsible for developing this style of treatment, decided that the most costly feature of depression was not sadness per se, but the slow, recurrent rumination on one's own worthlessness and failure—what Freud ([1917] 1976: 247) called the self-reproaches and self-revilings, the "dissatisfaction with the ego on moral grounds." It is what humans do: our minds wander, and unbidden, nagging thoughts pop up like gophers in the lawn. When people are depressed, those thoughts form a miserable chorus so relentless they recede from their status as thoughts and feel like facts about the world. A cognitive behavioral therapist asks clients not so much to remember their childhood or to marshal their anger but instead to pinpoint specific recurrent negative thoughts. The therapy asks people to pay attention to their thoughts—to observe them like a naturalist observing dolphins from a boat in the bay, clocking which animal swims by and how often and with whom. The client takes this data to the therapist, a literal list of observed thoughts, and together, client and therapist work out what is wrong about the recurrent thought ("you won't *really* die if you don't get any sleep tonight") and come up with sentences that could replace it when it reappears ("I'll just be a little tired in the morning"). In this approach, thought is a behavior you can change.

Cognitive behavioral therapy works. All therapy has its limits, as does prayer (Job could bless God's name after God had destroyed his crops and animals—but he could not bless God's name after God had blasted him with boils, and Job sat weeping in the ashes of his household, scratching at his sores). And yet despite limits, there is better empirical support for cognitive behavioral therapy than for any other psychotherapy (e.g., Butler et al. 2006; Hoffman et al. 2012; Tolin 2010).

One can say that the practices at the heart of cognitive behavioral therapy can also be found in prayer because prayer is above all else a behavior that alters the thoughts that one thinks. This is particularly striking in the practice of gratitude. When people pray about their troubles and state that God is good, they are describing their sorrows and reimagining them as gifts. They sit in peace and think about beauty, and they aim for joy. "Safely may I go about," the Navaho speaker says. "I have become your child" (Reichard 1944: 59).

Mindfulness and the Buddhist goal of detachment are related versions of this process. They work through learning to disattend, rather than to replace one kind of thought with another. Stories about the Buddha's practice are above all stories about thought, as in this excerpt from

Buddhaghosa, the famous fifth-century commentator on Buddhist texts and practices:

> When the Buddha arrived at an explanation according to the Vinaya, he did not ask [an offending monk] "what is your sensory contact, what is your feeling, what is your perception, what is your intention?" Rather, he primarily asked simply about his thought (*citta*): "monk, what was your thought?" And when the reply is "I had the thought to steal, Bhagavan," the Buddha does not say "the offense of stealing is of sensory contact, etc.," but rather that "the offense, monk, is in the thought to steal." And not only is this so of Vinaya teaching, but in other worldly teachings also he teaches primarily simply about thoughts. (Heim 2013: 134)

The practices laid out in the great texts of the Buddhist tradition are those that lead to scrupulous self-examination, and the effort is on shifting attention away from the self-interested act. One is to "jai yen," or work toward a cool heart, as Julia Cassaniti's Thai participants explained to her. When Cassaniti (2015) first went to Thailand, she did so aware that many observers felt that only monks understood terms like anicca (the impermanence of all things and all conditions), and that some observers believed that ordinary Buddhists repressed their anger and their grief. She observed instead that laypeople did genuinely appear to feel less grief-stricken and angry at moments that should have grieved or angered them, and she attributed this to their mindfulness-like practice. Mindfulness seems to lessen the force of negative emotions by teaching practitioners to attend to them differently: to observe them, rather than to feel them.

CONFESSION

Confession enables another form of cognitive restructuring: the ability to organize experience and to set small goals. To confess is to remember the past and to think through what one has done. To confess casts experience into language. It orders the past and gives it meaning, and that alone makes someone feel better. The psychologist James Pennebaker (1989) has found that merely writing down the details of an upsetting event lifts the writer's mood. To render the specifics of the past into language—and particularly into narrative—gives control to the one who uses the words. The murk grows less murky; the hurricane gale diminishes to a squall.

That is what people do when they pray. They think about the previous day. They think about their week. They run over what people have said to them and how they responded and the way that made them feel. They pray specifically and personally because the acts they pray about are specific and personal acts. Even if the specific prayer is scripted, the accompanying sotto voce commentary cannot be. You do not say "Lead us not into temptation, and deliver us from evil" without some detail about your life that flits across your mind unless the words are truly empty to you, unless you recite them so quickly you do not really hear them.

In the daily Jesuit Examen, developed by the brilliant sixteenth-century Ignatius of Loyola, the one who prays must exact "an account of self with regard to the particular matter decided upon for correction and improvement. He should run through the time, hour by hour or period by period, from the moment of rising until the present examination" (Loyola 1992: 25). It is a practice of inner examination. One focuses attention on thoughts, with the aim of making those thoughts feel less intentionally compelling, less important. One uses the imagination to place oneself in a difficult situation, to watch the scene unfold with detachment, and to scrutinize the small moments of one's day. One looks at one's life as if from the outside.

Does scrupulously attending to the past give one more control over one's behavior in the future? Augustine thought that only when one could see oneself clearly could one change. He exclaimed just prior to his conversion,

> You Lord, while [Ponticianus] was speaking, were turning me around so that I could see myself; you took me from behind my own back, which was where I had put myself during the time when I did not want to be observed by myself, and you set me in front of my own face so that I could see how foul a sight I was—crooked, filthy, spotted, and ulcerous. I saw and I was horrified, and I had nowhere to go to escape from myself. (2001: 163–64)

It is not a pretty read. It is not even (from an observer's perspective) particularly accurate. Yet Augustine was clear that this vivid, precise view of himself was necessary for the great change that he would make in his life because it gave him mastery over his own story. Freud went further: he asked his patients to speak as freely as they could, to allow recollection to slip past the censors we impose upon our own memories. He believed that if his patients could describe the past precisely, they would no longer be caught within the pincers of unconscious repetition.

Augustine, Ignatius, Freud, the Buddha—they were all aiming for comprehensive change: for a full, deep commitment to God, for the paralyzed hysteric to be set free. But notice that this focus on the concrete and particular creates achievable goals along the way. Reciting small details about how one has failed makes small successes more plausible. In an Examen, ticking off small sins on a grid, one does not pray to be perfect. One resolves to bite back that sharp retort, or to not indulge in an after-dinner snack or that second glass of wine. Thinking about missteps in the near past trains attention on the near future, and the near future is so much more manageable than the mountaintop ambition. It is a lesson I learn from writing. It is a terrible mistake to set out to write a book—or it is for me, anyway. My books are written paragraph by paragraph, each one drafted and redrafted, a flagstone set down along a path.

ASKING

To pray is to ask. People pray to be rewarded with olive oil and honey, for daily bread and the forgiveness of debt, for protection and for care. They pray about healing, and they pray about work. They pray about interviews and jobs and pregnancies. They pray about parking and football games. They want help. This is the psalm we call the *De profundis*: "Out of the depths have I cried unto thee, O Lord. Lord, hear my voice" (Psalm 130:1–2). Asking is not necessarily about getting. I have said that gratitude shifts attention from negative thoughts to positive thoughts, and confession organizes experience and sets small goals. Asking creates a third kind of cognitive restructuring: the assertion of hope.

To ask is powerful because it is an act. When a Dinka man (the Dinka are neighboring peoples to the Nuer in southern Sudan) is still far from home but the sun is low on the horizon, the man may stoop to tie grasses together to prevent the sun from sinking. This man, the anthropologist Godfrey Lienhardt explained, is not doing magic. He does not believe that the grass will hold back the sun. He also does not think that the act is meaningless. The man tied the grass together to make his hope real to himself by making it external in public space. "This 'mystical' action is not a substitute for practical or technical action, but a complement to it and preparation for it. The man who ties such a knot has made an external, physical representation of a well-formed mental intention. He has produced a model of his desires and hopes, upon which to base renewed practical endeavor" (1961: 283). To Lienhardt, this is the heart of prayer, whether spoken in the liturgy of a great cathedral or enacted in the dance of the !Kung. Prayer is an act that captures the attention and focuses the mind on hope. The action itself makes him feel effective, the way cleaning up your desk before you write a paper can make you feel effective, and that sense of efficacy itself can then spur the writing.

More specifically, to ask is a mental act that in its action asserts the capacity to act. The act of hoping is not in itself a metacognitive act, but deliberately choosing to hope is an act that trains attention on thought in a particular way. To pray is to make hope external, and the mere act of doing so can still one's panic. It can give a sense of anticipatory accomplishment—you have not yet achieved your goal, but you have done something with the aim of achieving your goal. This may lie behind Ted Kaptchuk's (et al. 2010) remarkable demonstration that when people were given an inert substance to treat their abdominal pain and told that the substance was a placebo—that it had no medical benefit—but that others had reported feeling better after taking it, these subjects also reported feeling better themselves. One thinks of the primary mechanism behind placebo as expectation: believe that the healer will heal, and he will. But Kaptchuk's experiment suggests that there is more than expectation involved. The *De profundis* suggests that it may be action itself: that to pray in the face of hopelessness is to assert that hope is real.

Asking also alters goals, because the moral expectations around the appropriate goal of prayer—one's sense of what it is right to pray for— will alter how one prays. Prayers for healing often include a shift in focus away from cure, the ostensible purpose of prayer, toward an acceptance of the illness. Often, those who pray not only ask for remission but also that God's will be done. For example, the anthropologist Anna Corwin

(2012) did her fieldwork in a Franciscan convent among nuns who had worked as missionaries, often abroad, before returning to the convent for retirement. One of those nuns, Sister Theresa, had been sent to Oceania. There she had contracted amoebiasis so thoroughgoing that by the time she sought medical attention, the disease had become incurable. For thirty years she had trouble walking. Parts of her infected body had been periodically removed through surgery; this included one of her feet. For years, Corwin wrote, Sister Theresa interpreted her pain as God's judgment, and she had prayed to Him for mercy. But her life spanned the sea change of Vatican II, the Catholic church's attempt to make God more accessible, more present. Before Vatican II, Sister Theresa explained to Corwin, she had been taught to pray as if God were far above her, a great and holy authority. Afterward, she was told that God resides in everything. She decided that this included her amoebas. She called a meeting of all the amoebas in her body and told them that she loved them. These days, every morning she stands in front of her mirror and "addresses all of God within herself." She still experiences pain, but the pain seems less significant. It no longer seems like God's punishment. Corwin found evidence that these nuns—riddled with tropical disease as some were—experienced greater well-being than their irreligious peers.

The anthropologist Gregory Simon provides a different kind of example in his study of daily Islamic prayer in western Sumatra. When people carry out these prescribed movements, he argues, they feel themselves both to be the bold individual striving in the world and also the docile subject who accepts God's will. They have willingly, deliberately, chosen to submit. They have done no more than what they must, but in choosing to do so, they feel alive. "The soul is freed of cares," one of his participants explains (2009: 260). We see the moral satisfactions of this conscious choice to constrain oneself in the surge of Islamic women who choose to veil (Brenner 1996; Mahmood 2005; Bowen 2007) and also in other ascetic practices—fasting, early waking, habit-wearing. In *Man's Search for Meaning*, Victor Frankl argued that one must deliberately choose to act even in the concentration camp, where guards regulate all behavior. To him, the capacity to choose to act, even on the smallest scale, is what gives life its meaning.

TO WHOM ONE PRAYS

The effects of prayer do not all depend on a god—on a someone who is addressed—yet of course many prayers are directed toward a listener: they are an act of talking to an invisible, or at least nonhuman, being. What is the consequence of that?

Buddhism is a useful place to begin because many Buddhist prayers are in fact addressed to someone, even though, theologically, there is no god. The Thai chants, for instance, are a request: "May they be happy." They are phrased as if there were one who can hear and will listen.

In her thoughtful essay comparing Buddhist and Christian prayer, the Buddhist scholar Rita Gross wrote that what matters about the addressee is not whether it exists, but how it creates as an opportunity to be heard. It is only North Americans, she writes, who get stuck on this problem of whether Buddhists feel that there is a listener who hears, because Buddhism has been remade in so peculiar a form in the North American context. "Even the forms of Buddhism that are most rigorous and uncompromising about ultimate nontheism have always recognized that super-human beings, invisible to ordinary human vision, do indeed 'exist'" (2002: 79–80). It is true that for many Buddhists there is no substantial, lasting, permanent self—and there are, ultimately, no invisible beings. But while these humans still feel that they have selves, they also still feel that there are spirits who listen—and that is important, Gross argues, because a listener makes prayers more effective for the one who prays.

The deep insight here is that talking to oneself is not as powerful as talking to another. This is the secret at the heart of confession, of Alcoholics Anonymous, of the face-to-face apology, the secret known to all teachers—that it changes you to speak in public space. The existence of an invisible other creates that public space. When you talk to someone, when you know that what you say is heard, you take ownership of your words more deeply. The words mean more. You listen more deeply to what you yourself have said.

It is also likely true that if you talk to an invisible other in the public space you create by addressing that being, the being feels more real. As the anthropologist Amy Cox Hall (2018: 1105) remarks, "Prayer [is] God *in potentia*." Knowing that you have spoken as if to a listener gives your sense of that listener more heft.

I believe that this is what Niloofar Haeri saw in her Tehrani women. They speak to God in informal, conversational prayer, more or less as if to a person. The formal prayers of Islam, as Haeri points out, include a sura that describes God as neither born nor as giving birth. God is thus, as Haeri puts it, "across an ontological divide." The god to whom one speaks informally is not as far away. That god feels more like a real person. In fact, the one who prays informally can find that the god feels so real one can get angry at what that god does. One of Haeri's participants, a retired high-school teacher she calls Mina, was berating God when her daughter overheard her:

> Once a serious problem came up for my daughter. I was very upset about it. It was night and after I finished my namaz, I went to my room and turned off the light and began to do du'a. I was crying and I wanted to know what I had done that my daughter would suffer like this. I just thought she is so young, she does not deserve such a terrible thing to happen to her. Well, apparently, my daughter was passing by and she heard me. So she entered the room and turned on the light and said with great distress: "Maman if you say these things to God, then your namaz is invalid." I said why, she said, "do you not say allaho akbar? What does that mean? That means God is generous and will take care of you. Either you believe in that or not."

Mina's daughter, who did not practice du'a diligently, could not conceive of a god at whom one could get mad. Another du'a practitioner, forced to marry a man she did not want, in a marriage she found infuriating, became so angry at God that she did not pray for years.

> I wanted to move back to Tehran with my family because my father's assignment [in the city where we lived with my husband] was over and they were moving back. So I tried to convince my husband to move with us, with our little son and my family. He refused, because I heard his father tell him, if you go with them, they will always say that the groom is eating off the hands of his father-in-law because you don't have a job there and you don't know anyone. So he refused to go with us. My own

father said, well you take your son and come with us, and I said "I am not going to have my child live fatherless." My husband's father had told him this thing and so when he told me he was not coming with us to Tehran at the last minute, after I had sold everything we had, I was extremely upset. After that, I did *qahr* [social avoidance] with God. I just said, this life is too difficult, I can't. Then for years I did not pray.

The idea that one can disagree with God, or even be angry with God, can feel heretical in the abstract. Yet in many faiths, this anger arises out of the intimacy with an invisible other who can feel and understand like a human. I met many evangelical Christians who spoke of feeling angry with God—and it seemed to me that the sense of anger helped them to feel more intimate with God. One woman even told me, with a rueful smile, that she and God had gone off to sulk at each other for a few days. In Judaism, the practice even has a name: "arguing with God."

I call this kindling when God feels a little more real to those who pray. These are tiny acts. Saying thank you, daily. Looking at the world around you and feeling glad. Thinking over your day, considering what you did wisely—and unwisely. Asking specifically about what steps to take next. Being miffed when God fails to answer one's prayers. Slowly, with tiny acts, a sense of presence builds.

When the kindling works and a god feels more real to someone, prayer may affect him or her for different reasons. Finally, then, to adoration.

ADORATION: CREATING A RELATIONSHIP IN WHICH YOU ARE LOVED

"You shall love the Lord your God with all your heart, with all your soul, and with all your might" (Deuteronomy 6:5). Unlike gratitude, asking, or confessing, what many people of faith call "adoration" is not about cognitive reframing. It is about attachment, or, in the language of social anthropology, social relationship. When God becomes real to people, God becomes a social relationship. The psychologist Uffe Schjoedt and his colleagues (2009) asked Christians to pray informally to God while in the fMRI scanner, and their brains behaved as if they were talking to a friend. (This did not happen when they simply recited the Lord's Prayer.) This social relationship has a direct impact on well-being. We know that people feel less lonely when they believe in God (loneliness is nearly as lethal as smoking [Holt-Lunstad, Smith, and Layton 2010]). In my own work (2013), the more people affirmed "I feel God's love for me, directly" on a standard survey, the less lonely they were, the less stressed they felt, and the fewer psychiatric vulnerabilities they displayed.

When that sense of an invisible other can be sustained, that other offers—to some extent—what a human friend might. The psychologist Shane Sharp (2010) set out to explore how prayer helped those who struggled with grief, fear, and anger by speaking with over sixty women from around the United States who had fled domestic violence in their homes. He asked them, as neutrally as he could, whether they had talked with God during their abuse and how it had been helpful. Almost all of them were Christians. Some were evangelical, some Catholic, a few Mormon, and some were spiritual-but-not-religious. He found five ways in which prayer helped to soothe the women's distress. Talking with God provided a person-like other to whom they could express negative emotions—above all, fear, anger, and shame. Talking with God provided a means for positive reappraisals: the women felt that God had a higher opinion of them than their partners did. Talking with God made them feel safe, as if they were in less danger than they were before they prayed. Talking with God was a distraction and a means to zone out, even during the abuse itself. And finally, talking to God made them feel more forgiving. Sharp wasn't sure all of these strategies were, in fact, ultimately helpful. He did not think that it was always wise for these women to minimize danger and forgive their assailants. But he thought that prayer made the women feel that they had a person in their corner who could help.

People do not get the emotional rewards of a loving social relationship through prayer unless they experience God as real to them, at least to some extent. They must feel that there is a particular God who pays attention and will respond—not in the misty future, but here and now in the world. It may be, in the end, that this feature—that God is a social relationship in the life of the person who prays—is prayer's most powerful and consequential feature. God—or rather, a human's understanding of God—can be a way to improve on reality. But for an invisible other to be real like that, the imagined representation of God—that daydream in the mind—must feel like more than a daydream. It must become a relationship.

This chapter has focused on the metacognitive effects of prayer. They result from thinking within the faith frame—thinking about one's own thinking from an outsider's perspective, in the public space where gods and spirits listen. Now we turn to the effects of kindling the feeling that these gods and spirits are real.

7

A GOD WHO RESPONDS

> At eight of a hot morning, the cicada speaks his first piece. He says of the world: heat. At eleven of the same day, he has not changed his note, but has enlarged his theme. He says of the morning: love. In the sultry middle of the afternoon, when the sadness of love and heat has shaken him, his symphonic soul goes into the great movement and he says: death. But the thing isn't over. After supper he weaves heat, love, death into a final stanza, subtler and less brassy than the others. He has one last heroic monosyllable at his command. Life, he says, reminiscing. Life.
>
> —E. B. White, "Life"

We began with the question of what we could learn by asking not whether people worship because they believe, but whether they believe because they worship. I pointed out that people of faith often did not behave as if gods and spirits mattered (when washing the dishes, feeding the dog, shrugging on a coat, and so forth) and that the challenge of faith was to keep gods and spirits in the forefront of awareness—to think within a faith frame in which gods and spirits matter. That, I suggested, was made easier when gods and spirits *felt* real. "Feeling real" is not the same as "believing in." Feeling real is more like an emotion (as Matthew Ratcliffe [2005] tells us). It is more like knowing that your mother loves you than believing that she is sitting in the den. Then I set out to describe the structure of real-making: the narratives, the absorption, the inner sense cultivation, the model of minds, and the events that these orientations and practices kindle into being. After this we came to the question: How does real-making change people? Prayer is one answer. Prayer is a determined attempt to use a faith frame to focus on a god. Here in this final chapter I focus on another. What happens when faith practices kindle a god or spirit into feeling real?

The answer is that gods and spirits respond. That is, what it means for gods and spirits to feel real is that humans feel a responsiveness, an aliveness—and this places them into a relationship that changes the humans. This sense of relationship doesn't happen to everyone, and in different religions it happens in different ways. Even if one begins from the faith perspective that gods and spirits are always communicating, it is clear that not all who are faithful hear, know, or feel what those gods and spirits mean to convey. They do not always feel that gods and spirits are interacting with *them*. This is why gods and spirits must be made real, and the reason it is so important to take seriously the difference between the realness of the everyday world and the realness of gods and spirits. Gods and spirits are invisible, immaterial, not accessible to the senses in ordinary ways. If humans are to feel the presence of these beings, they must know how to look, how to listen, and how to experience the event. They must learn how to know that spirits respond.

To be clear, these judgments are often fluid and open to doubt. In a hotel near the white cliffs of Dover, on a wet and windy weekend, I met a woman who talks with the dead. She is a medium. She claims to knows how to recognize when the dead make contact and how to communicate what they say to those who come to her for consultation. She says that anyone can do this, if they learn how—but that you must be taught, and you must not be credulous. She said that she was in a hotel on holiday when a water glass fell off the table. She thought it was the wind. But the glass fell a second time. When she asked the landlord whether anything had happened, he told her that a woman had just lost her husband on the beach. She knew then, she said, that a spirit had been trying to catch her attention—and she also said that if you are a good medium, your first instinct must be to doubt. It is what people say to assert that they are not foolish. The anthropologist Courtney Handman once described to me the human process of becoming sure of God as breaking through a door. There is a sense that God is on the other side of the door, yet people doubt that the humans have the right door or that they identify God rightly. And so, Handman remarked, they push the door farther and farther back: they decide that God is not in the icon, and then not in the wooden cross, perhaps not even (as Matthew Engelke [2007] described for one group of Christians) in the Bible itself, for all these doors can be false. Faiths change because humans want to connect with spirit, and it can be hard to be sure one has actually done so.

Yet many humans say that they do recognize a response. That response creates a relationship. I know that this statement can sound odd to skeptical observers, but it is what people say about their experiences, and frankly what you see on their faces. The most powerful but also most perplexing observation I have made in my work is that people of faith learn to identify gods and spirits as responding, that this responsiveness comes to feel like a relationship, and that this relationship changes people. Understanding this should change the way anthropologists think about religion. We should shift from our singular focus from belief, from the ideas people hold, to include the way gods and spirits become social relationships in human lives. In this final chapter, I will try to make sense of this claim and to reflect on its implications.

The first point is about specificity.

I was raised in a Unitarian church, in an era of progressive politics. As Unitarians, we believed that God was best understood through the parable in which six blind men encircled an elephant and described what they felt with their hands. They were all around the same elephant, but the man at its trunk felt a rope; the man at its leg, a tree; the man at its side, a wall; and so on. In the parable, the men fight because each takes the others to be lying. To Unitarians, the point of the story is that the quarrelling men share the same reality despite their differing evidence. We believed that God was understood in different cultures in different ways, but that these differences were superficial—overbeliefs, not the real stuff. Christians, Hindus, Jews, and Muslims knew the same God. We just stood at different parts of the elephant.

Our church was scarcely alone. America in the 1960s was heir to what Gary Wills (2019) calls the new piety of the 1950s. In 1947, polls had found that the most-respected leaders were ministers, priests, and rabbis. Billy Graham became a pastor to presidents and a celebrity. Americans began to describe their spiritual tradition as "Judeo-Christian." Aldous Huxley wrote *The Perennial Philosophy* to explain that all religions sprang out of the same source and the same experience, a mystical union with the "one." By the 1960s, there was great excitement about the common paths of different faiths. The Trappist monk Thomas Merton sold over six hundred thousand copies of a book about choosing his vocation, and he then went on to write admiring books about Zen Buddhism, Taoism, and Confucianism, extolling their practices and recommending them to his readers. In 1965, Vatican II decided that Catholics should develop relationships with people of other faiths. The first World Conference on Religion and Peace met in Kyoto, Japan, in 1970 to discuss "obstacles to peace in light of common religious principles" (see WCRP Proceedings 1969). It was as if all religions were part of a global kumbaya.

We are no longer in that idealistic moment. History does not teach us that cultural differences are window-dressing. In the last few decades societies around the world have been consumed in what have been called "culture wars" but are better described as a conflict between religions: the less conservative against the more conservative, liberal Christians against evangelicals, nonorthodox against orthodox, and permissive against restrictive, in the United States, Israel, the Middle East, Europe, Africa, and elsewhere. These are not so much arguments over cognitive propositions and abstract values as they are intense emotional fights over what leading a moral life demands from us. We are not so much arguing over what we believe but about who we are.

The intensity makes more sense when you understand people as having relationships as well as holding beliefs. Beliefs, after all, sound like things you can pick up and give away like a penny. You can change your mind about what you believe. People have all sorts of beliefs surrounding what they do and do not think about gods and spirits, some of which they can't put into words and some of which do not connect terribly well with what they actually do. But relationships change who you are.

A person acts, the other person responds, and because that second person is not identical to the first, he or she responds in unexpected ways. We are surprised by these others. Even if we choose exactly the spouse we want, because they seem perfect for the person that we are, we become someone different through the marriage. We form ourselves on the differentness of who they are, the obduracy of their otherness, and on the way they react, which is not what we would have done. The back-and-forth alters us—and we are surprised by the alteration. We did not necessarily imagine that we would become different in that way.

A reader might imagine that this is not true of a relationship with a god. Gods are not humans. They are invisible, immaterial, not present in an ordinary way. One might think that humans, being human, would simply make up the invisible others they want. One might suspect that people invent a god that simply reflects who they are already. And that characterization is not completely false, because people's sense of a god owes much to the hidden dynamics of their own inner landscapes.

But a god that cannot startle you does not feel real to people (see also Bialecki 2017). That is what a response feels like—that something happened that is not you and by which you are surprised, something that tells you that the cause of startlement came from beyond your inner world. The feeling of realness not only enables the relationship; in some sense, it *is* the relationship, because a true relationship cannot exist unless there is a responsive being—not just a face looking back in the mirror. This was Martin Buber's (1937) point. You cannot relate to an It. You relate to a You. In an I-It connection, the other is wholly passive. The I-Thou is a relationship of mutuality and reciprocity. The human who says "You," Buber wrote, stands in relation with another who is not himself, who responds.

Humans are changed by different dimensions of these relationships. They are changed by the basic sense of connection, through which a god can be known through social others. They are also changed because the god itself becomes a social other. In many ways people of faith relate to their god as if it were a person, and in the ordinary course of things relationships with other people change us. And more so than in many human relationships, people deliberately set out to work on themselves in order to deepen their connection to their god, thus causing change in themselves. I will emphasize positive changes here, because I am building an argument that real-making changes people in ways that may engage them in their faith. These relationships are particular histories of feelings and encounters, and they lead us to a moral conundrum that arises from the specificity of the god: that while a relationship with a benevolent god is often quite good for the individual, it does not at all follow that this god is good for the social whole.

I will walk through these different dimensions with observations from my own experiences of different faiths.

CONNECTION

At the shul for the newly orthodox, when I asked people why they came, the word people used most often was "connection." They felt connected to an imagined community that included not only all Jews living, but all Jews stretching back generation upon generation, "more numerous than the stars in the sky" (Genesis 22:17), as God promised to Abraham. They told me that at this shul, a traditional, orthodox shul, they were getting "the real thing"—that this was the way their ancestors had prayed for generations without number, even though most of the congregants neither understood the Hebrew nor even read it phonetically.

The mitzvoth then became the way they experienced that connection. People were excited when they felt a new inner compulsion to follow the commandments. For example, the fully observant orthodox woman dresses in skirts that fall beneath her knees and shirtsleeves that run past her elbows. She covers her hair with a hat outside her home or, more properly, with a wig. When women arrived for the first time in the shul, they came in all sorts of outfits. Once I stood next to a young woman in shorts and a tank top. What congregants described (if they came back) was that the desire to be observant came to them, and it no longer felt right to do as they had done. This was expected to happen gradually, in stages, and yet to grab you emotionally. It was meant to be a struggle and a joy. Here a middle-aged woman, a psychotherapist, reflects:

> I am wearing hats all the time now. I was wearing [a hat] just to shul. Then I started wearing it every time I went to shul whether it was ser-vices or not. Then in September, just before the High Holidays, I decided that I was going to commit to wearing a hat all the time when I go out. Sometimes I wear it in the house, too.
>
> [But] my family isn't committed to me being that consistent with it. Although they do appreciate me wearing the hat, they aren't ready for me to get a wig, for example. They are not quite ready for that yet.

You do one thing; you do another. Then you realize, as a middle-aged man told me, that you've run out of the easy steps, and the tougher ones, like keeping kosher, are just around the corner. "Then you realize," he continued, "that you've already made a commitment by taking those smaller steps. So do you back off? No. You take the next step."

It is true that to some extent people in the shul did experience God responding through spiritual presence events. The rabbi did not encourage people to discuss these moments. Mysticism, he said, could distract you from your true purpose, which was to live your life by God's commandments. (It is worth noting that this kind of orthodoxy emerges from a Lithuanian tradition in which deeds are everything, rather than from the Hasidic search for mystical meaning.) Yet people did report remarkable moments. Here the man above remembered,

> One day we were in shul [meaning, in the service], and [the rabbi] was davening [praying], he was doing musaf [a prayer service] in the latter part of the Saturday morning service, right after they had put the Torah away. He hit it right on the money. He had people walking out of shul saying that they had chills running down their spines. . . . It was amazing. I've experienced something like that only one other time, on Yom Kippur. I felt like I was alone in shul, that there was nobody else there. I felt like I was this high off the ground. Literally. It was extraordinary. . . . It was the most remarkable thing.

For this man, God became present in that special moment.

For most people, however, their primary experience of God was their experience of following the mitzvoth. That was how they felt connected to God, and their drama about what and when to follow became their relationship with God. For example, a young man told me that after he got into a fight with his wife, he vented his anger by violating the commandment about not using electricity on Shabbos. "I watched television last Saturday. Normally I don't. We don't use electricity. [But I did] and I wore my yarmulke [the head-covering worn by observant men] at the time. I love that! The dialectic, the dichotomies, all the problems, I *love* that." "Why?" I asked. "Because it makes me feel alive. . . . There is a choice to make." He was mad at his wife. He made himself feel better by doing something that—from his perspective—forced God to notice him, to recognize that he was there.

What seemed to matter was the choice to be part of that group that followed the mitzvoth—not whether you understood the text, not whether it made any sense that God forbade you to put a slice of American cheese on a hamburger. I met a young man, in his early thirties, struggling because the only house he and his wife could afford to buy was so far away that they would have to drive to shul on the sabbath, when the commandment (as interpreted by the rabbis) forbade the faithful to drive. I asked him whether he thought the mitzvoth came from God.

> I think some of them did. Yes. To figure out which parts did and which parts didn't, I get frustrated. But when it comes down to it, it doesn't matter. It was given to me by my parents, and I have these rhythms, these family connections. If I deny that the Torah came from Sinai, it doesn't matter because my forefathers thought it did.
>
> Who am I to break the connection because at any moment in time I am having these theological problems?

It helped me to understand the political commitment to Israel, which ran high in this shul. They understood Israel as part of the tradition—even if they had never visited the country, even if its policies might not have been those they might have chosen. It seemed to me that members of this shul imagined standing together in the presence of the same God, recognized as part of the whole. Who were they to break the connection?

THE EFFECTS OF CONNECTION

The most obvious point about the way connection changes people is that social connection changes bodies. This is the striking epidemiological finding that weekly church attendance has positive health effects. (Epidemiologists know most about the associations with attendance because frequency of attendance is the easiest variable to add into a large survey.) Attending services seems to boost the immune system and decrease blood pressure (Woods et al. 1999; Koenig and Cohen 2002). It may add two or three years to one's life (D. Hall 2006). One study found a seven-year difference in life expectancy, at age twenty, between those who never attended church and those who attended more than once a week (Hummer et al. 1999). Part of this story is that those who attend services have healthier behaviors: they may be more hesitant to drink, take drugs, or engage in risky sex. But that is not the whole story. In the 2012 edition of the *Handbook of Religion and Health*, the authors surveyed all the studies they could find. Despite differences in definition, measurement, outcome, and quality, across close to three thousand original data-based quantitative studies, they found that

> at least two thirds of these studies report that R/S [religious/spiritual] people experience more positive emotions (well-being, happiness, life satisfaction), fewer emotional disorders (depression, anxiety, suicide, substance abuse), more social connections (social support, marital stability, social capital), and live healthier lifestyles (more exercise, better diet, less risky sexual activity, less cigarette smoking, more disease screening, better compliance with treatment). This helps to explain why R/S people on average are physically healthier (less cardiovascular diseases, better immune and endocrine function, perhaps less cancer and better prognosis, and greater longevity). (Koenig, King and Carson 2012: 600–602)

Epidemiologists also find that social support matters to health, whether or not the social support has anything to do with religion. Social people are happy people. More socially isolated people are less healthy and more likely to die (Diener and Seligman 2002). Loneliness is as lethal as smoking (Cacioppo and Patrick 2008). Moreover, it is clear that there is a causal arrow that points from social support to health outcome, rather than the other way around (House, Landis, and Umberson 1988). To be sure, culture matters. The general effects appear to hold true of other countries and other faiths, but what counts as well-being shifts—social harmony in Japan, self-esteem in the United States (Ryff et al. 2014). Still, the greater the social support, the greater the well-being.

And of course, when someone joins a congregation, he or she has more social support. At the evangelical churches I know, people really did seem to look out for one another. They showed up with dinner when friends were sick and sat to talk with them when they were unhappy. Their help was sometimes surprisingly concrete. Perhaps a third of the church members belonged to housegroups that met weekly to talk about the Bible and their lives. One evening, a young woman in a group I had joined began to cry. Her dentist had told her that she needed a $1,500 procedure, and she didn't have the money. The other members of our small group—most of them students—simply covered the cost, by anonymous donation. A study conducted in North Carolina found that frequent churchgoers had larger social networks, with more contact with, more affection for, and more kinds of social support from those people than their unchurched counterparts (Ellison and George 1994).

It is no accident that Durkheim, who argued that the concept of God was really a symbol of society, was the son of a rabbi, from a long line of rabbis. The rules of practice created community in the shul in a way I have seen in no other faith. People related to God by relating to each other, and they experienced that sense of connection as a recognition by God. I saw in this congregation of newly orthodox Jews the most basic way that faith changes people: that the experience of connection with God—the following of the mitzvoth—becomes quite literally a connection to others. Every week—and usually twice a week—people ate at each other's houses. They could not eat at the home of anyone who did not keep kosher—anyone outside the group. As much as secular observers might think that those bonds would drive them nuts, from the bird's-eye distance that epidemiology provides, the intense bonds of religious participation are good for bodies. Religious practice and participation do deliver—to some extent—what people often pray for: health, happiness, and well-being.

Of course, those of faith gain more from their faith than the direct health benefits of human social contact. Gods and spirits can also be social relationships in their own right.

GODS ARE SOCIAL RELATIONSHIPS TOO

In the late 1980s, when I did my fieldwork, Bombay (as it was called then) was home to the great majority of the seventy-six thousand or so Parsi Zoroastrians in India, and symbolic homeland, perhaps, to another twenty or more thousand who have spread in the diaspora to Britain, Hong Kong, East Africa, Canada, and the United States. They were primarily a middle-class, well-educated community, often involved in law, medicine, and banking. They were descendants of the Zoroastrians who escaped an Islamized Persia in the tenth century and arrived eventually in Gujarat, where they settled into an agricultural life with some weaving and trading. When the British arrived, and particularly after the British acquired Bombay in the seventeenth century, the Parsis became involved with them as financiers and mediators and established their reputation for great business and political success during the following centuries. Their remarkable religion is one of the oldest monotheisms.

But for many of the Parsis I met, this ancient faith had become dry (Luhrmann, *The Good Parsi*). Throughout the nineteenth and early twentieth centuries, Parsis were strikingly eager to assume a Westernized identity, and they were particularly zealous as a community in proclaiming their religion's appropriateness to a modern, rational age. The Parsi literature of the period consistently presented the community as the most Westernized in India. The faith seemed to be collateral damage. I was struck by the number of Parsis who spontaneously and sadly said how little they knew about their religion and how they wished it meant more to them.

About a decade before I arrived, there arose a movement that promised to do just that. In 1977, a young, charismatic lecturer burst onto the scene like a rock 'n' roll star. Khojeste Mistree was handsome, intelligent, and dynamic, his accent very British, and he had just returned to Bombay from Oxford, where he had studied Zoroastrianism. With a friend, the scholar Alan Williams, he launched a series of talks on the religion that were phenomenally successful. Literally thousands of people crammed into the auditoriums. He spoke (in English) of Zoroastrianism's history and its importance for the modern Parsi. He explained, logically and clearly, in that appealing accent, the reasons behind the ancient prayers and rituals. He built a team that offered classes, gave lectures, produced a delightful children's book explaining the religion, made a major studio movie with that same aim, and recorded Parsi prayers and Gujarati songs. Their goal was not to convey knowledge simply for its own sake, but to invest those texts, their theology, and their rituals with meaning.

I saw that for his followers, the god of the texts (Ahura Mazda) began to feel like a person who responded to them. This was a big change for them. One woman, for example, was in her twenties when she first came across these new teachings. She had been raised in one of the few orthodox families, saying her prayers daily and following the rigid rules that govern menstruation (sleeping in a special bed, not touching any-thing that would be used outside of the menstrual period). Her mother's death, when she was nineteen, was devastating. "Everyone said, 'It's God's will, she was so dear to Him that He took her away.' That didn't make sense. It was a big problem for me." She tried to speak to God, but she did not feel that He answered. That changed after she began taking these classes. "I remember coming home so excited," she said. "I remember clearly the scene that evening, [my son] as a small child on the sofa, as if someone had come in with a new discovery, although all the time it had been there. It was such a relief to know, looking at the dirt and sickness, that God was not responsible." (Khojeste taught that the power of evil, personified as Ahriman, caused pain and misfortune.) Now God's intentions made sense to her. She could talk with Him.

Then there was a young man who was the kind of person who was at risk of feeling not very Parsi when growing up: he lived in a very secu-lar household, did not feel attached to the faith, and could well emigrate and marry a foreigner. He agreed to go on a trip to see different fire temples in Gujarat, north of Bombay. In one of them, the priest (das-tur) of that temple gave a talk about the fire as a person, and about Ahura Mazda as a friend (from a scholarly point of view, this stretches the texts). The young man told me he had never prayed with convic-tion before, but in this fire temple he tried, and for the first time he felt that someone was listening. That really meant something to him, and it made a big difference in his daily life, he said. He began to pray in a way he described as personally meaningful, to someone he expe-rienced as listening. He felt Zoroastrian in a way he had never done before.

THE INNER OTHER

Is the relation with a god a social relationship like any other? That is the hard part. We know that humans create imaginary companions with relative ease. For the most part, those who do are children. They often chatter away to their invisible friends, and they behave as if those friends are talking back. A man in his forties explained his childhood compan-ions to the psychologist Marjorie Taylor:

[Dewgy] was sort of a superdog. He was at least half human. He could talk and he liked to make jokes. When Digger [his invisible partner] got too serious, Dewgy and I would smile at each other and nod knowingly. (1999: 26)

Many psychologists think that these experiences help children understand other people more deeply (Fernyhough et al. 2019). The children are perfectly aware that their friend is only pretend. J. Bradley Wigger traveled to the Dominican Republic, Nepal, Malawi, and Kenya—to parts of the world that were as different from his Kentucky hometown as he could find. Everywhere, there were children who talked to invisible beings. These children knew that their imaginary friends were not real. Wigger tells a story about interviewing a young girl at some length about her two invisible friends. She crouched down to whisper to one and waved to call over another. At the end of the interview, Wigger offered her a sticker, and another two stickers for her friends. The child stared at him as if he was a little dim and retorted, "They're pretend!" (2019: 45).

Gods and spirits are different from invisible friends because people generally do not describe them as pretend, because they are shared, and because they have a more serious role in the person's life. This greater seriousness may be responsible for some of the ways the relationship changes the humans within them. I saw that people really worked at their relationships with their gods. In all the many faith communities I have known—witches, Zoroastrians, santeros, Jews, Catholics, and evangelicals—people have described to me having to learn how to recognize their gods, how to relate to them, and how to trust them. They have described periods in which they felt their gods deserted them and then came back. Many spoke of learning to experience their gods differently over the course of their experiences with faith.

How might we understand this? In *The Birth of the Living God*, the psychoanalyst Ana Maria Rizzuto described her experience with inpatients in Boston, back in the days when they could be admitted to the hospital for more than a year, often when they weren't even that ill. She asked these patients in-depth, probing questions about the way they experienced God and the way they experienced their families. She went out to meet some of their family members. She concluded that their God-concepts were not simply projections of some idealized father, as Freud had suggested, nor a simple reflection of a human parent. Instead, she argued that a person's internal representation of God was nearly as complex as an internal representation of a parent, that it drew on the important relationships and powerful experiences in the life of the individual, and that, once formed, the representation had all the psychic potential of a living person, even if it was experienced only in the privacy of the mind. She thought that her participants' God-concepts were created out of inner representations of humans, mostly of mothers and fathers. She argued that unlike the special stuffed toys that are so emotionally redolent, so comforting for young children but that just run out of meaning for most people as they age and are left to molder on a closet shelf, people's God-concepts are never sent to a psychic limbo. The process of creating them never stops. "Obviously," she wrote, "there are as many shapes for this [God] of ours as there are human beings. And there are as many ways of dealing with it as there are vicissitudes in the course of human life" (1979: 180). She thought that as people became psychically healthier, their God-concept became kinder and more humane.

I saw that prayer sessions in evangelical churches in effect set out to achieve this end. The same is likely true for prayer sessions in other faiths. In the evangelical churches I knew, congregants are prayed over repeatedly by other congregants. The persons receiving prayer are in distress, often visibly so; the people praying for them assert that they are loved by God. They repeat this again and again, week after week. In my experience, these churches quite clearly do not presume that congregants automatically experience God as loving. In fact, it's presumed that congregants have a hard time believing in God's love because they base their God-concepts on their parents, and few parents are ideal. I remember an evangelical man, the son of a brutal father, who said to me,

> I feel like God may want to test me in the future with something that's really devastating like becoming a paraplegic or something, or just something extremely devastating. I just feel like God would want me to experience all these things in life, you know, and I just feel like something may be around the corner that, you know, it's hard to explain.

He imagined that God would wallop him. It was what his dad had done. Those who prayed with him explicitly hoped that as they repeatedly described God to him as loving, he would come to feel loved, even though he had grown to manhood feeling as if he deserved to be beaten.

If someone's god-concept changes over time, this change happens in a way akin to a process Freud ([1914] 1984) called "working through"—the practice of repeating and elaborating the analyst's interpretations so that the analysand can understand them more deeply. In the faith setting, working through happens in what Henry Corbin (1969a) called "imaginal" relationships—one must use the imagination to be in these relationships, but the relationships are not understood as if they are merely imaginary.

IMAGINAL RELATIONSHIPS

In 1983–84, when I lived in London in order to participate in various groups whose members described themselves as practicing magic, what struck me most about these groups was their intense engagement with the imagination. Every week, people would meet together, close their eyes, and seek to imagine, with all the inner sensory vividness they could muster, narratives given to them by that evening's leader. Here is one such exercise, taken from a book (*The Spiral Dance*) that everyone in these circles read.

> Visualize a silver crescent moon, curving to the right. She is the power of beginning, of growth and generation. She is wild and untamed, like ideas and plans before they are tempered by reality. She is the blank page, the unplowed field. Feel your own hidden possibilities and latent potentials; your power to begin and grow. See her as a silver-haired girl running freely through the forest under the slim moon. She is Virgin, eternally unpenetrated, belonging to no one but herself. Call her name "Nimue!" and feel her power within you. . . .
>
> Visualize a round full moon. She is the mother, the power of fruition. She nourishes what the New Moon has begun. See her open arms, her full breasts, her womb burgeoning with life. Feel your own power to nurture, to give, to make manifest what is possible. She is the sexual woman: her pleasure in union is the moving force which sustains all life. Feel the power in your own pleasure, in orgasm. Her color is the red of blood, which is life. Call her name "Mari!" and feel your own ability to love.

Visualize a waning crescent curving to the left, surrounded by a dark sky. She is the Old Woman, the Crone who has passed menopause, the power of ending, of death. All things must end to fulfill their beginnings. The grain that was planted must be cut down. The blank page must be destroyed, for the work to be written. Life feeds on death—death leads on to life, and in that knowledge lies wisdom. The Crone is the Wise Woman, infinitely old. Feel your own age, the wisdom of evolution stored in every cell of your body. Know your own power to end, to lose as well as gain, to destroy what is stagnant and decayed. See the Crone cloaked in black under the waning moon: call her name "Anu!" and feel her power in your own death. (Starhawk 1979: 78–79)

These practices were explicitly oriented toward working through. They were structured to help practitioners to come to terms with the parts of their lives that were most difficult, and to come to experience them as a source of creativity. They did this through practices in which practitioners reenacted their relationships with gods and spirits in imagination again and again and again.

The women I met who were involved with Goddess spirituality wanted that experience of working through difficulty, and so they were very involved with the third aspect of the Goddess, with the Goddess as death, underworld, and destruction. They wanted a way to deal with loss, pain, failure. They wanted to reimagine loss as menstruation, in which blood and pain are intimately connected with birth and renewal. The hag (who sometimes menstruates) is the aspect of the Goddess about which people spoke with the greatest awe. They spoke of being initiated through her, of reaching the "deepest," "truest" aspect of themselves through her; they spoke with scorn of people who thought of the Goddess as "sweetness and light." The dark Goddess, the Crone, eats and destroys. She is the madness of the raging tiger, the mother bear's fury, Kali child-eater and Clytemnestra man-slayer, Medea, the Furies, and the witches on their blasted heath. She is darkness and despair.

When I was in London, a dog-eared book on the Goddess was passed from woman to woman within this network. Called *Descent to the Goddess* and written by Sylvia Brinton Perera, it focused on an ancient tale, the Sumerian myth of Ereshkigaal and Inanna written on clay tablets in the third millennium BC. In the Sumerian poem, Inanna decides to go into the underworld. Ereshkigaal, queen of the Great Below, becomes furious. She insists that the upper-world goddess be brought "naked and bowed low," as the Sumerians were laid in the grave. Ereshkigaal then kills Inanna and hangs her corpse on a peg, where it turns green and rots. Inanna will return, but her ordeal has been intense.

The women I knew in these groups loved this story. They spoke to me about the myth as the experience of being torn apart; they spoke of the experience of feeling the good girl within them—the Inanna-self— destroyed by their own Ereshkigaal-like raging anger and lust. They explained the experience of the myth as the experience of menstrual cramps so bad they couldn't think, of suicidal despair, of abortions, of madness, of losing jobs and lovers, of discovering their hatred of their mothers, their culture, their selves. They explained that they acted out the myth in their lives and that when they did so, their lives changed. One woman told me that she found herself counting rice grains on the kitchen table, losing her jewelry, feeling that she was rotting like meat— all stories from the myth—and that when she felt the myths through her body, she became pregnant, when previously she had failed.

I met Frances in one of these groups. She had come to magic as part of feminist awakening in her twenties. She had a medievalist's dream job in manuscript restoration, but she was frustrated with herself. She thought herself too unassertive, too compliant, and she chafed at the person she felt she'd become in a world dominated by men. As an adolescent, she had been intensely religious. She left Christianity, she said, because she could not tolerate a divine that made her own sexuality seem "filthy." Years later, she began to read about feminist spirituality and eventually found her way to the circles of people who called themselves magicians and witches. She sought the divine, but she also sought transformation. She wanted to be different. We spoke one evening of the dark Goddess:

> I think that the Inanna-Ereshkigaal thing is very important. It's a sort
> of shamanistic experience that each woman undergoes. If you look at it
> in psychoanalytical terms, she sheds all her ego defenses, takes all of those
> trappings, and, you know, peels the onion down to the core. And in the
> core, one encounters a sort of dark mirror, which is like a dark sister, and

this image of Inanna hanging on a peg, and rotting, is a peeling off of the outer trapping, that we have been conditioned to accept. If you rot like meat you lose everything. And it's so shamanistic, isn't it? You're sitting inside your own skeleton, your flesh rotting, everything. You have a core experience. And after that there's rebirth, and you go up. And you're given everything back, your clothes, your jewels, and then you go up, and she becomes Queen of Heaven.

You must rot like meat and peel the onion to the core. We live in a world, Frances argued, in which women learn to mask their essential natures. Women learn to be nice, to be good—not to show despair or lust or anger. Yet these feelings are real, she said, and we hide them below layers of social trappings. The dark Goddess brings up pain, Frances said, but it is the pain of encountering yourself, not the world, or at least of encountering that which the world has done to you. It is, Adrienne Rich–like, a diving into the deep of your internal self.

And that is what she did. Frances had set aside one of the two rooms of her flat as a shrine (her term) to the Goddess. Some sixty Goddess statuettes and pictures ranged the walls, each wall designated for a season and for the Goddess of that time: Nepthys, Hecate, and Persephone for winter, Isis and Aphrodite for summer. Tall, hand-painted murals of Egyptian deities dominated the room. Frances would perform rituals in the room and meditate in it. She chose to live among images of the Goddess because, she said, they enabled her to reach out for and remember certain ways of experiencing. "We don't have words for it, and we fumble along trying to articulate it, and it comes out sounding weird. . . . [The images are] a language, a language for feeling, and a way of working through the feeling with a landscape that's got physical marking points in it if you like, signposts, of the Goddess, that have different feeling states and emotional tones to them." When I knew her, the goddess she loved most was Sekhmet, the lion-headed Egyptian goddess associated with fire. Frances wanted Sekhmet's fire. She wanted to burn out her own diffidence and to blaze in her own right. Once I was present at a ritual she wrote about Sekhmet. She led participants (in their imaginations) through a hall of fire to face a terrifying but beautiful lion surrounded by flames. In her own practice, she did this again and again and again.

WORKING THROUGH

It is one of the oldest questions in anthropology. How do symbols and stories change us? In 1986, James Dow laid out an argument (building on an essay by Daniel Moerman [1979]) in which "symbolic healing" had four features: first, that the healer and patient share a mythic world; second, that the healer persuades the patient that the problem can be understood in the terms of the myth; third, that the healer gets the patient emotionally involved with the myth; and fourth, that the healer then manipulates the myth so that the patient feels changed by the manipulation. The idea was that when some mythic symbol (words, images, a story) came to feel emotionally real to the patient, someone else could affect the patient's experience by reworking the story.

The essay that captured the process for many anthropologists was Claude Lévi-Strauss's "The Effectiveness of Symbols." In it, Lévi-Strauss described a Cuna woman struggling in childbirth. He wrote that the shaman sang a song over her. The song recounted the woman's distress. It sang of the midwife's decision to call for him, that the midwife ran along the forest paths to find him, and that he came, burnt coca, and assembled the little wooden figurines he thought would help the woman in pain. Then the song left everyday reality behind. It went on to sing of good spirits (*ngellum*) who marched up the woman's birth canal and battled with the bad spirits of the goddess who stole the woman's soul. The spirits won the battle, and the child was born. Lévi-Strauss emphasized the way the shaman used details to help the woman feel her pain:

> Everything occurs as though the shaman were trying to induce the sick woman . . . to relive the initial situation through pain, in a very precise and intense way, and to become psychologically aware of its smallest details. ([1963] 1974: 188)

He wrote that details make the fantastic story equally compelling:

> The cure begins with a historical account of the events that preceded it, and some elements which might appear secondary . . . are treated with luxuriant detail as if they were, so to speak, filmed in slow motion. ([1963] 1974: 188)

He argued that when healing songs worked, they did so "in making explicit a situation originally existing on the emotional level and in rendering acceptable to the mind pains which the body refuses to tolerate" ([1963] 1974: 192).

The piece Dow missed is that the shaman's stories help the woman to imagine these good little spirits vividly—and that this vividness helps her to feel that they are present in her body. I would recast Dow's four steps like this:

1. *Expectation*: The shaman tells the suffering woman that the spirits will appear—now.
2. *Ambiguity*: The shaman moves the narrative from describing something real to the eye to describing something that can be seen only with the mind's eye, but he does not seem to distinguish between the reality of the immaterial and the material. He weaves them together, the technique that in modern literature is called magical realism.
3. *Vividness*: The shaman describes the visual details and sounds of the good spirits so that the woman can see them for herself— their pointed hats, their loud cries, their bristling, sharp-pointed spears.
4. *Engagement*: The shaman invites the woman to interact with the spirits. She feels that they are inside her, and she is able to respond to them in turn.

Only when the spirits become real can they work effectively.

In psychoanalysis, the central idea behind "working though" is that a person comes to take another person's interpretation of their inner experience as a true account of that inner experience—and because that interpretation initially feels implausible, the person being interpreted needs to engage with the interpretation again and again. Habits— including the habit of making sense of oneself—are hard to break. The point of the Cuna story is that the shaman's job is to make the spirits feel real inside the woman struggling with childbirth. Many critics have pointed out problems with this particular account (for example, Severi 1993), but the insight is that it takes effort to blur the boundary between outer representation and inner experience—and that when the blurring works, it can have consequences.

Dreams are inherently boundary-blurring. The dream belongs to the dreamer. It has the quality of "myness." Yet the dream also feels as if it can come from the outside—that the dreamer did not choose what to dream. In *Dreams That Matter*, the anthropologist Amira Mittermaier set out to understand the long tradition of dream interpretation in Cairo. She spoke with sheikhs known to have a gift for interpretation, with members of devotional groups, and with ordinary people. People would tell their dreams to those who could help them to understand them, and then they would dream again. Some dreams told them what to do. Some gave them insight. Dreams are remarkable human events: of the self, and yet not of the self—"a parole coming from elsewhere," as Stefania Pandolfo (1997: 184) puts it. That is, because dreams feel both personal and impersonal—like speech one has not spoken that nonetheless emerges from one's own inner world—they can become vivid symbols that lead to change. Mittermaier saw that in Cairo the practice of dreaming became for people the means to resolve conflicts and to make choices. Dreams became the means to learn—as one of Mittermaier's interlocutors insisted—to see beyond the everyday world into the divine reality that really counts.

Like the psychoanalyst, like the shaman, like Frances confronting Sekhmet, it is in blurring the boundary between inner and outer that the work gets done—and for the process to succeed, it must be enacted again and again. Even the shaman's battle (a one-off intervention) must use many stanzas, many tellings, many twists of plot.

A DARKER SIDE

Any sword can cut both ways. The vivid inner other that allows many Christians to feel embraced by love as intense as the gaze between mother and child can feel suffocating to those who find—whether because of their sexuality, their politics, or their families—that the god who has become so present also despises them. Kevin Flannelly and his colleagues (2010) observed that the more people pray to a god they feel loves them, the healthier they become; but the more they pray to a god they feel judges them, the more psychiatric symptoms they report.

Moreover, even though relationships with gods and spirits may change people in ways that can be good for their bodies and psyches, it does not follow that gods and spirits are necessarily good for societies. I have wrestled with the commitments of many conservative Christians; their judgments about how to care for the poor, for instance, seem not to be those that Jesus would have made. Some evangelicals report that they, too, are surprised by the moral commitments they have come to have, and that they understand those commitments to have arisen out of the ways they are in relationship with Jesus. For an anthropologist, this is the implication of James Laidlaw's *The Subject of Virtue*, where he argues that ethics should be understood as the way freedom unfolds within a specific social world, within the social relationships of that world. Once we treat God as a specific social actor, and not the expression of some global kumbaya, we confront the difficult truth that the moral understandings that emerge from those relationships may be different from our own.

JESUS THE CONSERVATIVE

The radical innovation of the evangelical Christianity that emerged after the tumult of the sixties lies in the claim that Jesus is a person—not only historically but now—and that he has a personal relationship with you in particular. This Jesus thinks, he feels, he loves, he weeps, and he gets angry, just the way he did in Palestine. You can ask him what shirt you should wear and what shampoo to buy. He's *alive*, and he wants to have the kind of friendship with you that you have with your best friend, only better. As a pastor told me, this living, breathing Jesus is "a compelling figure. He pisses me off. I don't agree with him. His teaching on divorce and marriage seems excessively strict. But he's messy. Complicated. He was a person. He was not flat."

A complicated Jesus raises many questions. In the Gospels, Jesus says, "Follow me." But he does not say how. The Gospels are a patchwork of anecdotes and sayings, retold in different ways by authors who seem to have been writing to different audiences. In one Gospel, Jesus tells those who recognize him not to tell anyone. In another, they are to proclaim him. He protects a prostitute from being stoned but then curses a fig tree for not bearing fruit, even though it's not the season for figs, and the poor tree withers and dies. His parables often make little sense, and his followers often didn't understand them. In one Gospel, his parents behave as if he has lost his mind. Again and again, Jesus seems to look out of the text directly at the reader and ask, "Who do you say I am?"

When someone discovers Jesus in an evangelical church, that person comes to him in the wake of two thousand years of interpretation and exegesis. It would be naïve to imagine that new converts truly grasp Jesus in a fresh and immediate way—and discover, by means of prayer and immersion in the scripture, who he is. Still, many newcomers—and even those who grow up in the church and later rediscover Jesus on their own, sometimes again and again—say that this is what it feels like.

Almost all modern evangelicals talk about faith as a *discovery process* in which you are always trying to understand who God is, and what He wants from you in particular. It is central to this process that Jesus is both perfect and also the complicated, messy person he is in the Gospels. He is both the angry young adult who threw out the moneychangers and the ideal friend. In housegroups, people sit with each other and talk about their experience of God/Jesus that week. Often, a member will describe how God confuses her in one way or another. Someone else will remind her how much God loves her, as if God couldn't be disappointed in her—and then go on to puzzle her way through another passage in which Jesus does something odd.

Because of this discovery process, evangelical Christians are always imagining themselves as who God wants them to be, rather than who they are. Faith becomes a matter of aspiration, not acceptance. The person you can be and should be is always emerging from the person who you are, and the Jesus you find can unsettle you.

One of the puzzles of evangelical Christianity is that the movement emerged in part out of a left-wing hippie Christian culture that traded LSD for speaking in tongues in the 1960s (Eskridge 2013). The mainstream culture called them "Jesus Freaks." For reasons that scholars still debate, evangelicals are now embedded firmly in the political right. Some explain the rightward shift as the outcome of conservative pastors who began to shepherd these hippie Christians (Shires 2007); some attribute it to the rage at the coastal elites they associate with left-wing politics (Hochschild 2016). I want to offer an account that emerges in one woman's insistence that her own transformation developed directly out of the relationship she developed with Jesus.

Betsy was, when I met her, a sixty-something-year-old, middle-class woman in Orange County, California. In her teens she became a leftist protester and then a hippie Christian during the Vietnam War, and soon after that, a middle-class, evangelical churchgoer. Once she settled into her church, what mainly troubled her about Democrats was their sense that people needed help from the government because they couldn't make it on their own. "God intends us to work," she told me. What she once thought of as rights—food, shelter, medical care—she now considered handouts. And she chastised the countercultural moocher she had been. "Back in the hippie days, we were all entitled. We all felt that. I think we all grow out of that. Hopefully."

Betsy told me that her rightward shift came out of her commitment to living a life in which you are seeking always to be better than you are. Evangelical Christians talk not so much about believing in God as if God were a yes-or-no proposition, but about walking and growing with God. They ask each other where they are "on their walk," by which they mean, are you becoming more confident about what God wants of you, and are you becoming more like the person He wants you to be?

For Betsy—this child of the sixties, someone who'd spent her teenage years with people dropping acid—this meant above all avoiding dependence, which she talked about as an addiction. In contemporary American evangelicalism, sin is modeled directly on substance abuse. "We are all addicts!" roared a leader at an evangelical conference I attended. He strode back and forth on the stage, pummeling the air with his fist, insisting that we turned to addiction to fill the emptiness inside, to deal with the loneliness, to cope with disappointing jobs and marriages. Betsy said, "I am all for those kinds of government programs that help people in the interim," she said. "It's when we become dependent on them—that's where we cross the line." Betsy never thought she'd end up as a Republican. When she was a hippie, she was all for the left-wing politics that supported the needy and dismantled the rich, the Robin Hood version of her counterculture. Now she has a near-visceral flinch at the idea of people depending upon help like a drug. And for her the culprits—the pushers, you might say—are the government, unions, and Democrats, all of them dispensing the kind of aid that ultimately, in her view, destroys the recipient. "I think welfare was good when it started," she tells me. "I think unions were good when they started. But I think they have just gone crazy. And now, we've created monsters. And I feel like the Democrats would just keep feeding these monsters."

Monsters: it is like a vision from Revelation, where the beast surged forth with demonic strength to grab the land, and the servants of the Lord rode out in armor to the battle. Here personal and spiritual growth are on the side of the angels, and government programs are on the side of the beast. "As we take handouts," Betsy explained to me, "we're stunting someone's growth. And that keeps them from progressing forward, being what they can be, what they want to be, what they were meant to be."

I understand that some readers might feel a near-visceral flinch of their own at the idea that Betsy's view constitutes a moral vision. I include her story to underscore the point I made before: individuals may benefit from developing a relationship with their god, but it does not follow that the way they imagine that god is a benefit for the social whole.

It also does not follow that all human-god relationships are good ones. Those in intimate relationships with an all-seeing god whom they take to despise them are in trouble. I have been making the case for how gods are made real, and so I have been emphasizing how the intense love people can feel, apparently from the air, can drive them forward. But the practices that can help to create intimacy between god and human can also build a god who makes someone miserable. When the inner other disapproves of you intensely, it can feel awful, worse than your own self-blame. It can feel as if you are jailed from within. Those who reach puberty as young evangelicals and discover that they cannot maintain chastity, or are drawn to the wrong gender, or cannot bear the politics that people around them hold can struggle for years to remake God in a way that feels safe. Human-human relationships are often difficult, and human-god relationships can be equally difficult. My goal here is to point out that when humans come to experience a god as responding, they experience a relationship—and that changes them. The epidemiological data suggest that on average, this is good for their bodies.

Now I want to add to this observation: human-god relationships are in many ways like real social relationships—and anthropology has not always taken that seriously.

RELATING TO PRESENCE

I have arrived at the same place as Robert Orsi, although I began from a different starting point. Orsi wrote *A History of Presence* to point out to Protestant readers that their emphasis on belief is a sectarian obsession. He spent his childhood in the Italian American Catholic working-class north Bronx. In college, he discovered the sober academic arguments that explained how religion arose from social needs and constructed the way people saw the world. He found these discussions to be untrue to his past. In his childhood, Jesus and Mary and the saints were real. When people got mad at St. Jude for not answering their prayers, they threw him into the back of the car so he could rethink what he had done. "There is the numinous, upside down on the floor of an old Chevy!" (2016: 98). To Orsi, the reality of God is a feeling, not a belief. He insists, repeatedly, that presence is simply there: that to understand the "abundant life" of a Catholic, you must understand how the more-than-ordinary is simply present in some objects and some people.

I have been insisting that gods must be made real in a way that matters—and I see in Orsi's work these processes of real-making as well. If a man born Catholic never prays, never confesses, never goes to Mass, that man will be much less likely to think that St. Jude gets the message when the man throws his statue to the floor. Like Orsi, I think that if you want to understand faith, you should focus on relationship as well as belief. "To be in relationship with special beings really present is as old as the species and as new as every human's infancy. This is how the world is religious today" (Orsi 2016: 251).

We scholars do not tend to talk about God that way. As the anthropologist Jon Bialecki (2014) points out, it is not uncommon for ethnographies to go on at length about what religious people do and say and think without mentioning how gods show up in their lives. As he puts it (2014: 33), "To be blunt, to ignore God as an agent in the world is not just to ignore or belittle the beliefs of many of our informants but to overlook an often vital mode of their engagement with the world." It is relatively rare to find an ethnography of how people experience gods and spirits—an ethnography, one might say, of God. That is a mistake. The lesson Bruno Latour has tried to teach us about nonhuman objects is that, in some fundamental sense, they are actors in people's lives. To be sure, in his work on religion, Latour (2005)—one of the sociologists most responsible for our understanding that scientific facts are socially constructed—oddly wants to remove God from the real-making processes he sees at work in science. I think that as a Catholic, he wants to protect God from being understood as in some sense constructed. But if we understand gods first and foremost as in relationships with humans, the real-making seems naturally part of the process. Relationships are what real-making generates: a sense that gods and spirits respond.

Of course beliefs matter. To return to the faith frame, the concept of "belief" captures an ontological commitment that is obviously important in understanding how gods and spirits make sense to humans. I introduced the faith frame as an analytic device to understand a mode of thinking in which gods and spirits matter, because it seemed evident to me that (as Neil Van Leeuwen argues) gods and spirits often don't matter in everyday ways of thinking about the world, even for people who understand themselves as devout. Beliefs about gods and spirits are different from beliefs about tables and chairs because beliefs about gods and spirits can be bracketed and set aside in ways that beliefs about the everyday world just can't be. The faith frame—that ontological attitude toward beliefs and spirits—needs to be anchored in place and made relevant by the human coming to feel that gods and spirits are real, which is ultimately more about relationships and less about true or false ideas. Together the faith frame and the practice of real-making cause gods and spirits to feel present.

I think that these are, ultimately, the stakes that Morten Pedersen, Martin Holbraad, Eduardo Viveiros de Castro, Aparecida Vilaça, and others have been arguing over in what has come to be called "the ontological turn" in anthropology. They have wanted the seemingly strange claims of Amazonian or Mongolian people not to be dismissed as false beliefs but understood as events. They have wanted a shift in perspective from (mistaken) interpretation to (actual) felt experience. The important point, they insist, is not whether women become jaguars but whether jaguar spirits are felt to be real in the world—and if we focus on belief, we tend to miss the experience. Anthropologists, as Joel Robbins (2012) points out, are often uncomfortable with the idea of the transcendent. They have preferred to understand religion as beliefs that do something functional (or dysfunctional) in the social world, much as anthropologists set out to understand witchcraft as enabling the expression of social conflict rather than as a felt confrontation with evil.

To understand gods and spirits as relationships is truer to the human experience of faith. It is also more respectful. I myself struggle personally with the idea of an invisible other somehow out there, sitting apart, a man with a beard in the sky. You might say that I do not believe that such a god exists. But I find it uncomfortable to characterize what one might call believers as having false beliefs. I find it more honest to proceed with what the philosopher Donald Davidson (1984) called the principle of charity: to set out to understand how a statement ("I believe in God") is true for someone within the context of our shared understanding. I set out to understand how gods and spirits can be real for someone without presuming that gods and spirits are present in the world like tables and chairs (if I did, I might have to conclude that their beliefs are false) and without presuming that their words are mere metaphors (if I did, I would imply that gods and spirits are not real for the person I am speaking with). This puzzle has been at the heart of my work for decades.

My solution has been to understand how gods and spirits are made real for people through human practices and come to be experienced as genuinely autonomous—as agents in people's lives. I have come to see that people have ontological commitments, faith frames, in which gods and spirits matter—but that those commitments must be made relevant by learning to feel that gods and spirits are real, sometimes in vividly sensory ways.

So there are two analytic stories. There is, first, the faith frame, the way people reason when they think that gods and spirits matter and how that ontological attitude works in the ecology of other beliefs, thoughts, and attitudes. Then, second, there is the story of the way the feeling of realness is kindled through practices, orientations, and the training of attention. The faith frame and the kindling support each other, but they set different puzzles to explore.

My approach has been to shift from the problem of whether there is a thing there in the world (God does or does not exist) to the puzzle of how a being becomes recognized and experienced through a variety of moments and experiences (gods and spirits come to feel real for people). To be clear: to focus on gods and spirits as real presences does not mean that those who study them must assume that they are truly there—the numinous upside down in the back of an old car. It means that our puzzlement must be not only about *why* people think gods and spirits are real but about *how* they become and are real for them. And we need to understand that when gods and spirits feel real to people, they have become beings that humans can love, argue with, and wrestle against. The deep anthropological puzzle about the human involvement with gods and spirits is how people come to feel intensely that invisible beings matter to their lives—how the invisible world comes close to humans and looks back, alive.

ACKNOWLEDGMENTS

This book has grown from many discussions over the years, and many papers presented and published. Indeed, it began as a collection of previously published essays and would have remained as such had Jennifer Cole not suggested that it would make more sense to build an argument; I am very grateful for our friendship and book discussions over the years. I owe a great deal to Ann Taves and Joel Robbins; I feel that my path has been formed through our conversations across the years. That is also true of Pascal Boyer. When we were at Cambridge together, he was developing his ideas about how belief was natural, as I was focusing in on how much people did to make spirit real; I have been thinking in relation to his work ever since. I learned every week with Dick Madsen about religion for years at UCSD and as we traipsed around to different faith gatherings. These days I walk every week with Hazel Markus, and her acute insight has sharpened these arguments. Conversations with Paul Harris, Sarah Iles Johnston, Rita Astuti, James Laidlaw, Jo Cook, Julia Cassaniti, Jon Bialecki, James Gross, Daniel Mason, and, more recently, Felicity Aulino, Josh Brahinsky, John Dulin, Vivian Dzokoto, Emily Ng, Rachel Smith, and Nikki Ross Zehnder have pushed me to think more deeply and clearly about these matters. This last group—the "Mind and Spirit crew," as we called ourselves—also read some of these chapters and made them better. I also had wonderful readers in Neil Van Leeuwen (who read every chapter and gave me great comments), Michael Lifshitz, G. E. R. Lloyd, and Kara Weisman, who also checked the statistics for chapter 5 and clarified my language. Ariel Mayse corrected some infelicities in my description of Orthodox Judaism. Conversations with Elaine Pagels were important; one with Elaine and Sarah Iles Johnston got me into church. When I tried out some of these ideas on Doug Medin, he told me about his Minnesotan grandmother. That conversation stayed with me as I wrote and rewrote chapter 1. Pascal Boyer and Amira Mittermaier read an early manuscript for the Press. Nancy Chu checked the references and in general gave wise and gentle advice. Sharon Broll again was an excellent editor. Fred Appel has been a fan of this book ever since he walked me to the train station in the rain at an anthropology conference and persuaded me that it belonged at Princeton. The Princeton team has been terrific. Hank Southgate's copyediting led to a much sharper argument, and Natalie Baan tightened the text even further. My father has been a very important reader. After my mother died, he distracted himself by reading each of these chapters again and again. He insisted that every sentence be clear. My husband Richard also read every chapter, with careful attention, and helped me give it bite. The joy I find in the world has much to do with him.

Versions of these chapters were presented as the 2006 Lewis Henry Morgan lectures; I am grateful to Thomas Gibson and Ernestine McHugh for their hospitality and questions, and to all the anthropologists at the University of Rochester. I gave another version as the 2011 Integration lectures at Fuller Theological Seminary (the Fuller Symposium on the Integration of Psychology and Theology). I would like particularly to thank Warren Brown and Bill Dyrness for their kindness and intellectual engagement. I put together the pilot work in the SSRC's New Directions in Prayer; Charles Hirschkind led the group I was in, and was a wise and kind soul in the midst of some agitated discussions. The John Templeton Foundation has funded many portions of this research. Their support has changed my life, and I am grateful.

I have leaned on previously published work in this book and borrowed paragraphs and sentences here and there: "The Ugly Goddess" (*History of Religions*, 2001); "Evil in the Sands of Time" (*Journal of Asian Studies*, 2002); "Metakinesis" (*American Anthropologist*, 2004); "The Absorption Hypothesis," coauthored with Howard Nusbaum and Ronald Thisted (*American Anthropologist*, 2010); "Blinded by the Right" (*Harpers*, 2013); "The Cultural Kindling of Spiritual Experiences," coauthored with Julia Cassaniti (*Current Anthropology*, 2014); "Knowing God" (*Cambridge Anthropology*, 2017); and "The Faith Frame" (*Contemporary Pragmatics*, 2018). I am deeply grateful to the reviewers and editors who helped me to improve the quality of those essays.

GENERAL NOTES ON METHODS

◆━◆

From 1998 to 2000, I spent time in four religious settings in San Diego: an orthodox shul, whose members were mostly people who had recently become observant; a conservative evangelical church; a Catholic church founded to serve an African American parish; and an Anglo-Cuban Santeria house. I did much of that work with my colleague Richard Madsen, and it gives me great pleasure to acknowledge his participation and inspiration here. In each setting, the religious leader (the rabbi, the pastor, the priest, and the madrina) knew of our presence, graciously welcomed us, and gave us permission to interview their congregants. We spent about a year each in the shul, the Catholic church, and the Santeria house, attending services and other events (service times did not overlap, but it was a busy schedule), and closer to six months subsequently in the evangelical church. In each setting, we interviewed ten congregants.

From 2003 to 2011, I participated primarily in two church settings: a Vineyard Christian Fellowship in Chicago, and another Vineyard on the San Francisco Peninsula. Each is one of many Vineyards in its geographical area. I attended each church regularly for two years and irregularly for longer periods. In addition, I attended a variety of local, regional, and national events. The pastors were aware of my presence as a researcher, and they supported the project and the work. Indeed, both churches were remarkably warm and supportive environments in which to ask questions. I interviewed well over fifty people with a digital recorder. I have well over a hundred hours of interviews and many, many notes. In most cases, I corrected the transcripts myself by listening to the interviews again. I read them repeatedly and obsessively.

At Stanford in 2007 and 2008, I ran a large project we called the Spiritual Disciplines Project. In that project, we interviewed around 130 people multiple times (we had a total of 129 initial interviews). The interviews were semistructured: we asked specific questions, with careful probing in follow-up questions. Participants were recruited through an advertisement seeking people "interested in spiritual transformation and the Christian spiritual disciplines," primarily through notices placed in church bulletins in four charismatic evangelical congregations on the San Francisco Peninsula (two were Vineyard churches and two were churches similar to the Vineyard). I was ably assisted by Christina Drymon, who conducted the interviews, entered the data, and kept the process organized—a Herculean task. She was replaced in time by Rachel Morgain, who listened to all four hundred or so hours of our interviews, corrected them for word-for-word accuracy, and coded them. We worked closely together during this process. Details of our methods are reported in Luhrmann 2012; Luhrmann and Morgain 2012; and Luhrmann, Nusbaum, and Thisted 2013. This work was funded by the John Templeton Foundation and by the National Science Foundation.

From 2013 to 2014, I worked overseas. In Chennai, I participated, by the invitation of the pastor, in the English-speaking services of the New Life Assembly of God church, and in Accra, again at the invitation of the pastor, I participated in one of the many International Gospel Church of Christ churches. In each setting, the bulk of the work for this project was done in a month. All who spoke with me agreed to be interviewed and were eager to share their understanding of God. This work was funded by the Social Science Research Council, from a grant from the John Templeton Foundation.

It is worth adding a comment about my decision to add more structured methods and analyze them statistically. I chose to do this because I began to look at differences between people, and those differences emerged more sharply when I added structured methods to support my ethnographic observations. No method gives us definitive access to the truth. But when similar patterns in the evidence emerge from more than one method, it helps to give one confidence.

All names are pseudonyms, and in some cases identifying details have been changed. Quotations have been edited to remove repetitions, hesitations, and phatic phrases. Almost all quotations come from transcripts. Following current anthropological conventions for protecting participants, I do not identify date and place for each quotation. In the text, I have chosen to use author-title citations for many books, but author-year for most scientific articles, in the interest of readerly ease. In general, biblical quotations are taken from the King James or New King James text.

We received Human Subjects approval for all work from the universities with which I was affiliated.

BIBLIOGRAPHIC ESSAYS AND NOTES

• → •

PREFACE

The theories of religion referred to in the preface are these: Freud, *The Future of an Illusion*; Durkheim, *The Elementary Forms of the Religious Life*; William James, *The Varieties of Religious Experience*; Edward Burnett Tylor, *Primitive Culture*; Pascal Boyer, *Religion Explained*; Justin Barrett, *Why Would Anyone Believe in God?*; Max Müller, *Lectures on the Science of Language*. Other notable, older anthropological theories include Sir George Frazer, *The Golden Bough*; Lucien Lévy-Bruhl, *Primitive Mentality*; and Mary Douglas, *Purity and Danger*. E. E. Evans-Pritchard's *Theories of Primitive Religion* is still well worth reading.

There is a new interest in the anthropology of "becoming," which resonates with my work here. This work draws its inspiration from Gilles Deleuze and is best expressed in an article by João Biehl and Peter Locke, "Deleuze and the Anthropology of Becoming" and in their edited collection, *Unfinished: The Anthropology of Becoming*.

CHAPTER 1: THE FAITH FRAME

I recognize that there is stubborn resistance to the notion that all humans distinguish between natural things and nonnatural things. Let me try to approach the argument another way. If a society affirms the existence of gods and spirits, that society will distinguish between events that are not the result of gods and spirits and those that are. Here is what Evans-Pritchard observed:

It is often asked whether primitive peoples distinguish between the natural and the supernatural, and the query may be here answered in a preliminary manner in respect to the Azande. The question as it stands may mean, do primitive peoples distinguish between the natural and the supernatural in the abstract? We have a notion of an ordered world conforming to what we call natural laws, but some people in our society believe that mysterious things can happen which cannot be accounted for by reference to natural laws and which therefore are held to transcend them, and we call these happenings supernatural. To us supernatural means very much the same as abnormal or extraordinary. Azande certainly have no such notions of reality. They have no conception of "natural" as we understand it, and therefore neither of the "supernatural" as we understand it . . . witchcraft is to Azande an ordinary and not an extraordinary, even though it may in some circumstances be an infrequent, event. It is a normal, and not an abnormal, happening. But if they do not give to the natural and supernatural the meanings which educated Europeans give to them, they nevertheless distinguish between them. For our question may be formulated, and should be formulated, in a different manner. We ought rather to ask whether primitive peoples perceive any difference between the happenings which we, the observers of their culture, class as natural and the happenings which we class as mystical. Azande undoubtedly perceive a difference between what we consider the workings of nature on the one hand and the workings of magic and ghosts and witchcraft on the other hand, though in the absence of a formulated doctrine of natural law they do not, and cannot, express the difference as we express it. (1937: 80–81)

The cognitive science of religion has a rich and active research agenda, with its own conferences and even its own journal: *Religion, Brain and Behavior*. Contributors include not only Thomas Lawson and Robert Mc-Cauley (*Rethinking Religion, Bringing Ritual to Mind*), Pascal Boyer (*The Naturalness of Religious Ideas, Religion Explained*), Stewart Guthrie (*Faces in the Clouds*), and Justin Barrett (*Why Would Anyone Believe in God?, Born Believers*), but also Jesse Bering (*The Belief Instinct*), Scott Atran (*In Gods We Trust*), Ara Norenzayan (*Big Gods*), Harvey Whitehouse (*Arguments and Icons*), and work by Benjamin Purzycki, Cristine Legare, Joe Henrich, Armin Geertz, Dimitris Xygalatas, Richard Sosis, and others. Helen De Cruz and Johan De Smedt provide an overview for theologians in *A Natural History of Natural Theology*. Webb Keane discusses relevant arguments in *Ethical Life*.

Neil Van Leeuwen has begun a series of experiments (now in conjunction with our own group) in which he teases out the relationship between "think" and "believe" more deeply. Working with Larisa Heiphetz and

Casey Lee Landers (2018), Van Leeuwen has found that people use the word "believe" more often with statements about religion and "think" more often with other statements. The team examined a large body of news articles and speeches and found that the phrase "believe that" was far more likely to occur in association with religious words than the phrase "think that." Then they asked students to complete sentences with either "think" or "believe." When the sentences referred to something overtly religious, participants were more likely to use the world "believe." The team argued that these observations support the finding that people conceive of thought and belief differently: that they are different kinds of cognitive commitments.

Jon Lanham (2020) recently pointed out that the difference between the ways anthropologists and psychologists think about belief is that anthropologists focus on behavior (for example, saying "I believe") and psychologists focus on cognitive capacity.

On the point about the categorical or continuum-based understanding of realness, see Master, Markman, and Dweck 2012.

The great theorists of play include Johan Huizinga (*Homo Ludens*), Roger Caillois (*Man, Play and Games*), Virginia Axline (*Dibs in Search of Self* and *Play Therapy*), D. W. Winnicott (*Playing and Reality* and *Psycho-Analytic Explorations*), and Gregory Bateson (*Steps to an Ecology of Mind*). Suzanne Gaskins (e.g., *Play and Development* with Artin Göncü and many individual essays), David Lancy (*Playing on the Mother-Ground*), Peter Stromberg (*Caught in Play*), and Wendy Haight and Peggy Miller (*Pretending at Home*) are among those anthropologists and psychologists who have been developing the empirical account of how play varies across cultures. Adam Seligman, Robert Weller, Michael Puett, and Bennett Simon's *Ritual and Its Consequences* is a closely related text. The classic philosophical statement of the value of the fictional, or nonreal, is Hans Vaihinger's *The Philosophy of 'As If.'*

CHAPTER 2: MAKING PARACOSMS

Robert Silvey, a researcher at the BBC, developed the concept of "paracosm," but the term was invented by Ben Vincent, one of the participants in his 1976 study. The study itself appears in David Cohen and Stephen

MacKeith, *The Development of Imagination: The Private Worlds of Childhood*. See also Gavin Flood (*Mapping Invisible Worlds*) and the wonderful work of Marjorie Taylor (e.g., *Imaginary Companions*) and Mary Watkins (*Invisible Guests, Waking Dreams*). Taylor's work directly addressing paracosms is Marjorie Taylor, Candice M. Mottweiler, Emilee R. Naylor, and Jacob G. Levernier's "Imaginary Worlds in Middle Childhood: A Qualitative Study of Two Pairs of Coordinated Paracosms" and "Paracosms: The Imaginary Worlds of Middle Childhood."

One of the best guides to the understanding of imagination, particularly imagination in childhood, is Paul Harris (*The Work of the Imagination*). There is also a remarkable overview in the *Oxford Handbook of the Development of Imagination*, edited by Marjorie Taylor (in which work by Paul Harris, Suzanne Gaskins, and others appears). Another useful, if dated, volume is *Imagining the Impossible*, edited by Karl Rosengren, Carl Johnson, and Paul Harris. Jacqueline Woolley, also a significant contributor to discussions about things that are fantastical, has essays in both volumes.

There are now many fine ethnographies of contemporary Christianity. Excellent books on the Vineyard include Jon Bialecki's *A Diagram for Fire*. The new anthropologists of evangelical Christianity include Joel Robbins (*Becoming Sinners*), James Bielo (*The Social Life of Scriptures, Emerging Evangelicals*), Courtney Handman (*Critical Christianity*), Bambi Schieffelin ("Christianizing Language and the Dis-placement of Culture in Bosavi, Papua New Guinea"), Annelin Eriksen, Michelle MacCarthy, and Ruy Llera Blanes (*Going to Pentecost*), Simon Coleman (*The Globalisation of Charismatic Christianity*), Matthew Engelke (*A Problem of Presence*), Webb Keane (*Christian Moderns*), and Naomi Haynes (*Moving by the Spirit*). Anthropologists of Catholicism include Maya Mayblin (*Gender, Catholicism, and Morality in Brazil*) and Anna Corwin (*Holding the Hand of God*). I have learned a great deal about modern paganism from Sabina Magliocco (*Witching Culture*) and about Judaism from Yoram Bilu (*With Us More Than Ever*), Michal Kravel-Tovi (*When the State Winks*), Elizabeth Ehrlich (*Miriam's Kitchen*), and through conversations with Ariel Mayse. *The Social Life of Spirits*, edited by Ruy Blanes and Diana Espírito Santo, is a remarkable collection on spirit possession.

The new approach to understanding myth and religion through narrative theory, and understanding narrative theory through religion and myth, is brilliantly described by Sarah Iles Johnston (*The Story of Myth*), Joshua Landy (*How to Do Things with Fictions*), James Wood (*How Fiction Works*), and Blakey Vermeule (*Why Do We Care about Literary Characters?*).

Ann Taves also discusses special worlds in *Religious Experience Reconsidered* and in *Revelatory Events*.

CHAPTER 3: TALENT AND TRAINING

In the anthropological community, "discipline" is often associated with bodily discipline. Michel Foucault spoke of technologies of the self, practices that individuals used to alter their own minds and bodies so as to transform their lives, but he tended to draw attention to techniques of bodily transformation. In *Genealogies of Religion*, Talad Asad used the concept to explore the ways in which medieval monks' practices transformed them, themes that his students Saba Mahmood (*Politics of Piety*) and Charles Hirschkind (*The Ethical Soundscape*) developed to understand the ways Muslim men and women created themselves as political subjects. These practices of ethical transformation resonate strongly with the prayer practices described here.

There is a different scholarly genealogy that lays out the specific mental practices that are used to alter thoughts and feelings. At the heart of this tradition sits Frances Yates (*The Art of Memory, Giordano Bruno and the Hermetic Tradition*), the great historian of the Renaissance. The medievalist Mary Carruthers described the way monks' practices enabled them to alter their inner experiences (*The Craft of Thought*). One of the new young scholars in this tradition is Paul Dilley (*Monasteries and the Care of Souls in Late Antique Christianity*), who presents these practices of monks in the Egyptian desert in remarkable detail. Rebecca Lester (*Jesus in Our Wombs*) gives a similarly detailed account of contemporary Mexican nuns.

Among my favorite texts on these training practices is Richard Noll's "Mental Imagery Cultivation as a Cultural Phenomenon." I remember reading this article when it was published in 1985 and thinking that he had captured something deeply important. Jon Christopher Crocker's *Vital Souls* remains one of the most detailed accounts of shamanic training among nonmodern shamans; Stephen Beyer's *The Cult of Tara* is likewise still one of the most detailed accounts of practice in Tibetan Buddhism (and see his *Singing to the Plants*, a similar book about ayahuasca). Jonathan Garb (*Shamanic Trance in Modern Kabbalah*) is beginning to do the same in his work on Kabbalah, following in the footsteps of Elliot Wolfson (*Through a Speculum That Shines*), Moshe Ideal (*Hasidism: Between Ecstasy and Magic*), and of course Gershom Scholem.

My work on absorption and inner sense cultivation is described in more detail in *When God Talks Back* and in related scientific papers. Michael Lifshitz, Michiel van Elk, and I recently published an overview of the relationship between absorption and spiritual experience more broadly (2020).

Now we move into the domain of statistics. These numbers are a conventional expression of the closeness of the relationship between two observations, in this case, a subject's absorption score (0–34) and the score of the other measure, which varies depending on the scale. The "r" symbol marks the correlation coefficient between two variables, the correlation being a mathematical operation. The r ranges between −1 (for a strict negative correlation) and +1 (for a strict positive correlation), 0 corresponding to the absence of correlation. The higher the absolute value of r, the closer the relationship. The p-value, between 0 and 1, is the probability for the observed correlation value under the null hypothesis model of no actual dependency between the variables. For example, $r = 0.15$, $p = 0.25$ means that the positive correlation observed (0.15), or a higher value, would be expected to be observed a quarter of the time if there were no association between the two variables. When p is less than, or equal to, .05, the convention is to reject the null hypothesis and to therefore describe the relationship as "significant." So $p = .05$ means that the probability of this, or a more extreme, observation would be 5 percent under the null model of no association.

On the Sensory Delight Scale: In 2018, we asked around 250 participants on Amazon's MTurk to take this scale and others. The Sensory Delight Scale correlated highly with the Absorption Scale ($r = .854$, $n = 252$, $p < .001$); highly with a list of spiritual events like hearing God's voice and having a vision ($r = .736$, $n = 252$, $p < .001$); and highly with the revised

Launay Slade, a list of secular hallucination-like events (r = .743, n = 252, p < .001). In the spring of 2016, we asked just over a hundred people on Amazon's MTurk to take this scale and others. The Sensory Delight Scale correlated highly with the Absorption Scale (r = .873, n = 114, p < .001); with the Daily Spiritual Experiences Scale (r = .487, n = 103, p < .001); with the Thalbourne "Sheep-Goat," a list of statements about paranormal phenomenon (one is asked whether one believes each statement in turn) (r = .552, n = 112, p < .001); and with the Connectedness to Nature Scale, which asks about spiritual connectedness to nature (r = .501, n = 51, p < .001). Cordelia Erickson-Davies named the scale.

Here are the papers in which these scales were first presented: the Absorption Scale (Tellegen and Atkinson 1974); Sensory Spiritual Events (Luhrmann, n.d.); Launay Slade Revised (McCarthy and Fernyhough 2011); Daily Spiritual Experiences (Underwood and Teresi 2002); Thalbourne Sheep-Goat (Thalbourne and Delin 1993); Connectedness to Nature (Mayer and Frantz 2004).

CHAPTER 4: HOW THE MIND MATTERS

Anthropologists have had many arguments about dualism, but some of the debates seem to be diseases of language. It is hard to deny that humans are conscious, and it is simply difficult to believe that humans everywhere do not distinguish between inner awareness and matters of the body. One sees this clearly in Astuti and Harris (2008), and it is supported by much other work. Among the more recent essays is Weisman, Dweck, and Markman (2017). They presented children with a series of pictures (a beetle, a child, a cell phone, etc.) and asked whether the object in the picture could get hungry, sad, do math, and so forth. Even very young children answered as if they distinguished between mental and bodily actions. This work has been repeated in five more countries. In all of them, children and adults distinguish between mental and bodily action. What appears to be culturally variable is how emotions are categorized.

People who have written about charismatic Christianity in Ghana include Birgit Meyer (*Translating the Devil*), Bruno Reinhardt (e.g. 2014), and John Dulin (forthcoming). Good histories of Ghanaian

Pentecostalism and Christianity in general can be found in work by Emmanuel Larbi (*Pentecostalism: The Eddies of Ghanaian Christianity*) and Cephas Omenyo (*Pentecost outside Pentecostalism*). Along with Asamoah-Gyadu's work (*African Charismatics, Contemporary Pentecostal Christianity*), Paul Gifford's sociological analysis of these churches (*Ghana's New Christianity*) is clear and incisive.

Far less has been written about charismatic Christian South India, although see Nathaniel Roberts, *To Be Cared For*. The standard history is Michael Bergunder, *The South Indian Pentecostal Movement in the Twentieth Century*.

To supplement my interviews in Chennai and in Accra, in 2013 and 2014 I arranged for Christian undergraduates in Chennai (Women's Christian College), in Accra (Central University), and at Vanguard College in Los Angeles to fill out some surveys on spiritual experience.

One question was this: Have you ever heard an audible voice when you were alone, or a voice that no one else present could hear, like someone calling your name? The participant was to circle "true" or "false." (This question followed the Absorption Scale, which uses a true-false answer key.) At Vanguard, 44 percent of the 59 students answered "true," while 57 percent of the 30 students in Chennai answered "true," and 90 percent of the 29 students in Accra said "yes." On another page, there was a religious version of this question: Have you ever heard God speak to you in a way you felt you heard outside your head? The answer key was $0 =$ never, $1 =$ once, $2 =$ several times, $3 =$ fairly often, $4 =$ very often. For the 59 Southern Californian students, the mean response was 1.4 ($M = 1.44$, $SD = 1.15$); for the 30 students in Chennai, the mean response was 1.7 ($M = 1.70$, $SD = 1.34$); for the 30 students in Accra, the mean was over 2 ($M = 2.17$, $SD = 1.12$).

We also gave the students a scale (Posey and Losch 1983) that asked about auditory events more generally (one question asked them whether they had heard God's voice). These fourteen questions were structured like this:

"Last summer I was hanging up clothes in the backyard. Suddenly I heard my husband call my name from inside the house. He sounded like something was wrong and was loud and clear. I ran in. . . . But he was out in the garage and he hadn't called at all. Obviously I guess I made it up. . . .

But it sounded like a real voice and it was my husband's." Has this or something similar happened to you?

The answer key was yes or no. Again, the US Vanguard students reported the least experience ($M = 4.53$, $SD = 2.83$); the students at the Women's Christian College in Chennai reported somewhat more ($M = 5.67$, $SD = 3.57$); and the students at Central University in Accra, the most ($M = 8.04$, $SD = 3.17$).

This pattern (US lowest, Ghana highest, India in the middle) did not hold for other scales, such as the Trait Meta-Mood Scale (Salovey et al. 1995), a standard scale that asks about the awareness of feelings (US $M = 144.35$, $SD = 17.04$; India $M = 134.37$, $SD = 14.2$; Ghana $M = 127.57$, $SD = 13.46$). In other words, these responses do not simply express a "yes bias" from students in Accra. Instead, they express a consistent pattern: that despite using different methods and different participants, people in Accra consistently identified themselves as having more audible experiences of God than people in Chennai, and those in Chennai more than those in the United States.

CHAPTER 5: EVIDENCE FOR THE WAY GODS AND SPIRITS RESPOND

General note: William James is infinitely subtle. In his conclusion to *The Varieties of Religious Experience*, he does describe the way each of us creates our own reality. In fact, he writes as if those realities are quite distinct. Nevertheless, the entire book is structured to make the point that the common features of the mystical experience lead to true insight about what, in his Conclusion, he called "the more."

Study 1 methods: In 2011, Julia Cassaniti returned to the small valley community in Northern Thailand where she had been doing ethnographic fieldwork since 2002. The Thai community with which she works is made up of people with spiritual lineages that differ slightly from each other, but the community grouped them all under the umbrella of Theravada Buddhism. People in this community are middle- and lower-class farmers and small-business owners. Julia interviewed twenty people who were actively involved in Buddhist practice. She translated and had back-translated the questions that I had asked of Christians in the Spiritual Disciplines Project. Back-translation is the practice of having a translated document translated back into its original tongue by a different translator, to see if the translation retains the original sense. While some ideas were more difficult to translate into Thai than others, for the most part Julia felt that the questions she asked were similar to the ones asked in the Spiritual Disciplines Project. The exceptions were these: rather than asking about "demonic" presence, she asked, "Do you ever feel like a bad spirit(s) come near you?"; she did not use the term "Holy Spirit" or "slain in the spirit"; and rather than asking about "God," she asked about "spirits" or "spiritual." As in the Spiritual Disciplines Project, the question was asked as stated and then probed with follow-up questions. We compared her interviews to those done with Vineyard church members in the Spiritual Disciplines Project.

Study 2 methods: This emerged from the Spiritual Disciplines Project, described above and in more depth in Luhrmann 2012; Luhrmann and Morgain 2012; and Luhrmann, Nusbaum, and Thisted 2013. For the observations reported here, I looked at the initial interviews done with 129 Christians in their first visit. Christina Drymon asked all of them the same questions, and probed if they said yes. For the most part, the interviews lasted around an hour and a half each. Rachel Morgain then coded the interviews. She made an initial judgment about whether the individual did indeed have the experience that was the target of the question, then worked with me to discuss individual cases. This gave us two judgments: what the person said, and whether we thought that the person was actually reporting the experience we had asked about. In all cases, we coded yes, maybe, and no. We coded voices and visions together as a group (Rachel, myself, and my two postdoctoral fellows at the time, Julia Cassaniti and Jocelyn Marrow). In general, we coded generously. If someone gave an example that seemed like it might be an instance, we marked it as a yes. We only marked a voice or a vision as a yes if the interview participant gave some clear indication that he or she experienced the event as outside of his or her mind.

The data:

First: *Events that are named but that have no particular bodily markers are most common; events that depend on bodily affordances are next common; and anomalous events are least common, and are not always identified as spiritual when they occur.*

Of those we interviewed, 96 percent said that they heard from God in any way (not necessarily audibly); 93 percent said that they had heard from God through circumstances (for example, when another person made a comment that seemed surprisingly apt to something they were thinking about); and 90 percent said "yes" to hearing God through scripture. We judged that 37 percent experienced the overwhelming emotion of crying, when the crying seemed spiritual to them; we judged that only 31 percent experienced the sense of being shot through with an electrical bolt that they associated with the Holy Spirit; and we judged that 21 percent experienced the sudden muscle weakness that they associated with being "slain in the spirit." Anomalous events were even less common: we judged that fewer had experienced a powerful event like a mystical experience (17 percent), sleep paralysis (26 percent), or out-of-body event (12 percent). (Sleep paralysis, although an anomalous event, is fairly common; being "slain in the spirit" seems not to have been part of the local expectations of the experience of God.) Here, I am counting only those people for whom we judged that the answer to our question was yes.

Second: Proclivity mattered.

In this group, people who scored more highly in absorption were significantly more likely to report having had a variety of spiritual and otherwise extraordinary experiences, as judged by a simple linear regression to predict these experiences with their response to the absorption score. These included auditory hallucination-like events ($F[1,126] = 16.069$, $p < .001$, with an R^2 of .113); visual hallucination-like events ($F[1,126] = 23.185$, $p < .001$, with an R^2 of .156); thoughts from God—not thoughts about God, but thoughts God had placed in their mind as a communication from Him ($F[1,126] = 11.618$, $p = .001$, with an R^2 of .084); images from God, placed in the mind as communications ($F[1,126] = 9.093$, $p = .003$, with an R^2 of .067); feelings and sensations from God, also given by God as communications ($F[1,126] = 4.168$, $p = .043$, with an R^2 of .032); and the presence of God ($F[1,124] = 3.976$, $p = .048$, with an R^2 of .031).

These are small effects, partly because the answer scale was short ($0 = no$, $1 = maybe$, $2 = yes$), and partly because the events are so common for these charismatic evangelical Christians. Still, the effect is consistent.

When the events become less frequent (and more strikingly anomalous), the role of absorption strengthens. Absorption predicted the events we judged to be mystical ($F[1,124] = 6.608$, $p = .011$, with an R^2 of .051); the events we judged to be like out-of-body events ($F[1,123] = 17.755$, $p < .001$, with an R^2 of .126); the events we judged to be like near-death experiences ($F[1,124] = 6.201$, $p = .014$, with an R^2 of .048); and the events we judged to be sleep paralysis ($F[1,123] = 5.185$, $p = .025$, with an R^2 of .04).

Absorption did not predict all experiences of God, including whether someone had heard from God at all ($F[1,127] = .832$, $p = .364$, with an $R^2 = .007$); whether someone had heard from God through circumstances ($F[1,125] = .270$, $p = .604$, with an R^2 of .002); whether someone had heard from God through scripture ($F[1,126] = .000$, $p = .987$, with an R^2 of .000). These experiences are very common; 90 percent or more of our participants said that they had had these experiences. Absorption also did not predict whether someone spoke in tongues, an act that seems to depend as much on the culture of the church as on individual proclivity ($F[1,123] = 1.156$, $p = .284$ with an R^2 of .009).

All told, absorption was a significant positive predictor ($p < .05$) for all of the anomalous "core" experiences included in our interview and for most of the less common ones, although not for the ones so common that the great majority of people reported them. In the interest of transparency, let me add that there were four questions we asked that we felt worked so badly that I simply did not include the data—for example, asking whether people had experienced "Holy Terror" (these Christians just looked at us with astonishment when they heard the question). Setting those four questions aside, absorption predicted 11 out of 14 of our items with $p < .05$.

Absorption was also correlated with how *frequently* people had (or said they had had) spiritual experiences, including the frequency with which people experienced thoughts from God ($r = .335$, $n = 115$, $p < .001$); experienced feelings and sensations associated with God ($r = .283$, $n = 113$, $p = .002$); had images from God ($r = .302$, $n = 110$, $p = .001$); and had voice-like events ($r = .194$, $n = 114$, $p = .039$) or vision-like events ($r = .334$, $n = 114$, $p < .001$), as well as how meaningful they judged those voice- and vision-like events to be (judged on a five-point scale; voice: $r = .379$, $n = 114$, $p = .039$; vision: $r = .271$, $n = 127$, $p = .002$). All told, absorption was significantly correlated ($p < .05$) with 10 out of 17 of the frequency judgments included in our interview (here including the 3 very common experiences of hearing from God at all, hearing through circumstance, and hearing through scripture).

Third: These events are habituated for the group. Local expectations shape the kinds of events people experience.

To reiterate, one should not feel too confident of the rates for these unusual experiences because different studies use different methods to reach their rates. Related to this, one cannot compare these rates statistically. In my current work with the Mind and Spirit Project, we hope, with time, to produce numbers that may help us triangulate more effectively. Nonetheless, the numbers we have place estimates of mystical experiences in the general population at one in a hundred or less (Thomas and Cooper 1980; Wulff 2000). We undoubtedly coded more inclusively than we might have done, but even so, our rates are much higher than that. When people value such experiences and expect to encounter God vividly through them, they seem to have them more often.

The general population rates for sleep paralysis are about 25–33 percent (as reported in Adler 2011), and for US charismatic Christians, who did not value these experiences or, for the most part, interpret them as demonic (in this sample, at least), the rate was about the same. For out-of-body events, five studies have found a rate of about 10 percent (reported in Alvarado 2000). Again, for the charismatic Christians in our sample, who did not interpret these as spiritual events, the rates were about the same. The rates for voices vary depending upon measure and approach (see Luhrmann 2012). A recent analysis of the rates of auditory hallucinations in the general population found a rate of 6–7 percent (Baumeister et al. 2017).

Fourth: These events become habituated for individuals, and often an initial experience is more powerful than those that come after.

We added up answers to all the questions we asked people about anomalous experiences that had taken place before their first interview, and then, one month later, about whether they had experienced any events during that month. These were questions about whether they'd experienced voices, visions, a sense of God's presence, out-of-body events, mystical events, sleep paralysis, overwhelming emotion, a rush of power (a Holy Spirit experience), or muscle cataplexy (a "slain in the spirit" experience). People who had more experiences in the past also tended to have more experiences during the month (r = 491, n = 108, p < .001). The effect remains significant when one controls for absorption (r = .467, n = 107, p < .001). That is, kindling is not absorption by another name. It is more as if absorption boosts the floor of the capacity to have the experience. We did not find evidence of an interaction between absorption and other factors (like practice) that increases the frequency of spiritual events, although we may have had too few participants to find one.

Finally: Anomalous events are associated with each other. If someone has had one, he or she is more likely to have another.

Cronbach's Alpha is often used to evaluate the closeness of association between items. For voices, visions, presence, mystical experiences, out-of-body experiences, sleep paralysis, intense emotional experiences from God, adrenaline rushes (Holy Spirit experiences that feel like electricity), and cataplexy ("slain in the spirit" experiences), the Cronbach's Alpha, which can range from 0 (meaning no association) to 1 (meaning perfect association), was .653. This suggests that if someone has had one of these events, he or she is indeed more likely to have another.

Biomedical essays on kindling include Delgado and Sevillano 1961; Goddard 1967; Goddard and Douglas 1975; Gaito 1974; McNamara et al. 1980; Kendler, Thornton, and Gardner 2000; Gilbert 2001; and Post 2007.

The history of psychiatric diagnosis is rich and fascinating. I have told some of that story in *Of Two Minds*, but that book described the shift from psychoanalytic noncategorization to the DSM. The account of the shift from the DSM to RDoc is presented with an excellent overview of classification by Zachar and Kendler 2017.

David Hufford's *The Terror That Comes in the Night* made famous not only the condition of sleep paralysis, but also a folklore method for understanding whether a folk story had roots in physiology. He collected a wide variety of folkloric examples, quantified them, categorized them, interviewed living people with similar experiences, and consulted the scientific literature on sleep physiology. He concluded that the Old Hag syndrome and medieval and early modern European stories of incubi and succubi were ultimately rooted in a physiological phenomenon, yet that cultural factors heavily determined the ways in which the experience was described and interpreted. More recently, Shelley Adler (*Sleep Paralysis*) has documented the "nocebo" effect of sleep paralysis, particularly among the Hmong, who interpret sleep paralysis as a precursor of death and sometimes indeed appear to die as a result of the experience. See Hinton, Hufford, and Kirmayer 2005.

The idea that there are constrained patterns in what is deemed religious is most famously associated with William James's *Varieties of Religious Experience*. He was not sui generis: at the time, other scholars like Edwin Starbuck, James Leuba, and George Coe shared his ambitions. Rudolf Otto's *The Idea of the Holy* sets out on a similar path. More recent contributions include Alister Hardy's *The Spiritual Nature of Man*, a fascinating categorization of the thousands of reports people sent in response to newspaper solicitations for the spiritual experiences of ordinary people. *Varieties of Anomalous Experience*, edited by Etzel Cardeña, Steven Jay Lynn, and Stanley Krippner, is another quite interesting collection, summarizing what we know about the frequency and consistency of mystical states, out-of-body phenomena, near-death experiences, and so forth. Wayne Proudfoot's *Religious Experience* reminds us how cautious we must be in interpreting these claims. Ann Taves (*Religious Experience Reconsidered, Revelatory Events*) is doing some of the best contemporary work on the topic.

CHAPTER 6: WHY PRAYER WORKS

Roughly 55 percent of Americans say that they pray every day and 78 percent say that they pray at least sometimes (Pew 2008). The sociologist Margaret Poloma distinguishes four types of prayer: ritual (the rote, recited script); conversational prayer (the informal chat); petitionary prayer (a request); and meditative prayer (nearly wordless contemplation). In the fall of 1988, she persuaded George Gallup to include questions about prayer in a US national survey. They found that nearly nine in ten people prayed. Half of them at least occasionally recited memorized prayers, and half of them used contemplative prayer—they said that they spent time thinking about God or just feeling his presence. Almost half of them asked for material things, but almost all of them talked to God informally in their own words (Poloma and Gallup 1991: 26). A 2006 Pew Research Center survey of over 35,000 people in the United States 18 and older (The US Religious Landscape Survey) found that 55 percent prayed daily; 16 percent weekly; 6 percent monthly; and 23 percent seldom or never.

In his unfinished dissertation on prayer (*On Prayer*), Marcel Mauss suggested that prayer has a history: that as the person becomes more individualized, so too does prayer practice, and the understanding of what acts in prayer shifts inward from the exactness of the liturgy to the intention of the one who enacts. Relatively few anthropologists since have written about prayer, although that is changing. More recently, anthropologists have drawn attention to the structured form prayer has as a linguistic performance (Capps and Ochs 2002); that it is a special kind of language, intended for special ends (Shoaps 2002; Keane 1997a; Baquedano-Lopez 2008); that it becomes a manner of encountering modernity (Robbins 2001); and that there are unintended political consequences from its use by colonizers (William Hanks, *Converting Words*; Jean Comaroff, *Body of Power, Spirit of Resistance*). Philip and Carol Zaleski's *Prayer: A History* is well worth consulting.

A brief comment on Robertson Smith: he was trying not to focus on an exchange system but to move beyond it. It is nonetheless hard to read him without assuming that this is what he was describing; and certainly those views were adopted by Tylor and Frazer. See Jones 1981.

Two cognitive scientists who have explored the way Melanesian navigation works are Thomas Gladwin (*East Is a Big Bird*) and Edwin Hutchins (*Cognition in the Wild*).

The idea that religion is fundamentally about the regulation of emotion is not central to the way that many anthropologists have thought about religion, but there is a group of anthropologists—among them, Amy Cox Hall ("Living on a Prayer"), Joanna Cook (*Meditation in Modern Buddhism*), Rebecca Lester (*Jesus in Our Wombs*), and Thomas Csordas (*The Sacred Self*)—who have led the way in describing how prayer changes the self. Jerome Frank (*Persuasion and Healing*) argued over fifty years ago that religious healing and psychotherapy both worked for the same reason: they persuaded the suffering subject that the priest/healer/therapist had the authority to heal him, and that subject and healer shared a symbolic system within which healing could occur. But Frank was focused on healing—and his discussion is often relegated to the discussion of symbolic healing as something that religion happens to be good for, rather than being central to what religion is.

"Metacognition" is a word that has come to serve many purposes, particularly in education, but is being explored through anthropology, philosophy, and psychology as an act of thinking about thinking. The famous article "Metacognition and Cognitive Monitoring" was written by John Flavell in 1979. Anthropologists associated with metacognition include Martin Fortier, Joanna Cook, and Jonathan Mair. A useful overview from a number of disciplinary perspectives, including an early version of this chapter, is Joëlle Proust and Martin Fortier, eds., *Metacognitive Diversity.*

Well-being is a very broad field. For a more exacting consideration of the nature of well-being, the reader might consult Steve Derné's *Sociology of Well-Being.*

The research on the efficacy of mindfulness is now substantial. Reviews include Cresswell (2017) and Dahl, Lutz, and Davidson (2015). As is true for much science, as research has developed, so have the observations that in the general population the effects of meditation may be more modest than once thought. Nevertheless, it does appear that mindfulness can have significant benefits for those suffering from depression, anxiety, pain, and substance abuse. Joanna Cook (2016, 2018) provides a helpful anthropological perspective on the differences in how mindfulness is understood and enacted in disparate cultural settings, as does Julia Cassaniti, *Remembering the Present.*

Many people quote this as Blaise Pascal's dictum: Get down on your knees and pray, and you will believe. He never said that. Here is the correct quotation (2004: 202):

> Proofs only convince the mind; custom provides our strongest and most firmly believed proofs. . . . We must acquire an easier belief, which is that of habit.

CHAPTER 7: A GOD WHO RESPONDS

Both on a cellular level and in the brain, the invisible other is experienced as a social relationship. That is, we know that the nature of one's relationship with God affects immune function and loneliness, and we know that the act of talking with God looks (from the point of view of an fMRI machine) like talking with a friend (Schjoedt et al. 2009; Woods et al. 1999; Paloutzian and Ellison 1982). Moreover, people certainly talk as if they have social relationships with their gods. They talk about speaking with their gods, being teased, comforted, encouraged, chastised, and so forth.

In 1953, D. W. Winnicott invented the term "transitional object" to capture that which was not quite part of a child's body but not part of external reality, neither separate from the self nor identical to the self, "an area of experiencing to which inner reality and external life both contribute" (1953: 90). He argued that this in-between realness enabled children to use toys to substitute for their mothers in their absence, and to feel that love emanated from toys despite their awareness that the bear is not "really" alive. Winnicott also argued that this was the psychic domain from which creativity, art, and religion were born—that gods, in effect, worked the way teddy bears did.

Self-psychologists have a name for the mental construct this trust creates in the mind: a "self-object." This is a term coined by the Chicago analyst Heinz Kohut (1971), who argued that what made intensive long-term psychotherapy effective was that patients learned to experience the empathic therapist as an internal "object" that was loving, caring, and concerned with what was best for them. A patient who was helped by therapy was able to act and think and feel as if always aware of that therapist's loving concern, as if the patient became the person created within that responsive, attentive relationship. From this perspective, the ideal self-object is a cross between a coach and a teddy bear, always available, never intrusive, whose emotional presence keeps hope alive and self-doubt at bay.

In her study of a Mexican convent, Rebecca Lester (2005) described a trajectory through which religious practice might create God as a soothing self-object, that wise internal teddy bear coach. She set out a seven-stage process through which postulants—women (really, girls) who have not professed their vows—travel across the course of a year if they come to experience their vocation as rightly chosen. The seven-stage process is not simply a movement toward the acceptance of a vocation but also a process of coming to have a relationship with God.

1. *Brokenness*: the postulant acknowledges a sense of discomfort as a call from God to become a nun.

2. *Belonging*: the postulant comes to feel socially integrated within the convent.
3. *Containment*: the postulant comes to experience her body as complete within and contained within the convent walls.
4. *Regimentation*: the postulant learns to enact certain practices that she experiences as remaking her rebellious, desiring human body into one more suitable for God.
5. *Internal critique*: the postulant chooses to subject herself to intense self-scrutiny, and identifies her faults as the source of the broken relationship with God.
6. *Surrender*: the postulant chooses to turn herself, faults and all, over to God.
7. *Recollection*: the postulant comes to experience herself as truly present with God.

The sequence depends first and foremost on "brokenness." The postulant deliberately makes herself feel badly, and again and again practices replacing that feeling with a sense of being in relationship with a loving God. See also Johanna Richlin (2019) on the way God works as a therapeutic presence for Brazilian immigrants in the United States, and Thomas Csordas, *The Sacred Self*.

Meanwhile, on the way presence can be understood as an interaction, see a very interesting essay by Cordelia Erickson-Davis and Anna Corwin (2020) and work by Herbert Clark, *Using Language*, where he argues that interaction generates presence.

Having said that anthropologists tend to treat God as a belief and to not write ethnographies about the way God works as a relationship, it is with pleasure that I report that Amira Mittermaier is writing an ethnography of God.

BIBLIOGRAPHY

Abram, David. 1996. *The Spell of the Sensuous: Perception and Language in a More-Than-Human World*. New York: Random House.

Adler, Shelley. 2011. *Sleep Paralysis: Night-mares, Nocebos, and the Mind-Body Connection*. New Brunswick, NJ: Rutgers University Press.

Alvarado, Carlos. 2000. "Out of Body Experiences." In *Varieties of Anomalous Experience: Examining the Scientific Evidence*, edited by Etzel Cardeña, Steven Jay Lynn, and Stanley Krippner, 183–218. Washington, DC: American Psychological Association.

Appadurai, Arjun. 1996. *Modernity at Large: Cultural Dimensions of Globalization*. Minneapolis: University of Minnesota Press.

Asad, Talal. 1993. *Genealogies of Religion: Discipline and Reasons of Power in Christianity and Islam*. Baltimore: Johns Hopkins University Press.

Asamoah-Gyadu, J. Kwabena. 2005. *African Charismatics: Current Developments within Independent Indigenous Pentecostalism in Ghana*. Leiden: Brill.

———. 2013. *Contemporary Pentecostal Christianity: Interpretations from an African Context*. Eugene, OR: Wipf and Stock.

Astuti, Rita. 2001. "Are We All Natural Dualists?" *Journal of the Royal Anthropological Institute* 7: 429–47.

———. 2007. "What Happens after Death?" In *Questions of Anthropology*, edited by Rita Astuti, John Parry, and Charles Stafford, 227–47. LSE Monographs on Anthropology 76. London: Berg Publishers.

———. 2009. "Revealing and Obscuring River's Pedigree: Biological Inheritance and Kinship in Madagascar." In *Kinship and Beyond: The Genealogical Model Reconsidered*, edited by Sandra Bamford and James Leach, 214–36. Oxford: Berghahn Books.

Astuti, Rita, and Paul Harris. 2008. "Understanding Mortality and the Life of the Ancestors in Rural Madagascar." *Cognitive Science* 32 (4): 713–40.

Atran, Scott. 2002. *In Gods We Trust: The Evolutionary Landscape of Religion*. Oxford: Oxford University Press.

Atran, Scott, and Jeremy Ginges. 2012. "Religious and Sacred Imperatives in Human Conflict." *Science* 336 (18): 855–57.

Atran, Scott, Hammad Sheik, and Angel Gomez. 2014. "For Cause and Comrade: Devoted Actors and Willingness to Fight." *Cliodynamics* 5 (1). https://escholarship.org/uc/item/6n09f7gr.

Augustine. 2001. *Confessions*. Translated by Rex Warner. New York: Signet Classic.

Axline, Virginia. (1947) 1989. *Play Therapy: The Inner Dynamics of Childhood*. Edinburgh: Churchill Livingstone.

———. 1964. *Dibs in Search of Self*. New York: Ballantine Books.

Baquedano-Lopez, Patricia. 2008. "Prayer." *Journal of Linguistic Anthropology* 9 (1–2): 197–200.

Barrett, Justin L. 2004. *Why Would Anyone Believe in God?* Walnut Creek, CA: AltaMira Press.

———. 2012. *Born Believers: The Science of Children's Religious Beliefs*. New York: Simon and Schuster.

Bartlett, Robert. 2008. *The Natural and the Supernatural in the Middle Ages*. Cambridge: Cambridge University Press.

Bateson, Gregory. (1972) 2000. *Steps to an Ecology of Mind*. Chicago: University of Chicago Press.

Baumeister, David, Ottilie Sedgwick, Oliver Howes, and Emmanuelle Peters. 2017. "Auditory Verbal Hallucinations and Continuum Models of Psychosis: A Systematic Review of the Healthy Voice-Hearer Literature." *Clinical Psychology Review* 51: 125–41.

Beck, Aaron. 1976. *Cognitive Therapy and the Emotional Disorders*. New York: Meridian.

Berger, Peter. 1967. *The Sacred Canopy: Elements of a Sociological Theory of Religion*. New York: Anchor.

Bergunder, Michael. 2008. *The South Indian Pentecostal Movement in the Twentieth Century*. Grand Rapids, MI: William B. Eerdmans.

Bering, Jesse. 2012. *The Belief Instinct: The Psychology of Souls, Destiny, and the Meaning of Life*. New York: W. W. Norton & Company.

Berkman, Lisa F., Thomas Glass, Ian Brisette, and Teresa E. Seeman. 2000. "From Social Integration to Health: Durkheim in the New Millennium." *Social Science and Medicine* 51 (6): 843–57.

Beyer, Stephen. 1978. *The Cult of Tara: Magic and Ritual in Tibet*. Oakland: University of California Press.

———. 2009. *Singing to the Plants: A Guide to Mestizo Shamanism in the Upper Amazon*. Albuquerque: University of New Mexico Press.

Bialecki, Jon. 2014. "Does God Exist in Methodological Atheism? On Tanya Luhrmann's *When God Talks Back* and Bruno Latour." *Anthropology of Consciousness* 25 (1): 32–52.

———. 2017. *A Diagram for Fire: Miracles and Variation in an American Charismatic Movement*. Oakland: University of California Press.

Biehl, João, and Peter Locke. 2010. "Deleuze and the Anthropology of Becoming." *Current Anthropology* 51 (3): 317–51.

———, eds. 2017. *Unfinished: The Anthropology of Becoming*. Durham, NC: Duke University Press.

Bielo, James, ed. 2009a. *The Social Life of Scriptures: Cross-Cultural Perspectives on Biblicism*. New Brunswick, NJ: Rutgers University Press.

———. 2009b. *Words upon the Word: An Ethnography of Evangelical Group Bible Study*. New York: New York University Press.

———. 2011. *Emerging Evangelicals: Faith, Modernity, and the Desire for Authenticity*. New York: New York University Press.

Bilu, Yoram. 2013. "'We Want to See Our King': Apparitions in Messianic Habad." *Ethos* 41 (1): 98–126.

———. Forthcoming. *With Us More Than Ever: Making the Absent Rebbe Present in Messianic Chabad*. Stanford: Stanford University Press.

Blanes, Ruy, and Diana Espírito Santo, eds. 2013. *The Social Life of Spirits*. Chicago: University of Chicago Press.

Blech, Benjamin. 1992. *Understanding Judaism: The Basics of Deed and Creed*. New York: Jacob Aronson.

Bloch, Maurice. 2008. "Why Religion Is Nothing Special but Is Central." *Philosophical Transactions of the Royal Society B.* 363: 2055–61.

Boudry, Maarten, and Jerry A. Coyne. 2016. "Disbelief in Belief: On the Cognitive Status of Supernatural Beliefs." *Philosophical Psychology* 29 (4): 601–15.

Bowen, John. 2007. *Why the French Don't Like Headscarves: Islam, the State, and Public Space.* Princeton, NJ: Princeton University Press.

Boyer, Pascal. 1994. *The Naturalness of Religious Ideas: A Cognitive Theory of Religion.* Oakland: University of California Press.

———. 2001. *Religion Explained: The Evolutionary Origins of Religious Thought.* New York: Basic Books.

———. 2008. "Religion: Bound to Believe?" *Nature* 455 (23): 1038–39.

———. 2013. "Why 'Belief' Is Hard Work: Implications of Tanya Luhrmann's *When God Talks Back.*" *HAU: Journal of Ethnographic Theory* 3 (3): 349–57.

Bradley, Marion Zimmer. 1983. *The Mists of Avalon.* New York: Knopf.

Brenner, Suzanne. 1996. "Reconstructing Self and Society: Javanese Muslim Women and 'the Veil.'" *American Ethnologist* 23 (4): 673–97.

Briggs, Jean. 1998. *Inuit Morality Play: The Emotional Education of a Three-Year-Old.* New Haven, CT: Yale University Press.

Brooks, David. 2012. "Op-Ed: The Power of the Particular." *New York Times*, June 25.

Buber, Martin. 1937. *I and Thou.* Translated by Ronald Gregor Smith. New York: Charles Scribner and Sons.

Butler, Andrew C., Jason. E. Chapman, Evan M. Forman, and Aaron T. Beck. 2006. "The Empirical Status of Cognitive-Behavioral Therapy: A Review of Meta-Analyses." *Clinical Psychology Review* 26 (1): 17–31.

Cacioppo, John, and William Patrick. 2008. *Loneliness: Human Nature and the Need for Social Connection.* New York: W. W. Norton & Company.

Caillois, Roger. 1960. *Man and the Sacred.* Translated by Meyer Barash. New York: Free Press.

———. 1961. *Man, Play and Games.* Translated by Meyer Barash. Glencoe, IL: Free Press.

Capps, Lisa, and Elinor Ochs. 2002. "Cultivating Prayer." In *The Language of Turn and Sequence*, edited by Cecelia Ford, Barbara Fox, and Sandra Thompson, 39–55. New York: Oxford University Press.

Cardeña, Etzel, Steven Jay Lynn, and Stanley Krippner, eds. 2000. *Varieties of Anomalous Experience: Examining the Scientific Evidence.* Washington, DC: American Psychological Association Press.

Carruthers, Mary. 1998. *The Craft of Thought: Meditation, Rhetoric, and the Making of Images.* Cambridge: Cambridge University Press.

Cassaniti, Julia. 2015. *Living Buddhism: Mind, Self, and Emotion in a Thai Community.* Ithaca, NY: Cornell University Press.

———. 2018. *Remembering the Present: Mindfulness in Buddhist Asia.* Ithaca, NY: Cornell University Press.

Cassaniti, Julia, and T. M. Luhrmann. 2011. "Encountering the Supernatural: A Phenomenological Account of Mind." *Religion and Society* 2: 37–53. https://doi.org/10.3167/arrs.2011.020103.

———. 2014. "The Cultural Kindling of Spiritual Experiences." *Current Anthropology* 55 (S10): S333–43.

Chentsova-Dutton, Yulia E., and Vivian Dzokoto. 2014. "Listen to Your Heart: The Cultural Shaping of Interoceptive Awareness and Accuracy." *Emotion* 14 (4): 666–78.

Christian, William, and Gábor Klaniczay, eds. 2009. *The "Vision" Thing: Studying Divine Intervention*. No. 18. Budapest: Collegium Budapest Workshop Series.

Clark, Herbert. 1996. *Using Language*. Cambridge: Cambridge University Press.

Cohen, David, and Stephen MacKeith. 1991. *The Development of Imagination: The Private Worlds of Childhood*. Concepts in Developmental Psychology. New York: Routledge.

Coleman, Simon. 2000. *The Globalisation of Charismatic Christianity: Spreading the Gospel of Prosperity*. Cambridge: Cambridge University Press.

Comaroff, Jean. 1985. *Body of Power, Spirit of Resistance: The Culture and History of a South African People*. Chicago: University of Chicago Press.

Cook, Joanna. 2011. *Meditation in Modern Buddhism: Renunciation and Change in Thai Monastic Life*. Cambridge: Cambridge University Press.

———. 2016. "Mindful in Westminster: The Politics of Meditation and the Limits of Neoliberal Critique." *HAU: Journal of Ethnographic Theory* 6 (1): 141–61.

———. 2018. "Paying Attention to Attention." *Anthropology of This Century* 22. http://aotcpress.com/articles/paying-attention-attention/.

Corbin, Henry. 1969a. *Alone with the Alone: Creative Imagination in the Sūfism of Ibn 'Arabī*. Translated by Ralph Manheim. Princeton, NJ: Princeton University Press.

———. 1969b. *Creative Imagination in the Sūfism of Ibn 'Arabī*. Translated by Ralph Manheim. Princeton, NJ: Princeton University Press.

Corwin, Anna. 2012. "Changing God, Changing Bodies: The Impact of New Prayer Practices on Elderly Catholic Nuns' Embodied Experience." *Ethos* 40 (4): 390–410.

———. Forthcoming. *Holding the Hand of God: How Catholic Nuns Become Models of Successful Aging*. New Brunswick: Rutgers University Press.

Corwin, Anna, and Cordelia Erickson-Davies. 2020. "Experiencing Presence: An Interaction Model of Perception." *HAU: Journal of Ethnographic Theory* 10 (1): 166–82.

Covington, Dennis. 1995. *Salvation on Sand Mountain: Snake Handling and Redemption in Southern Appalachia*. New York: Penguin.

Cresswell, J. David. 2017. "Mindfulness Interventions." *Annual Review of Psychology* 68: 491–516.

Crocker, J. Christopher. 1985. *Vital Souls: Bororo Cosmology, Natural Symbolism, and Shamanism*. Tucson: University of Arizona Press.

Csordas, Thomas. 1993. "Somatic Modes of Attention." *Cultural Anthropology* 8 (2): 135–56.

———. 1994. *The Sacred Self: A Cultural Phenomenology of Charismatic Healing*. Oakland: University of California Press.

Dahl, Cortland J., Antoine Lutz, and Richard J. Davidson. 2015. "Reconstructing and Deconstructing the Self: Cognitive Mechanisms in Meditation Practice." *Trends in Cognitive Sciences* 19 (9): 515–23.

Davidson, Donald. 1984. *Inquiries into Truth and Interpretation*. Oxford: Oxford University Press.

Davidson, Richard J., Jon Kabat-Zinn, Jessica Schumacher, Melissa Rosenkranz, Daniel Muller, Saki Santorelli, Ferris Urbankowski, Anne Harrington, Katherine Bonus, and John Sheridan. 2003. "Alterations in Brain and Immune Function Produced by Mindfulness Meditation." *Psychosomatic Medicine* 65 (4): 564–70.

Davies, Owen. 2003. "The Nightmare Experience, Sleep Paralysis, and Witchcraft Accusations." *Folklore* 114 (2): 181–203.

De Cruz, Helen, and Johan De Smedt. 2014. *A Natural History of Natural Theology: The Cognitive Science of Theology and Philosophy of Religion*. Cambridge, MA: MIT Press.

Delgado, José M. R., and Manuel Sevillano. 1961. "Evolution of Repeated Hippocampal Seizures in the Cat." *Electroencephalography and Clinical Neurophysiology* 13 (5): 722–33. https://doi.org/10.1016/0013-4694(61)90104-3.

Derné, Steve. 2016. *Sociology of Well-Being: Lessons from India*. Delhi: SAGE Publications.

Descola, Philippe. (2005) 2013. *Beyond Nature and Culture*. Translated by Janet Lloyd. Chicago: University of Chicago Press.

Desjarlais, Robert, and C. Jason Throop. 2011. "Phenomenological Approaches in Anthropology." *Annual Reviews in Anthropology* 40: 87–102.

Diener, Ed, and Martin E. P. Seligman. 2002. "Very Happy People." *Psychological Science* 13 (1): 81–84.

Dillard, Annie. (1974) 2016. *Pilgrim at Tinker Creek*. New York: Harper Collins.

Dilley, Paul. 2017. *Monasteries and the Care of Souls in Late Antique Christianity: Cognition and Discipline*. Cambridge: Cambridge University Press.

Doostdar, Alireza. 2018. *The Iranian Metaphysicals: Explorations in Science, Islam, and the Uncanny*. Princeton, NJ: Princeton University Press.

Douglas, Mary. (1966) 2002. *Purity and Danger: An Analysis of Concepts of Pollution and Taboo*. London: Routledge and Keegan Paul.

Dow, James. 1986. "Universal Aspects of Symbolic Healing: A Theoretical Synthesis." *American Anthropologist* 88 (1): 56–69.

Dulin, J. 2020. "Vulnerable Minds, Bodily Thoughts, and Sensory Spirits: Local Theory of Mind and Spiritual Experience in Ghana." Special Issue: *Mind and Spirit: A Comparative Theory*, edited by T. M. Luhrmann. *Journal of the Royal Anthropological Institute* 26 (S1): 61–76. https://doi.org/10.1111/1467-9655.13241.

———. Forthcoming. "When High Gods and Low Gods Speak to 'the Mind': The God-Thoughts of Indigenous Religious Specialists and Charismatic Christians in Ghana." *American Anthropologist*.

Durkheim, Émile. (1912) 2001. *The Elementary Forms of Religious Life*. Translated by Karen E. Fields. Oxford: Oxford University Press.

Dyrness, William. 2004. *Reformed Theology and Visual Culture: The Protestant Imagination from Calvin to Edwards*. Cambridge: Cambridge University Press.

———. 2008. *Senses of the Soul: Art and the Visual in Christian Worship*. Eugene, OR: Wipf and Stock.

Dzokoto, V. 2010. "Different Ways of Feeling: Emotion and Somatic Awareness in Ghanaians and Euro-Americans." *Journal of Social, Evolutionary, and Cultural Psychology* 4 (2): 68–78.

Dzokoto, Vivian. 2020. "*Adwenhoasem*: An Akan Theory of Mind." Special Issue: *Mind and Spirit: A Comparative Theory*, edited by T. M. Luhrmann. *Journal of the Royal Anthropological Institute* 26 (S1): 77–94. https://doi.org/10.1111/1467-9655.13242.

Ehrlich, Elizabeth. 1997. *Miriam's Kitchen*. New York: Penguin.

Ellison, Christopher. 1991. "Religious Involvement and Subjective Well-Being." *Journal of Health and Social Behavior* 32: 80–99.

Ellison, Christopher, and Linda George. 1994. "Religious Involvement, Social Ties and Social Support in a Southeastern Community." *Journal for the Scientific Study of Religion* 33 (1): 46–61.

Engelke, Matthew. 2007. *A Problem of Presence: Beyond Scripture in an African Church.* Oakland: University of California Press.

Eriksen, Annelin. 2018. "Going to 'Pentecost': How to Study Pentecostalism—in Melanesia, for Example." *Journal of the Royal Anthropological Institute* 24 (1): 164–80.

Eriksen, Annelin, Michelle MacCarthy, and Ruy Llera Blanes. 2019. *Going to Pentecost: An Experimental Approach to Studies in Pentecostalism.* London: Berghahn Books.

Eskridge, Larry. 2013. *God's Forever Family.* Oxford: Oxford University Press.

Evans, Jonathan St B. T. 1984. "Heuristic and Analytic Processes in Reasoning." *British Journal of Psychology* 75 (4): 451–68.

Evans-Pritchard, E. E. 1937. *Witchcraft, Oracles and Magic among the Azande.* Oxford: Clarendon Press.

———. 1956. *Nuer Religion.* Oxford: Oxford University Press.

———. 1965. *Theories of Primitive Religion.* Oxford: Clarendon Press.

Fernyhough, Charles. 2016. *The Voices Within: The History and Science of How We Talk to Ourselves.* New York: Basic Books.

Fernyhough Charles, Ashley Watson, Marco Bernini, Peter Moseley, and Ben Alderson-Day. 2019. "Imaginary Companions, Inner Speech, and Auditory Verbal Hallucinations: What Are the Relations?" *Frontiers in Psychology* 10: Article 1665. https://doi.org/10.3389/fpsyg.2019.01665.

Festinger, Leon, Henry Riecken, and Stanley Schechter. (1956) 2009. *When Prophecy Fails: A Social and Psychological Study of a Modern Group That Predicted the Destruction of the World.* New York: Harper and Row.

Field, Margaret, and Taft Blackhorse Jr. 2002. "The Dual Power of Metonymy in Navaho Prayer." *Anthropological Linguistics* 44 (3): 217–30.

Flannelly, Kevin J., Kathleen Galek, Christopher Ellison, and Harold Koenig. 2010. "Beliefs about God, Psychiatric Symptoms, and Evolutionary Psychology." *Journal of Religion and Health* 49: 246–61.

Flavell, John. 1979. "Metacognition and Cognitive Monitoring: A New Area of Cognitive-Developmental Inquiry." *American Psychologist* 34 (10): 906–11.

Flood, Gavin, ed. 1993. *Mapping Invisible Worlds.* Edinburgh: Edinburgh University Press.

Fortes, Meyer. 1970. *Time and Social Structure and Other Essays.* London: Athlone Press.

———. 1987. *Religion, Morality and the Person: Essays on Tallensi Religion.* Cambridge: Cambridge University Press.

Foster, Richard. 2006. *Celebration of Discipline: The Path to Spiritual Growth.* New York: HarperSanFrancisco.

Frank, Jerome. 1961. *Persuasion and Healing: A Comparative Study of Psychotherapy.* Baltimore: Johns Hopkins University Press.

Frankl, Victor. 1959. *Man's Search for Meaning.* Translated by Ilse Lasch. Boston: Beacon Press.

Frazer, James George. (1922) 1994. *The Golden Bough: A Study in Magic and Religion.* Oxford: Oxford University Press.

Freston, Paul. 2013. "The Future of Pentecostalism in Brazil: The Limits to Growth." In *Global Pentecostalism in the 21st Century,* edited by Robert Hefner, 63–90. Bloomington: Indiana University Press.

Freud, Sigmund. (1914) 1984. *On Metapsychology.* Penguin Freud Library. London: Penguin.

———. (1917) 1976. "Mourning and Melancholia." In *The Standard Edition of the Complete Psychological Works of Sigmund Freud,* translated by James Strachey, 14:237–58. New York: W. W. Norton.

———. (1927) 1989. *The Future of an Illusion.* Edited and translated by James Strachey. New York: W. W. Norton & Company.

Friston, Karl. 2010. "The Free-Energy Principle: A Unified Brain Theory?" *Nature Reviews Neuroscience* 11: 127–38. https://doi.org/10.1038/nrn2787.

Gade, Anna. 2004. *Perfection Makes Practice: Learning, Emotion, and the Recited Qur'ān in Indonesia.* Honolulu: University of Hawai'i Press.

Gaito, John. 1974. "The Kindling Effect." *Physiological Psychology* 2 (1): 45–50.

Garb, Jonathan. 2011. *Shamanic Trance in Modern Kabbalah.* Chicago: University of Chicago Press.

Gaskins, Suzanne. 2014. "Pretend Play as Culturally Constructed Activity." In *The Oxford Handbook on the Development of Imagination,* edited by Marjorie Taylor, 224–47. Oxford: Oxford University Press.

Gavriyuk, Paul, and Sarah Coakley, eds. 2011. *The Spiritual Senses: Perceiving God in Western Christianity.* Cambridge: Cambridge University Press.

Geertz, Armin W. 2017. "Religious Bodies, Minds and Places: A Cognitive Science of Religion Perspective." In *Spazi e luoghi sacri: Espressioni ed esperienze di vissuto religioso,* edited by Laura Carnevale, 35–52. Biblioteca Tardoantica 11. Bari: Edipuglia.

Geertz, Clifford. 1988. *Works and Lives: The Anthropologist as Author.* Stanford: Stanford University Press.

Gelman, Susan A., and Gail D. Heyman. 1999. "Carrot-Eaters and Creature-Believers: The Effects of Lexicalization on Children's Inferences about Social Categories." *Psychological Science* 10 (6): 489–93.

Gendler, Tamar. 2008. "Alief and Belief." *Journal of Philosophy* 105 (10): 634–63.

Geschiere, Peter. 2013. *Witchcraft, Intimacy, and Trust: Africa in Comparison.* Chicago: University of Chicago Press.

Geurts, Kathryn. 2002. *Culture and the Senses: Bodily Ways of Knowing in an African Community.* Oakland: University of California Press.

Gibson, James. 1986. *The Ecological Approach to Visual Perception.* New York: Psychology Press.

Gifford, Paul. 2004. *Ghana's New Christianity: Pentecostalism in a Globalising African Economy.* London: Hurst and Company.

Gilbert, M. E. 2001. "Does the Kindling Model of Epilepsy Contribute to Our Understanding of Multiple Chemical Sensitivity?" *Annals of the New York Academy of Sciences* 933 (1): 68–91.

Gladwin, Thomas. 1995. *East Is a Big Bird: Navigation and Logic on Puluwat Atoll.* Cambridge, MA: Harvard University Press.

Goddard, G. V. 1967. "Development of Epileptic Seizures through Brain Stimulation at Low Intensity." *Nature* 214 (3): 1020–21.

Goddard, G. V., and R. M. Douglas. 1975. "Does the Engram of Kindling Model the Engram of Normal Long Term Memory?" *Canadian Journal of Neurological Sciences* 2 (4): 385–94.

Golomb, Claire, and Regina Kuersten. 1996. "On the Transition from Pretence Play to Reality: What Are the Rules of the Game?" *British Journal of Developmental Psychology* 14 (2): 203–17.

Göncü, Artin, and Suzanne Gaskins, eds. 2006. *Play and Development: Evolutionary, Sociocultural, and Functional Perspectives.* Mahwah, NJ: Lawrence Erlbaum.

Gopnik, Alison. 1996. "The Scientist as Child." *Philosophy of Science* 63 (4): 485–514.

Graybeal, Lynda, and Julia Roller (with Richard Foster). 2006. *Connecting with God: A Spiritual Formation Guide.* Englewood, CO: Renovaré, Inc.

Gross, Rita M. 2002. "Meditation and Prayer: A Comparative Inquiry." *Buddhist-Christian Studies* 22: 77–86.

Guarnaccia, Peter J., Glorisa Canino, Marita Rubio-Stipec, and Milagros Bravo. 1993. "The Prevalence of Ataques de Nervios in the Puerto Rico Disaster Study: The Role of Culture in Psychiatric Epidemiology." *Journal of Nervous and Mental Disease* 181 (3): 157–65.

Guarnaccia Peter J., Roberto Lewis-Fernandez, Igda Martinez Pincay, Patrick Shrout, Jing Guo, Maria Torres, Glorisa Canino, and Margrita Alegria. 2010. "Ataque de Nervios as a Marker of Social and Psychiatric Vulnerability: Results from the NLAAS." *International Journal of Social Psychiatry* 56 (3): 298–309.

Guarnaccia, Peter J., Melissa Rivera, Felipe Franco, and Charlie Neighbors. 1996. "The Experiences of Ataques de Nervios: Towards an Anthropology of Emotion in Puerto Rico." *Culture, Medicine, and Psychiatry* 20 (3): 343–67.

Guerrero, Silva, Ileana Enesco, and Paul L. Harris. 2010. "Oxygen and the Soul: Children's Conception of Invisible Entities." *Journal of Cognition and Culture* 10: 123–51.

Guthrie, Stewart. 1993. *Faces in the Clouds: A New Theory of Religion.* Oxford: Oxford University Press.

Haeri, Niloofar. Forthcoming. *Say What Your Longing Heart Desires: Women, Prayer and Poetry in Iran.* Stanford: Stanford University Press.

Haight, Wendy, and Peggy Miller. 1992. *Pretending at Home: Early Development in a Sociocultural Context.* Albany: State University of New York Press.

Hall, Amy Cox. 2018. "Living on a Prayer: Neo-Monasticism and Socio-Ecological Change." *Religion* 48 (4): 1096–151.

Hall, Daniel E. 2006. "Religious Attendance: More Cost-Effective Than Lipitor?" *Journal of the American Board of Family Medicine* 19 (2): 130–39.

Handelman, Don. 2008. "Afterword: Returning to Cosmology—Thoughts on the Positioning of Belief." *Social Analysis* 52 (1): 181–95.

Handman, Courtney. 2014. *Critical Christianity: Translation and Denominational Conflict in Papua New Guinea.* Oakland: University of California Press.

Hanks, William. 2010. *Converting Words: Maya in the Age of the Cross.* Oakland: University of California Press.

Harding, Susan. 2000. *The Book of Jerry Falwell.* Princeton, NJ: Princeton University Press.

Hardy, Alister. 1979. *The Spiritual Nature of Man: A Study of Contemporary Religious Experience*. Oxford: Clarendon Press.

Harris, Paul. 2000. *The Work of the Imagination*. Oxford: Wiley-Blackwell.

———. 2012. *Trusting What You're Told: How Children Learn from Others*. Cambridge, MA: Harvard University Press.

Harris, Paul L., Linda Abarbanell, Elisabeth S. Pasquini, and Suzanne Duke. 2007. "Imagination and Testimony in the Child's Construction of Reality." *Intellectica* 2–3 (46–47): 69–84.

Harris, Paul, Emma Brown, Crispin Marriott, Semantha Whittall, and Sarah Harmer. 1991. "Monsters, Ghosts and Witches: Testing the Limits of the Fantasy-Reality Distinction in Young Children." *British Journal of Developmental Psychology* 9 (1): 105–23.

Harris, Paul, and Kathleen Corriveau. 2014. "Learning from Testimony about Religion and Science." In *Trust and Skepticism: Children's Selective Learning from Testimony*, edited by Elizabeth Robinson and Shiri Einav, 28–41. New York: Psychology Press.

Harris, Paul L., and Melissa Koenig. 2007. "Imagination and Testimony in Cognitive Development: The Cautious Disciple." In *Imaginative Minds*, edited by Ilona Roth. Oxford: Oxford University Press.

Harris, Paul, Elisabeth S. Pasquini, Suzanne Duke, Jessica J. Asscher, and Francisco Pons. 2006. "Germs and Angels: The Role of Testimony in Young Children's Ontology." *Developmental Science* 9 (1): 76–96.

Haynes, Naomi. 2017. *Moving by the Spirit: Pentecostal Social Life on the Zambian Copperbelt*. Oakland: University of California Press.

Heelas, Paul, and Andrew Lock. 1981. *Indigenous Psychologies: The Anthropology of the Self*. New York: Academic Press.

Heim, Maria. 2013. *The Forerunner of All Things: Buddhaghosa on Mind, Intention, and Agency*. Oxford: Oxford University Press.

Heiphetz, Larisa, Casey Lee Landers, and Neil Van Leeuwen. 2018. "Does 'Think' Mean the Same Thing as 'Believe'? Linguistic Insights into Religious Cognition." *Psychology of Religion and Spirituality*. Advance online publication. https://doi.org/10.1037/rel0000238.

Henrich, Joseph, Steven J. Heine, and Ara Norenzayan. 2010. "The Weirdest People in the World?" *Behavior and Brain Sciences* 33 (2–3): 61–83.

Hinton, Devon, David Hufford, and Laurence Kirmayer. 2005. "Culture and Sleep Paralysis." *Transcultural Psychiatry* 42 (1): 5–10.

Hirschkind, Charles. 2006. *The Ethical Soundscape: Cassette Sermons and Islamic Counterpublics*. New York: Columbia University Press.

Hochschild, Arlie. 2016. *Strangers in Their Own Land*. New York: The New Press.

Hoffman, Stefan, Anu Asnaani, Imke Vonk, Alice Sawyer, and Angela Fang. 2012. "The Efficacy of Cognitive Behavioral Therapy: A Review of Meta-analyses." *Cognitive Therapy and Research* 36 (5): 427–40.

Holbraad, Martin. 2009. "Ontology, Ethnography, Archaeology: An Afterword on the Ontography of Things." *Cambridge Archaeological Journal* 19 (3): 431–41.

Holbraad, Martin, and Morton Axel Pedersen. 2017. *The Ontological Turn*. Cambridge: Cambridge University Press.

Holt-Lunstad, Julianne, Timothy B. Smith, and J. Bradley Layton. 2010. "Social Relationships and Mortality Risk: A Meta-analytic Review." *PLoS Medicine* 7 (7): e1000316. https://doi.org/10.1371/journal.pmed.1000316.

Horton, Donald, and R. Richard Wohl. 1956. "Mass Communication and Para-Social Interaction: Observations on Intimacy at a Distance." *Psychiatry* 19 (3): 215–29. https://doi.org/10.1080/00332747.1956.11023049.

Horton, Robin. 1993. *Patterns of Thought in Africa and the West: Essays on Magic, Religion and Science.* Cambridge: Cambridge University Press.

House, James S., Karl R. Landis, and Debra Umberson. 1988. "Social Relationships and Health." *Science* 241 (4865): 540–45. https://doi.org/10.1126/science.3399889.

Hufford, David. 1982. *The Terror That Comes in the Night: An Experience-Centered Study of Supernatural Assault Traditions.* Philadelphia: University of Pennsylvania Press.

———. 1995. "Beings without Bodies: An Experience-Centered Theory of the Belief in Spirits." In *Out of the Ordinary*, edited by B. Walker, 11–45. Logan: Utah State University Press.

Huizinga, Johan. (1938) 1971. *Homo Ludens: A Study of the Play-Element in Culture.* Boston: Beacon Press.

Hummer, Robert, Richard Rogers, Charles Nam, and Christopher Ellison. 1999. "Religious Involvement and US Adult Mortality." *Demography* 36 (2): 273–85.

Hurlburt, Russell. 2011. *Investigating Pristine Inner Experience: Moments of Truth.* Cambridge: Cambridge University Press.

Huson, Paul. 1970. *Mastering Witchcraft: A Practical Guide for Witches, Warlocks, and Covens.* New York: G. P. Putnam's.

Hutchins, Edwin. 1995. *Cognition in the Wild.* Cambridge, MA: MIT Press.

Huxley, Aldous. 1945. *The Perennial Philosophy.* New York: Harper and Brothers.

Idel, Moshe. 1995. *Hasidism: Between Ecstasy and Magic.* Albany: State University of New York Press.

James, William. (1902) 1999. *The Varieties of Religious Experience: A Study in Human Nature.* New York: Modern Library.

———. (1935) 1970. *Essays in Pragmatism.* New York: Free Press.

Jaynes, Julian. 1976. *The Origin of Consciousness in the Breakdown of the Bicameral Mind.* Boston: Houghton Mifflin.

Johnston, Sarah Iles. 2015a. "The Greek Mythic Story World." *Arethusa* 48 (3): 283–311.

———. 2015b. "Narrating Myths." *Arethusa* 48 (2): 173–218.

———. 2018. *The Story of Myth.* Cambridge, MA: Harvard University Press.

Jones, Nev, and T. M. Luhrmann. 2015. "Beyond the Sensory: Findings from an In-Depth Analysis of the Phenomenology of 'Auditory Hallucinations' in Psychosis." *Psychosis* 8 (3): 191–202.

Jones, Robert Alun. 1981. "Robertson Smith, Durkheim, and Sacrifice: An Historical Context for *The Elementary Forms of the Religious Life*." *Journal of the History of the Behavioral Sciences* 17: 184–205.

Kahneman, Daniel. 2003. "Maps of Bounded Rationality: Psychology for Behavioral Economics." *American Economic Review* 93 (5): 1449–75.

———. 2011. *Thinking Fast and Slow.* New York: Farrar, Straus and Giroux.

Kaptchuk, Ted J., Elizabeth Friedlander, John M. Kelley, M. Norma Sanchez, Efi Kokkotou, Joyce P. Singer, Magda Kowalczykowski, Franklin G. Miller, Irving Kirsch, and Anthony J. Lembo. 2010. "Placebos without Deception: A Randomized Controlled Trial in Irritable Bowel Syndrome." *PLoS ONE* 5 (12): e15591. https://doi.org /10.1371/journal.pone.0015591.

Keane, Webb. 1997a. "Religious Language." *Annual Review of Anthropology* 26: 47–71.

———. 1997b. *Signs of Recognition: Power and Hazards of Representation in an Indonesian Society.* Oakland: University of California Press.

———. 2006. *Christian Moderns: Freedom and Fetish in the Mission Encounter.* Oakland: University of California Press.

———. 2015. *Ethical Life: Its Natural and Social Histories.* Princeton, NJ: Princeton University Press.

Kendler, Kenneth, Laura M. Karkowski, and Carol A. Prescott. 1999. "Causal Relationship between Stressful Life Events and the Onset of Major Depression." *American Journal of Psychiatry* 156 (6): 837–41.

Kendler, Kenneth, Laura Thornton, and Charles Gardner. 2000. "Stressful Life Events and Previous Episodes in the Etiology of Major Depression in Women: An Evaluation of the 'Kindling' Hypothesis." *American Journal of Psychiatry* 157 (8): 1243–51.

Keng, Shian-Ling, Moria J. Smoski, and Clive J. Robins. 2011. "Effects of Mindfulness on Psychological Health: A Review of Empirical Studies." *Clinical Psychology Review* 31 (6): 1041–56. https://doi.org/10.1016/j.cpr.2011.04.006.

Kierkegaard, Søren. (1847) 1948. *Purity of Heart.* Translated by D. V. Steere. New York: Harper.

Knight, Gareth. (1975) 2010. *Experience of the Inner Worlds: A Course in Christian Qabalistic Magic.* Cheltenham: Skylight Press.

Koenig, Harold, and Harvey Jay Cohen, eds. 2002. *The Link between Religion and Health: Psychoneuroimmunology and the Faith Factor.* New York: Oxford University Press.

Koenig, Harold, Dana King, and Verna Benner Carson. 2012. *Handbook of Religion and Health.* Oxford: Oxford University Press.

Kohut, Heinz. 1971. *The Analysis of the Self: A Systematic Approach to the Psychoanalytic Treatment of Narcissistic Personality Disorders.* Chicago: University of Chicago Press.

Kraepelin, Emil. 1921. *Manic-Depressive Insanity and Paranoia.* Edinburgh: E & S Livingstone.

Kravel-Tovi, Michal. 2017. *When the State Winks: The Performance of Jewish Conversion in Israel.* New York: Columbia University Press.

Kravel-Tovi, Michal, and Yoram Bilu. 2008. "The Work of the Present: Constructing Messianic Temporality in the Wake of Failed Prophecy among Chabad Hasidim." *American Ethnologist* 35 (1): 64–80.

Kripke, Saul. 1980. *Naming and Necessity.* Cambridge, MA: Harvard University Press.

Laidlaw, James. 2012. "Ontologically Challenged." *Anthropology of this Century* 4. http:// aotcpress.com/articles/ontologically-challenged.

———. 2013. *The Subject of Virtue.* Cambridge: Cambridge University Press.

Lamott, Anne. 2012. *Help, Thanks, Wow.* London: Riverhead Books.

Lancy, David. 1996. *Playing on the Mother-Ground: Cultural Routines for Children's Development.* New York: Guilford Press.

Landy, Joshua. 2012. *How to Do Things with Fictions*. Oxford: Oxford University Press.

Lanham, Jon. 2020. "Belief." *The Immanent Frame*, January 31, 2020. https://tif.ssrc.org /2020/01/31/belief-lanman/.

Larbi, Emmanuel Kingsley. 2001. *Pentecostalism: The Eddies of Ghanaian Christianity*. Accra: CPCS.

Larsen, Timothy. 2016. *The Slain God*. Oxford: Oxford University Press.

Latour, Bruno. 2005. "'Thou Shall Not Freeze-Frame' or How Not to Misunderstand the Science and Religion Debate." In *Science, Religion, and the Human Experience*, edited by James D. Proctor, 27–48. New York: Oxford University Press.

Lawrence, Brother. 1982. *The Practice of the Presence of God*. New York: Whitaker House.

Lawson, Thomas E., and Robert N. McCauley. 1990. *Rethinking Religion: Connecting Cognition and Culture*. Cambridge: Cambridge University Press.

———. 2002. *Bringing Ritual to Mind: Psychological Foundations of Cultural Forms*. Cambridge: Cambridge University Press.

Legare, Cristine, E. Margaret Evans, Karl S. Rosengren, and Paul Harris. 2012. "The Co-Existence of Natural and Supernatural Explanations across Culture and Development." *Child Development* 83 (3): 779–93.

Legare, Cristine H., and Susan A. Gelman. 2008. "Bewitchment, Biology, or Both: The Co-Existence of Natural and Supernatural Explanatory Frameworks across Development." *Cognitive Science* 32 (4): 607–42.

Lester, Rebecca. 2005. *Jesus in Our Wombs: Embodying Modernity in a Mexican Convent*. Oakland: University of California Press.

Levine, Robert. 1973. "Patterns of Personality in Africa." *Ethos* 1 (2): 123–52.

Levinson, Stephen. 2006. "On the Human Interaction Engine." In *The Roots of Human Sociality*, edited by Stephen Levinson and Nicholas Enfield, 39–69. London: Berg.

Lévi-Strauss, Claude. (1963) 1974. "The Effectiveness of Symbols." In *Structural Anthropology*, translated by Claire Jacobson, 186–205. New York: Basic Books.

Lévy-Bruhl, Lucien. 1923. *Primitive Mentality*. Translated by Lilian A. Claire. London: London, Allen & Unwin.

———. (1926) 1979. *How Natives Think*. Translated by Lilian A Claire. New York: Knopf.

———. (1949) 1975. *The Notebooks on Primitive Mentality*. Translated by Peter Rivière. New York: Harper & Row.

Lewis, C. S. (1952) 1980. *Mere Christianity*. New York: Penguin.

———. 1962. *The Weight of Glory*. London: Geoffrey Bless.

Lienhardt, Godfrey. 1961. *Divinity and Experience: The Religion of the Dinka*. Oxford: Clarendon Press.

Lifshitz, Michael, Michiel van Elk, and T. M. Luhrmann. 2019. "Absorption and Spiritual Experience: A Review of Evidence and Potential Mechanisms." *Consciousness and Cognition* 73. https://doi.org/10.1016/j.concog.2019.05.008.

Lillard, Angeline. 1998. "Ethnopsychologies: Cultural Variations in Theory of Mind." *Psychological Bulletin* 123 (1): 3–32.

Lindquist, Galina, and Simon Coleman. 2008. "Introduction: Against Belief?" *Social Analysis: The International Journal of Social and Cultural Practice* 52 (1): 1–18.

Lloyd, G. E. R. 2018. *The Ambivalences of Rationality*. Cambridge: Cambridge University Press.

Lohmann, Roger Ivar, ed. 2003. *Dream Travelers: Sleep Experiences and Culture in the Western Pacific*. New York: Palgrave Macmillan.

Lord, Albert B. (1960) 2019. *The Singer of Tales*. Edited by David F. Elmer. Cambridge, MA: Harvard University Press.

Loyola, Ignatius. 1992. *The Spiritual Exercises*. Translated by Joseph Tetlow. New York: Crossroad Publishing Company.

Luhrmann, T. M. 1989. *Persuasions of the Witch's Craft: Ritual Magic in Contemporary England*. Cambridge, MA: Harvard University Press.

———. 2000. *Of Two Minds: An Anthropologist Looks at American Psychiatry*. New York: Vintage.

———. 2006. *The Good Parsi*. Cambridge, MA: Harvard University Press.

———. 2011a. "Hallucinations and Sensory Overrides." *Annual Review of Anthropology* 40: 71–85.

———. 2011b. "Towards an Anthropological Theory of Mind." *Journal of the Finnish Anthropological Association* 36 (4): 5–13.

———. 2012. *When God Talks Back: Understanding the American Evangelical Relationship with God*. New York: Alfred A. Knopf.

———. 2013. "Making God Real and Making God Good: Some Mechanisms through Which Prayer May Contribute to Healing." *Transcultural Psychiatry* 50 (5): 707–25.

———. 2017. "Knowing God." *Cambridge Journal of Anthropology* 35 (2): 125–42.

———. n.d. The Spiritual Events Scale.

Luhrmann, T. M., and Rachael Morgain. 2012. "Prayer as Inner Sense Cultivation: An Attentional Learning Theory of Spiritual Experience." *Ethos* 40 (4): 359–89.

Luhrmann, T. M., Howard Nusbaum, and Ron Thisted. 2010. "The Absorption Hypothesis: Learning to Hear God in Evangelical Christianity." *American Anthropologist* 112 (1): 66–78.

———. 2013. "'Lord, Teach Us to Pray': Prayer Practice Affects Cognitive Processing." *Journal of Cognition and Culture* 13 (1–2): 159–77.

MacDonald, Paul. 2003. *History of the Concept of Mind*. Vol. 1, *Speculations about Soul, Mind and Spirit from Homer to Hume*. London: Ashgate.

Magliocco, Sabina. 2004. *Witching Culture: Folklore and Neo-Paganism in America*. Philadelphia: University of Pennsylvania Press.

Mahmood, Saba. 2005. *Politics of Piety: The Islamic Revival and the Feminist Subject*. Princeton, NJ: Princeton University Press.

Mair, Jonathan. 2013. "Cultures of Belief." *Anthropological Theory* 12 (4): 448–66.

Makari, George. 2015. *Soul Machine: The Invention of the Modern Mind*. New York: W. W. Norton & Company.

Malinowski, Bronislaw. 1954. *Magic, Science and Religion*. New York: Doubleday.

Markus, Hazel, and Shinobu Kitayama. 1994. "A Collective Fear of the Collective: Implications for Selves and Theories of Selves." *Personality and Social Psychology Bulletin* 20 (5): 568–79.

Marrow, J. 2019. "To Make Her Understand with Love: Expectations for Emotion Work in North Indian Families." In *Psychology of Women under Patriarchy*, edited by H. Matthews and Adriana Manago, 71–90. New Mexico: School for Advanced Research Advanced Seminar Series.

Master, Allison, Ellen Markman, and Carol Dweck. 2012. "Thinking in Categories or along a Continuum: Consequences for Children's Social Judgments." *Child Development* 83 (4): 1145–63.

Mauss, Marcel. 2003. *On Prayer.* Edited by W. S. F. Pickering. Oxford: Berghahn Books.

Mayblin, Maya. 2010. *Gender, Catholicism, and Morality in Brazil: Virtuous Husbands, Powerful Wives.* New York: Palgrave Macmillan.

Mayer, F. Stephen, and Cynthia M. Frantz. 2004. "The Connectedness to Nature Scale: A Measure of Individuals' Feeling in Community with Nature." *Journal of Environmental Psychology* 24 (4): 503–15.

McCarthy-Jones, Simon, and Charles Fernyhough. 2011. "The Varieties of Inner Speech: Links between the Quality of Inner Speech and Psychopathological Variables in a Sample of Young Adults." *Consciousness and Cognition* 20 (4): 1586–93. https://doi.org/10.1016/j.concog.2011.08.005.

McCauley, Robert. 2013. *Why Religion Is Natural and Science Is Not.* Oxford: Oxford University Press.

McCauley, Robert, and E. Thomas Lawson. 2009. *Bringing Ritual to Mind: Psychological Foundations of Cultural Forms.* Cambridge: Cambridge University Press.

McNamara, James, M. Constant Byrne, Richard Dasheiff, and J. Gregory Fitz. 1980. "The Kindling Model of Epilepsy: A Review." *Progress in Neurobiology* 15 (2): 139–59.

Mead, Margaret. 1930. *Growing Up in New Guinea: A Comparative Study of Primitive Education.* New York: Blue Ribbon Books.

Medin, Douglas, and Scott Atran. 2004. "The Native Mind: Biological Categorization, Reasoning and Decision Making in Development and across Cultures." *Psychological Review* 111: 960–83.

Medin, Douglas, Hillarie Schwartz, Sergey Blok, and Lawrence Birnbaum. 1999. "The Semantic Side of Decision Making." *Psychonomic Bulletin and Review* 6 (4): 562–69.

Meyer, Birgit. 1999. *Translating the Devil: Religion and Modernity among the Ewe in Ghana.* Edinburgh: University of Edinburgh Press.

———. 2015. "How to Capture the 'Wow': R. R. Marett's Notion of Awe and the Study of Religion." *Journal of the Royal Anthropological Institute* 22 (1): 7–26.

Mezzenzana, Francesca. 2018. "Encountering Supai: An Ecology of Spiritual Perception in the Ecuadorian Amazon." *Ethos* 46 (2): 275–95.

Miles, Jack. 1995. *God: A Biography.* New York: Knopf.

Miller, Donald E. 1997. *Reinventing American Protestantism: Christianity in the New Millennium.* Oakland: University of California Press.

Mines, Mattison. 1994. *Public Faces, Private Lives: Community and Individuality in South India.* Oakland: University of California Press.

Mittermaier, Amira. 2010. *Dreams That Matter: Egyptian Landscapes of the Imagination.* Oakland: University of California Press.

Moerman, Daniel. 1979. "The Anthropology of Symbolic Healing." *Current Anthropology* 20 (1): 59–66.

Monroe, Scott M., and Kate L. Harkness. 2005. "Life Stress, the 'Kindling' Hypothesis, and the Recurrence of Depression: Considerations from a Life Stress Perspective." *Psychological Review* 112 (2): 417–45.

Müller, F. M. 1864. *Lectures on the Science of Language.* New York: Scribner, Armstrong and Co.

Needham, Rodney. 1972. *Belief, Language and Experience*. Chicago: University of Chicago Press.

Neisser, Ulrich. 1976. *Cognition and Reality: Principles and Implications of Cognitive Psychology*. New York: W. H. Freeman.

Nelson, Richard. 1983. *Make Prayers to the Raven: A Koyukon View of the Northern Forest*. Chicago: University of Chicago Press.

Niebuhr, Reinhold. 1955. *The Self and the Dramas of History*. New York: Charles Scribner and Sons.

Noll, Richard. 1985. "Mental Imagery Cultivation as a Cultural Phenomenon: The Role of Visions in Shamanism, with Commentary." *Current Anthropology* 26 (4): 443–61.

Norenzayan, Ara. 2013. *Big Gods: How Religion Transformed Cooperation and Conflict*. Princeton, NJ: Princeton University Press.

Obeyesekere, Gananath. 2012. *The Awakened Ones: Phenomenology of Visionary Experience*. New York: Columbia University Press.

Omenyo, Cephas. 2002. *Pentecost outside Pentecostalism: A Study of the Development of Charismatic Renewal in the Mainline Churches in Ghana*. Zoetermeer: Boekencentrum.

Orsi, Robert. (2006) 2013. *Between Heaven and Earth: The Religious Worlds People Make and the Scholars Who Study Them*. Princeton, NJ: Princeton University Press.

———. 2012. "The Problem of the Holy." In *The Cambridge Companion to Religious Studies*, edited by Robert Orsi, 84–108. Cambridge: Cambridge University Press.

———. 2016. *A History of Presence*. Cambridge, MA: Harvard University Press.

Otto, Rudolf. (1917) 1958. *The Idea of the Holy*. Translated by John W. Harvey. Oxford: Oxford University Press.

Paloutzian, R. F., and C. W. Ellison. 1982. "Loneliness, Spiritual Well-Being and the Quality of Life." In *Loneliness: A Sourcebook of Current Theory, Research and Therapy*, edited by L. A. Peplau and D. Perlman, 224–36. New York: John Wiley & Sons.

Pandolfo, Stefania. 1997. *Impasse of the Angels*. Chicago: University of Chicago Press.

Parkin, David, ed. 1991. *The Anthropology of Evil*. New York: Wiley Blackwell.

Pascal, Blaise. 2004. *Pensées*. Translated by Roger Ariel. Indianapolis, IN: Hacket Publishing.

Pedersen, Morten Axel. 2011. *Not Quite Shamans*. Ithaca, NY: Cornell University Press.

Pennebaker, James. 1989. "Confession, Inhibition, and Disease." *Advances in Experimental Social Psychology* 22: 211–44.

Perera, Sylvia Brinton. 1981. *Descent to the Goddess*. Toronto: Inner City Books.

Pew Forum on Religion and Public Life. 2008. "US Religious Landscape Survey." https://www.pewforum.org/religious-landscape-study/frequency-of-prayer/.

Pew Research Center. 2006. *Spirit and Power: A Ten Country Survey of Pentecostals*. Washington, DC: Pew Research Center.

Poloma, Margaret, and George Gallup Jr. 1991. *Varieties of Prayer: A Survey Report*. Philadelphia: Trinity Press International.

Posey, Thoma, and Mary Losch. 1983. "Auditory Hallucinations of Hearing Voices in 375 Normal Subjects." *Imagination, Cognition and Personality* 3 (2): 99–113.

Post, R. M. 2007. "Kindling and Sensitization as Models for Affective Episode Recurrence, Cyclicity, and Tolerance Phenomena." *Neuroscience and Biobehavioral Reviews* 31 (6): 858–73.

Powell, Lynda, Leila Shahabi, and Carl Thoresen. 2003. "Religion and Spirituality: Linkages to Physical Health." *American Psychologist* 58 (1): 36–52.

Proudfoot, Wayne. 1985. *Religious Experience*. Oakland: University of California Press.

Proust, Joëlle, and Martin Fortier, eds. 2018. *Metacognitive Diversity: An Interdisciplinary Approach*. Oxford: Oxford University Press.

Purzycki, Benjamin G., Daniel N. Finkel, John Shaver, Nathan Wales, Adam B. Cohen, and Richard Sosis. 2012. "What Does God Know? Supernatural Agents' Access to Socially Strategic and Non-Strategic Information." *Cognitive Science* 36: 846–69.

Radcliffe-Brown, Alfred. (1922) 2013. *The Andaman Islanders: A Study in Social Anthropology*. Cambridge, MA: Cambridge University Press.

Ratcliffe, Matthew. 2005. "The Feeling of Being." *Journal of Consciousness Studies* 12 (8): 43–60.

Reichard, Gladys Amanda. 1944. *Prayer: The Compulsive Word*. New York: J. J. Augustin.

———. 1950. *Navaho Religion: A Study of Symbolism*. Princeton, NJ: Princeton University Press.

Reichel-Dolmatoff, Gerardo. 1975. *The Shaman and the Jaguar: A Study of Narcotic Drugs among the Indians of Colombia*. Philadelphia: Temple University Press.

Reinhardt, Bruno. 2014. "Soaking in Tapes: The Haptic Voice of Global Pentecostal Pedagogy in Ghana." *Journal of the Royal Anthropological Association* 20: 315–36.

Reisman, Paul. 1977. *Freedom in Fulani Social Life: An Introspective Ethnography*. Chicago: University of Chicago Press.

Richlin, Johanna. 2019. "The Affective Therapeutics of Migrant Faith: Evangelical Christianity among Brazilians in Greater Washington, DC." *Current Anthropology* 60 (3): 369–90.

Rizzuto, Ana Maria. 1979. *The Birth of the Living God*. Chicago: University of Chicago Press.

Robbins, Joel. 2001. "God Is Nothing but Talk: Modernity, Language, and Prayer in a Papua New Guinea Society." *American Anthropologist* 103 (4): 901–12.

———. 2004a. *Becoming Sinners: Christianity and Moral Torment in a Papua New Guinea Society*. Oakland: University of California Press.

———. 2004b. "The Globalization of Pentecostal and Charismatic Christianity." *Annual Review of Anthropology* 33: 117–43.

———. 2006. "Anthropology and Theology: An Awkward Relationship?" *Anthropological Quarterly* 78 (2): 285–94.

———. 2012. "Transcendence and the Anthropology of Christianity." *Suomen Antropologi: Journal of the Finnish Anthropological Society* 37 (2): 5–23.

———. n.d. "Opacity of Mind, Imagining Others, and the Coordination of Action: Melanesianist Reflections on the Ethics of Trust." Unpublished manuscript.

Robbins, Joel, and Alan Rumsey. 2008. "Cultural and Linguistic Anthropology and the Opacity of Other Minds." *Anthropological Quarterly* 8 (2): 407–20.

Roberts, Nathaniel. 2016. *To Be Cared For: The Power of Conversion and Foreignness of Belonging in an Indian Slum*. Oakland: University of California Press.

Rosengren, Karl, Carl Johnson, and Paul Harris, eds. 2000. *Imagining the Impossible: Magical, Scientific, and Religious Thinking in Children*. Cambridge: Cambridge University Press.

Ryff, Carol D., Gayle D. Love, Yuri Miyamoto, Hazel Rose Markus, Katherine B. Curhan, Shinobu Kitayama, Jiyoung Park, Norito Kawakami, Chiemi Kan, and Mayumi

Karasawa. 2014. "Culture and the Promotion of Well-Being in East and West: Understanding Varieties of Attunement to the Surrounding Context." In *Increasing Psychological Well-Being in Clinical and Education Settings: Interventions and Cultural Contexts*, edited by G. A. Fava and C. Ruini, 1–19. New York: Springer. https://doi .org/10.1007/978-94-017-8669-0.

Salovey, Peter, John D. Mayer, Susan Lee Goldman, Carolyn Turvey, and Tibor P. Palfai. 1995. "Emotional Attention, Clarity, and Repair: Exploring Emotional Intelligence Using the Trait Meta-Mood Scale." In *Emotion, Disclosure and Health*, edited by James W. Pennebaker, 125–54. Washington, DC: American Psychological Association.

Schieffelin, Bambi. 2014. "Christianizing Language and the Dis-Placement of Culture in Bosavi, Papua New Guinea." *Current Anthropology* 55 (S10): S226–37.

Schjoedt, Uffe, Hans Stødkilde-Jørgensen, Armin W. Geertz, and Andreas Roepstorff. 2009. "Highly Religious Participants Recruit Areas of Social Cognition in Personal Prayer." *Social Cognitive and Affective Neuroscience* 4 (2): 199–207.

Seligman, Adam, Robert Weller, Michael Puett, and Bennett Simon. 2008. *Ritual and Its Consequences: An Essay on the Limits of Sincerity*. Oxford: Oxford University Press.

Severi, Carlos. 1993. "Talking about Souls: On the Pragmatic Construction of Meaning in Cuna Chants." In *Cognitive Aspects of Religious Symbolism*, edited by Pascal Boyer, 165–81. Cambridge: Cambridge University Press.

Sharp, Shane. 2010. "How Does Prayer Help Manage Emotions?" *Social Psychology Quarterly* 73 (4): 417–37.

Shires, Preston. 2007. *Hippies of the Religious Right*. Houston: Baylor.

Shoaps, Robin. 2002. "'Pray Earnestly': The Textual Construction of Personal Involvement in Pentecostal Prayer and Song." *Journal of Linguistic Anthropology* 12 (1): 34–71.

Shulman, David. 2012. *More Than Real: A History of the Imagination in South India*. Cambridge, MA: Harvard University Press.

Silvey, Robert, and Stephen MacKeith. 1998. "The Paracosm: A Special Form of Fantasy." In *Organizing Early Experience: Imagination and Cognition in Childhood*, edited by D. C. Morrison, 173–97. New York: Baywood.

Simon, Gregory. 2009. "The Soul Freed of Cares? Islamic Prayer, Subjectivity, and the Contradictions of Moral Selfhood in Minangkabau, Indonesia." *American Ethnologist* 36 (2): 258–75.

Smith, Jonathan Z. 1982. *Imagining Religion: From Babylon to Jonestown*. Chicago: University of Chicago Press.

Smith, Robertson. (1889) 1956. *Lectures on the Religion of the Semites*. New York: Meridian.

Snell, Bruno. (1953) 1960. *The Discovery of the Mind: The Greek Origins of European Thought*. New York: Dover.

Sosis, Richard, and Joseph Bulbulia. 2011. "The Behavioral Ecology of Religion: The Benefits and Costs of One Evolutionary Approach." *Religion* 41 (3): 341–62.

Spelke, Elizabeth, and Katherine Kinzler. 2007. "Core Knowledge." *Developmental Science* 10 (1): 89–96.

St. John of the Cross. 2010. *Ascent of Mount Carmel*. Translated by E. Allison Peers. San Bernadino, CA: Bottom of the Hill Publishing.

Starhawk. 1979. *The Spiral Dance*. New York: Harper and Row.

Stromberg, Peter. 2009. *Caught in Play: How Entertainment Works on You*. Stanford: Stanford University Press.

Strunk, William, Jr., and E. B. White. 1959. *The Elements of Style*. New York: Macmillan.

Taves, Ann. 2009a. "Channeled Apparitions: On Visions That Morph and Categories That Slip." *Visual Resources* 25 (1–2): 137–52.

———. 2009b. *Religious Experience Reconsidered: A Building-Block Approach to the Study of Religion and Other Special Things*. Princeton, NJ: Princeton University Press.

———. 2016. *Revelatory Events: Three Case Studies of the Emergence of New Spiritual Paths*. Princeton, NJ: Princeton University Press.

Taves, Ann, and Egil Asprem. 2016. "Experience as Event: Event Cognition and the Study of (Religious) Experiences." *Religion, Brain & Behavior* 7 (1): 43–62. https://doi.org/10.1080/2153599X.2016.1150327.

———. 2020. "The Building Block Approach: An Overview." In *Building Blocks of Religion: Critical Applications and Future Prospects*, edited by Göran Larsson, Jonas Svensson, and Andreas Nordin, 5–25. London: Equinox.

Taylor, Charles. 2007. *A Secular Age*. Cambridge, MA: Harvard University Press.

Taylor, Marjorie. 1999. *Imaginary Companions and the Children Who Create Them*. Oxford: Oxford University Press.

———. 2013. *The Oxford Handbook of the Development of Imagination*. Oxford: Oxford University Press.

Taylor, Marjorie, Candice Mottweiler, Naomi Aguiar, Emilee Naylor, and Jacob G. Levernier. 2018. "Paracosms: The Imaginary Worlds of Middle Childhood." *Child Development* 91 (4): 1–15. https://doi.org/10.1111/cdev.13162.

Taylor, Marjorie, Candice M. Mottweiler, Emilee R. Naylor, and Jacob G. Levernier. 2015. "Imaginary Worlds in Middle Childhood: A Qualitative Study of Two Pairs of Coordinated Paracosms." *Creativity Research Journal* 27 (2): 167–74. https://doi.org/10.1080/10400419.2015.1030318.

Tellegen, Auke. 1981. "Practicing the Two Disciplines for Relaxation and Enlightenment." *Journal of Experimental Psychology: General* 110 (2): 217–26.

Tellegen, Auke, and Gilbert Atkinson. 1974. "Openness to Absorbing and Self-Altering Experiences ('Absorption'), a Trait Related to Hypnotic Susceptibility." *Journal of Abnormal Psychology* 83 (3): 268–77.

Thalbourne, Michael, and Peter Delin. 1993. "A New Instrument for Measuring the Sheep-Goat Variable: Its Psychometric Properties and Factor Structure." *Journal of the Society for Psychical Research* 59 (832): 172–86.

Thomas, Eugene, and Pamela Cooper. 1980. "Incidence and Psychological Correlates of Intense Spiritual Experiences." *Journal of Transpersonal Psychology* 12 (1): 75–85.

Thomas, Keith. 1971. *Religion and the Decline of Magic: Studies in Popular Beliefs in Sixteenth and Seventeenth Century England*. New York: Scribner.

Tien, Allen. 1991. "Distribution of Hallucinations in the Population." *Social Psychiatry and Psychiatric Epidemiology* 26 (6): 287–92.

Tolin, David. 2010. "Is Cognitive-Behavioral Therapy More Effective Than Other Therapies? A Meta-Analytic Review." *Clinical Psychology Review* 30 (6): 710–20.

Toren, Christina. 2007. "How Do We Know What Is True? The Case of Mana in Fiji." In *Questions of Anthropology*, edited by Rita Astuti, Jonathan Parry, and Charles Stafford, 227–48. Oxford: Berg.

Tsai, Jeanne L. 2007. "Ideal Affect: Cultural Causes and Behavioral Consequences." *Perspectives on Psychological Science* 2 (3): 242–59.

Tsai, Jeanne, Jennifer Louie, Eva Chen, and Yukiko Uchida. 2007. "Learning What Feelings to Desire: Socialization of Ideal Affect through Children's Storybooks." *Personality and Social Psychology Bulletin* 33 (1): 17–30.

Turner, Victor. 1967. *The Forest of Symbols: Aspects of Ndembu Ritual*. Ithaca, NY: Cornell University Press.

Tylor, Edward Burnett. (1871) 2010. *Primitive Culture*. Cambridge: Cambridge University Press.

Underwood, Lynn, and Jeanne Teresi. 2002. "The Daily Spiritual Experience Scale: Development, Theoretical Description, Reliability, Exploratory Factor Analysis, and Preliminary Construct Validity Using Health-Related Data." *Annals of Behavioral Medicine* 24 (1): 22–33.

Vaihinger, Hans. 1925. *The Philosophy of 'As If': A System of the Theoretical, Practical and Religious Fictions of Mankind*. Translated by C. K. Ogden. New York: Harcourt, Brace and Co.

Van Leeuwen, Neil. 2014. "Religious Credence Is Not Factual Belief." *Cognition* 133 (3): 698–715.

Vardenoe, Kirk. 1996. *Jasper Johns: A Retrospective*. New York: Museum of Modern Art.

Vermeule, Blakey. 2010. *Why Do We Care about Literary Characters?* Baltimore: Johns Hopkins University Press.

Verren, Helen. 2001. *Science and an African Logic*. Chicago: University of Chicago Press.

Veyne, Paul. 1988. *Did the Greeks Believe in Their Myths? An Essay on the Constitutive Imagination*. Chicago: University of Chicago Press.

Vilaça, Aparecida. 2013. "Two or Three Things That I Know about Talking to the Invisible." *HAU: Journal of Ethnographic Theory* 3 (3): 359–63.

———. 2016. *Praying and Preying: Christianity in Indigenous Amazonia*. Oakland: University of California Press.

Virkler, Mark, and Patti Virkler. 1986. *Dialogue with God*. Gainsville: Bridge-Logos.

Vitebsky, Piers. 2005. *The Reindeer People: Living with Animals and Spirits in Siberia*. New York: Mariner Books.

Viveiros de Castro, Eduardo. 2011. "Zeno and the Art of Anthropology: Of Lies, Beliefs, Paradoxes, and Other Truths." *Common Knowledge* 17 (1): 128–45.

Wacker, Grant. 2003. *Heaven Below: Early Pentecostals and American Culture*. Cambridge, MA: Harvard University Press.

Warren, Rick. 2002. *The Purpose Driven Life*. Grand Rapids, MI: Zondervan.

Watkins, Mary. 1976. *Waking Dreams*. Newark, NJ: Gordon and Breach.

———. 1986. *Invisible Guests: The Development of Imaginal Dialogues*. Hillsdale, NJ: Analytic Press.

Weil, Simone. (1947) 2002. *Gravity and Grace*. Translated by E. Crawford and Mario von der Ruhr. New York: Routledge.

Weisman, Kara, Carol Dweck, and Ellen Markman. 2017. "Rethinking People's Conceptions of Mental Life." *Proceedings of the National Academy of Sciences* 114 (43): 11374–79.

White, E. B. 1990. "Life." In *Writings from The New Yorker, 1925–1976*, edited by Rebecca Dale, 3. New York: Harper Perennial.

White, Geoffrey, and John Kirkpatrick, eds. 1985. *Person, Self, and Experience: Exploring Pacific Ethnopsychologies*. Oakland: University of California Press.

Whitehouse, Harvey. 2000. *Arguments and Icons: Divergent Modes of Religiosity*. Oxford: Oxford University Press.

Wigger, J. Bradley. 2019. *Invisible Companions: Encounters with Imaginary Friends, Gods, Ancestors, and Angels*. Stanford: Stanford University Press.

Wilde, Oscar. 1940. *The Importance of Being Earnest and Other Plays*. London: Penguin.

Wills, Gary. 2019. "Shallow Calls to Shallow." Review of Mary Gordon, *On Thomas Merton*. *Harpers*, April.

Winnicott, D. W. 1953. "Transitional Object and the Transitional Phenomena: A Study of the First Not-Me Possession." *International Journal of Psycho-Analysis* 53 (2): 89–97.

———. 1971. *Playing and Reality*. London: Tavistock Publications.

———. 2010. *Psycho-Analytic Explorations*. London: Routledge.

Winzeler, Robert. 2007. *Anthropology and Religion: What We Know, Think, and Question*. Lanham, MD: AltaMira Press.

Wolfson, Elliot. 1994. *Through a Speculum That Shines: Vision and Imagination in Medieval Jewish Mysticism*. Princeton, NJ: Princeton University Press.

Wood, James. 2008. *How Fiction Works*. New York: Farrar, Straus and Giroux.

Woods, Teresa, Michael Antoni, Gail Ironson, and David Kling. 1999. "Religiosity Is Associated with Affective and Immune Status in Symptomatic HIV-Infected Gay Men." *Journal of Psychosomatic Research* 46 (2): 165–76.

"World Conference on Religion and Peace Proceedings." *Contemporary Religions in Japan* 10, nos. 3–4 (1969): 204–315. Accessed March 20, 2020. https://www.jstor.org/stable/30233040.

Wulff, David. 2000. "Mystical Experience." In *Varieties of Anomalous Experience: Examining the Scientific Evidence*, edited by Etzel Cardeña, Steven Jay Lynn, and Stanley Krippner, 397–440. Washington, DC: American Psychological Association.

Xygalatas, Dimitrios, and William McCorkle, eds. 2013. *Mental Culture: Classical Social Theory and the Cognitive Science of Religion*. London: Routledge.

Yates, Frances. 1964. *Giordano Bruno and the Hermetic Tradition*. Chicago: University of Chicago Press.

———. (1966) 2014. *The Art of Memory*. New York: Random House.

Zachar, Peter, and Kenneth Kendler. 2017. "The Philosophy of Nosology." *Annual Review of Clinical Psychology* 13: 49–71.

Zaleski, Philip, and Carol Zaleski. 2005. *Prayer: A History*. Boston: Houghton Mifflin.

INDEX

Printed in the USA
CPSIA information can be obtained
at www.ICGtesting.com
JSHW032004100624
64551JS00017B/637